About Island Press

Island Press, a nonprofit organization, publishes, markets, and distributes the most advanced thinking on the conservation of our natural resources—books about soil, land, water, forests, wildlife, and hazardous and toxic wastes. These books are practical tools used by public officials, business and industry leaders, natural resource managers, and concerned citizens working to solve both local and global resource problems.

Founded in 1978, Island Press reorganized in 1984 to meet the increasing demand for substantive books on all resource-related issues. Island Press publishes and distributes under its own imprint and offers these services to other nonprofit organizations.

Support for Island Press is provided by Apple Computer, Inc., Mary Reynolds Babcock Foundation, Geraldine R. Dodge Foundation, The Energy Foundation, The Charles Engelhard Foundation, The Ford Foundation, Glen Eagles Foundation, The George Gund Foundation, William and Flora Hewlett Foundation, The Joyce Foundation, The John D. and Catherine T. MacArthur Foundation, The Andrew W. Mellon Foundation, The Joyce Mertz-Gilmore Foundation, The New-Land Foundation, The J. N. Pew, Jr. Charitable Trust, Alida Rockefeller, The Rockefeller Brothers Fund, The Florence and John Schumann Foundation, The Tides Foundation, and individual donors.

About the Union of Concerned Scientists

The Union of Concerned Scientists (UCS) is an independent nonprofit organization of scientists and other citizens concerned about the impact of advanced technology on society. UCS's energy programs focus on national energy policy, transportation, global warming, and nuclear power safety. UCS is a nationally respected advocate of energy strategies that minimize risks to public health and safety, provide for efficient and cost-effective use of energy resources, and minimize damage to the global environment.

Steering a New Course

STEERING A NEW COURSE

■

TRANSPORTATION, ENERGY, AND THE ENVIRONMENT

DEBORAH GORDON

UNION OF CONCERNED SCIENTISTS

ISLAND PRESS

Washington, D.C. ❑ *Covelo, California*

Library of Congress Cataloging-in-Publication Data

Gordon, Deborah, 1959–
    Steering a new course : transportation, energy, and the environment / Deborah Gordon.
        p. cm.
    Includes bibliographical references and index.
    ISBN 1-55963-135-X (alk. paper). — ISBN 1-55963-134-1 (alk. paper : pbk.)   1. Transportation, Automotive—United States. 2. Transportation, Automotive—Environmental aspects—United States.   3. Automobiles—United States—Fuel consumption. 4. Transportation and state—United States.   I. Title.
HE5623.G67   1991
388'.068—dc20   91-24401
                                                                            CIP

PHOTO CREDITS
Page 7 Highway Users Federation; 8 Ford Motor Company; 9 Highway Users Federation; 12 American Public Transit Association; 13 Highway Users Federation; 15 Highway Users Federation; 17 American Public Transit Association; 122 Volvo Corporation; 128 American Public Transit Association; 133 American Public Transit Association; 135 French Rail Inc.; 136 Thyssen Aktiengesellschaft; 138 American Public Transit Association; 138 Taxi 2000 Corporation; 141 American Association of Railroads; 142 American Association of Railroads; 143 RoadRailer Inc.; 145 American Public Transit Association; 150 American Public Transit Association; 155 American Public Transit Association

Text Design and Typesetting
Desktop Publishing & Design, Boston, MA

Printed on recycled, acid-free paper

♻

Manufactured in the United States of America

10   9   8   7   6   5   4   3   2   1

Contents

Tables

Figures

Acknowledgments

I would like to thank Dr. Arthur Rosenfeld (Lawrence Berkeley Laboratory) for first piquing my interest in transportation policy and for his continuing support of my work.

My special thanks to the several individuals who reviewed this study and provided their comments and particularly useful suggestions: Andy Clarke (Bicycle Federation of America); Charles Komanoff (Charles Komanoff Associates); Charles Lave (University of California-Irvine, Department of Economics); Marc Ledbetter (American Council for an Energy-Efficient Economy); Marcia Lowe (WorldWatch Institute); James MacKenzie (World Resources Institute); Jim Grieshaber-Otto (House of Commons, Ottawa, Ontario); Frank Pane (United Technologies—Pratt & Whitney); Harriet Parcells (National Association of Railroad Passengers); Michael Replogle (Montgomery County, Maryland, Planning Department); Marc Ross (University of Michigan, Department of Physics); Daniel Sperling (University of California-Davis, Department of Civil Engineering and Environmental Studies); and James Sweeney (Stanford University, Engineering Economic Systems).

I am especially grateful to Steve Casler of Allegheny College, who willingly gave his time and shared his data with me on indirect transportation energy.

I would also like to thank Warren Leon, director of public education for the Union of Concerned Scientists, who helped write Chapter 1 on the history of transportation in 20th-century America, and Howard Ris, Jr., executive director of UCS, for his many helpful comments. I am indebted to Steven Krauss, senior editor at UCS, for his invaluable editorial skills; to UCS intern Jim Greiner for gathering photographs and checking citations; and to my other colleagues at UCS for their ongoing support and useful suggestions.

D.G.

Steering a New Course

Introduction

The United States faces a transportation crisis. To a citizenry grown weary of domestic crises—the savings-and-loan debacle, the deficit, the environment, crime, drugs, homelessness—one more may seem less than earthshaking. Yet anyone who drives, and that includes most of us, will feel the effects of this crisis personally.

What we are facing is the deterioration of our transportation system across the board—cars, trucks, trains, and airplanes. As the infrastructure becomes increasingly unable to handle the spiraling volume of traffic, cracks that have already appeared will widen. Worsening congestion will soon make transportation an even more tedious, aggravating exercise than it already often is, while a killing dependence on foreign oil will make supplies of it increasingly unreliable and exorbitantly expensive. And without innovative strategies aimed at reducing the number of miles driven, cars and trucks will continue to pollute air, water, and land.

The breakdown of the transportation system will not occur tomorrow, or even next year. Without corrective action, however, a serious disintegration of service is likely by the end of the decade. One of the most ominous warnings is the alarming increase in congestion. The US General Accounting Office has calculated that if present trends continue, road congestion in the United States will *triple* in only 15 years even if capacity is increased by 20 percent, a goal that is unlikely to be achieved (GAO 1989a).

Already two-thirds of the rush-hour travelers on urban interstate highways experience delays. Americans spend one billion hours a year stuck in traffic, wasting two billion gallons of gasoline and costing the economy anywhere from $10 billion to $30 billion—enough to fund the entire federal environmental program. By the time congestion triples, it will cost the nation up to $50 billion a year, more than the federal government now spends on low-income housing, veterans benefits, and the war on drugs, combined.

Traffic has gotten worse because there are simply too many passenger cars and trucks being driven too many miles, with too few people in them, for our roads to handle. An estimated one-half of all trips Americans take, and at least three-quarters of all commutes, are made by a single person alone in a car. To accommodate this habit, we now own enough cars to put every American in one—and no one would have to sit in the back seat. We drove those vehicles nearly two trillion miles last year, and the number is growing at the rate of 3 percent a year.

Gridlock will become a way of life not only on the road but in the air. Airports are severely crowded, and the situation is getting worse. In 1990, 16 airports were considered congested by Federal Aviation Administration standards, and 42 more will be by 2020 (Owen 1988).

Another unmistakable sign of crisis is our increasing dependence on foreign oil, a problem that has come to the forefront with the Iraqi invasion of Kuwait. The United States must now import fully half its oil. We could cut this habit substantially by increasing fuel efficiency and holding the volume of travel constant. For example, by increasing the efficiency of all US automobiles from the current average of 18 miles per gallon to 21, while simultaneously holding total miles traveled steady, the United States could eliminate the need for all imports of Iraqi and Kuwaiti oil.

As congestion and foreign-oil dependence reach critical proportions, a third indicator also warns of trouble in our transportation system: the degradation of the environment. Cars and trucks are the largest single source of air pollution and a major contributor to global warming. They emit carbon monoxide, nitrogen oxides, reactive hydrocarbons (forming smog), and the principal greenhouse gas, carbon dioxide—the latter at the rate of 20 pounds for every gallon of gasoline burned. Despite continuing gains in pollution control and efficiency improvements, overall emissions of pollutants are projected to increase by almost 40 percent by 2010 because we are driving more and under more congested conditions.

Motor vehicles pollute not only the air but also our water and land. Oil spills contaminate our waterways. And motor vehicles require large amounts of irreplaceable land; in cities, upwards of one-third of the land is taken up by cars, trucks, roads, and parking lots. Nationwide, more land is now devoted to the automobile than to housing.

The pollution, congestion, and damage to health caused by our dependence on motor vehicles are the hidden costs of our transportation system. Yet drivers do not pay these costs directly. The price we pay for transportation is artificially low because fuel remains relatively inexpensive and nearly all roads are free of charge. But this should not obscure the fact that as a society we are paying these hidden costs. And as the costs continue to mount, we will pay them increasingly with our time, health, and welfare.

This book makes bold recommendations for policymakers seeking to ameliorate a host of problems associated with the US transportation sector. Because our recommendations cannot consider specific local characteristics, it is important to evaluate the synergistic effects of a package of policies that are tailored to address particular needs.

We begin by looking at the history of US transportation in the 20th century. Chapter 1 traces the rise of the automobile, the decline of mass transit, the construction of the interstate highway system, and the oil crises of the 1970s, which inspired dramatic gains in automotive efficiency. Unfortunately, with oil prices falling to record lows in the late 1980s, those gains began to erode.

Chapter 2 analyzes current and projected future patterns of passenger and freight transportation. Transportation demands (both passenger and freight) are discussed first because these variables can and should be modified. The work commute and the role of heavy trucks are detailed, since these demands stress the system. In analyzing transportation supplies, both energy use (direct and indirect) and system costs (real and hidden) are considered. The chapter then looks at future trends, examining the implications of a "business-as-usual" course.

Chapter 3 examines the difference in transportation services in various countries. The cost of transportation, the greater emphasis on bicycling, walking, and trains as compared to the United States, and greenhouse-warming policies of other nations are among the topics discussed.

Chapter 4 provides the link between transportation, air pollution, and global warming. Each major air pollutant and greenhouse gas is discussed as to its health effects and the relative share produced by transportation sources. In addition, health costs and vehicle emissions are documented.

Chapter 5 surveys alternative transportation fuels and sets out criteria for evaluating the various fuels. Each is then assessed on the basis of these criteria: cost and availability; hardware modifications; resource base and secure supply; fuel properties and safety concerns; greenhouse-gas and other emissions; and existing government policies.

Ultra-fuel-efficient vehicles are the subject of Chapter 6. Fuel-efficiency technologies, both currently available and under development, are examined. The chapter concludes with a discussion of the relationships between fuel efficiency and safety, and fuel efficiency and vehicle speed.

The range of innovative strategies available to address transportation-sector problems is presented in Chapter 7. Options include mass-transit advancements; intermodal freight (truck-plus-train and other combinations); improvements to fleet vehicles; new strategies to manage transportation demand and the transportation system; regional-development strategies; and state-of-the-art transportation technologies.

Culminating the discussion of the first seven chapters, Chapter 8 presents a comprehensive survey of policy options available to decision makers by answering two questions: Which strategies hold the most promise?, and What policy tools should be used to induce the necessary changes? Four policy tools are considered: regulations, economic incentives (such as taxation), information (education as well as testing and demonstration programs), and quasi-governmental measures (such as private-sector involvement in planning). Examples of each of these policy tools serve as the basis of the recommendations.

The concluding chapter discusses the question of who is best suited to formulate and implement the recommended policies. What is offered is a master list of policy recommendations for each level of government—federal, state, regional, and local. Objectives are set out with the goal of developing a sustainable transportation system that can preserve our mobility (by providing more choices for travel) while reducing transportation's social costs. Specific policies follow each objective. While further analysis is required to determine precisely which policies suit specific regions, it is clear that no single policy can solve all of the problems attributed to the transportation sector; thus an array of creative policies is required.

1 The History of American Transportation in the 20th Century

The main theme in the story of transportation in 20th-century America has been the triumph of gasoline-powered motor vehicles, and especially the private automobile. The automobile achieved dominance remarkably swiftly—in a single generation—and has then extended that dominance. Today, there are over 185 million passenger cars and light trucks on the road. These vehicles consume 85 percent of all the energy used for transporting people (Davis et al. 1989).

The Rise of the Automobile

At the turn of the century, automobiles were still oddities. Cars were perceived as recreational vehicles, and their owners had to fit into a road system dominated by pedestrians, horse-drawn carriages, and bicycles. In Vermont, for example, motorists were required to hire "a person of mature age" to walk an eighth of a mile in front of their car carrying a red flag (Leuchtenburg 1958). As late as 1909, when American automakers produced 124,000 cars, two million horse-drawn carriages were manufactured (Rae 1984, Lynd and Lynd 1929).

Horses and cars delivered mail in the early 1900s.

In fact, during the first decade of the new century, a different transportation innovation, the interurban street railway, was spreading faster than motor vehicles and played a (temporarily) larger role in reshaping the American transportation system. Street railways, or trolleys, were introduced into American cities in the 1850s and were initially pulled by horses. After Richmond, Virginia, built the first electric streetcar system in 1887, electric trolleys quickly displaced the horse-drawn vehicles. In addition to carrying commuters from downtown locations to nearby suburbs, trolleys began to link more distant communities, and an entire interurban street railway network grew. From 2,107 miles of track in 1900, the electric interurban

Moving assembly line, Ford Motor Company, 1913.

railways reached a peak of 15,580 miles in 1916 (Flink 1988). Trolleys enabled workers to live farther from their jobs and allowed more frequent passenger travel between communities in a region. For freight and long-distance travel, steam-powered railroads and boats remained the main carriers.

The automobile did not initially displace either trolleys or trains, but it was an immediate threat to horses. Cars were not only faster and more efficient than horses, they were also cheaper to operate. They were especially attractive to farmers and others in rural areas, where train service was irregular and distances were great. Consequently, before World War I, proportionately more farmers than city dwellers purchased cars.

Urbanites nevertheless saw advantage in using motor vehicles for the main tasks assigned to horses—the shipment of goods within the city and private transportation for the well-to-do. Although the car may threaten public health at the end of the 20th century, at the beginning it was seen as a clear environmental improvement over the horse. "In New York City alone at the turn of the century," historian James Flink points out, "horses deposited on the streets every day an estimated 2.5 million pounds of manure and 60,000 gallons of urine, accounting for about two-thirds of the filth that littered the city's streets. Excreta from horses in the form of dried dust irritated nasal passages and lungs, then became a syrupy mass to wade through and track into the home whenever it rained" (Flink 1988).

Automobile ownership spread much faster in the United States than elsewhere. As early as 1913, when Henry Ford introduced the moving assembly line, American car manufacturers were producing almost half a million cars a year, 80 percent of world production. During the next decade and a half, yearly car production increased tenfold (Rae 1984). Just before the 1929 stock-market crash, over 26 million motor vehicles were registered in the United States. This meant that there was one car for every five Americans, and more than half of the nation's families owned a car. In contrast, there was only one car for every 43 people in Great Britain and one car for every 325 people in Italy (Leuchtenburg 1958). Thus in only three decades the car had become a ubiquitous symbol of American prosperity. The automobile industry had become America's premier industry. It had taken on a structure and shape that would last for decades, with 80 percent of car sales dominated by the three largest makers—Ford, General Motors, and Chrysler (Flink 1988).

Why did so many Americans buy cars so quickly compared with Europeans? The population was more scattered and density was lower, so many Americans did not have access to satisfactory public transit. For them, the automobile filled a need for faster and more convenient travel. Because average incomes were higher and wealth was distributed more equally than in Europe, more people could afford cars to fill this need (Cochran 1972).

But the rapid spread of an automobile-dominated culture cannot be explained entirely by such rational, practical, economic factors. More

intangible considerations involving consumer preferences, advertising, and political attitudes also played a role. For example, the automobile was not necessarily incompatible with a well-developed urban mass-transit system. Yet as the trolley system and the car-based culture

Federal highway construction in the 1930s.

grew in the first decades of the new century, they both required extensive public assistance, but only motor vehicles received it.

Motor-vehicle manufacturers needed government help, since they produced a product that required the use of government-owned facilities—the roads. In 1909, less than 10 percent of the roads were surfaced. But then the nation went on a road-building and road-paving binge as citizens pressured the government for roads so they could make good use of the new technology of motor vehicles. By 1930, a system of interconnected concrete roads spanned the continent (Flink 1988).

Road building was such a monumental task that all levels of government got involved. Although local governments continued to play the largest role, accounting for 53 percent of highway funds in 1927, the states and federal government also participated (Leuchtenburg 1958). With the 1916 Federal Aid Road Act, the national government committed itself to improving post roads. Later, the Federal Highway Act of 1921 provided matching grants to the states to help with the establishment of a nationwide system of highways.

Although the initial road-building efforts were financed primarily from general government revenues, enthusiasm for the automobile was so great that motorists willingly accepted a significant user fee, the gasoline tax. Between 1919 and 1929, every state passed such a tax, most often of three or four cents a gallon. As historian John Burnham notes, the public's seeming willingness to "pay their own way" encouraged government officials to accelerate road-improvement efforts: "Never before in the history of taxation has a major tax been so generally accepted in so short a period" (1961).

The Decline of Mass Transit

In contrast, streetcars and other mass-transit systems languished. Up to 1918, urban transit ridership was growing faster than the urban population, but most mass-transit systems were unpopular (Yago 1984). Streetcars and subways were run as private corporations, so company profits were inevitably a higher priority than public service. Many streetcar companies used their rail lines to promote their own suburban real-estate ventures and avoided building lines to other growing communities. Some streetcar companies used political pressure, economic favors, and bribery to gain influence over local elected officials and thereby improve their own financial position at the public's expense (Bottles 1987).

Much of the public consequently distrusted the mass-transit companies and considered them corrupt. When the companies began to experience financial difficulties after 1914 and argued that they could not expand their service to remain competitive, most citizens were not anxious to help. Transit companies' responses to rapidly changing consumer demand were generally tardy, hesitant, and uncoordinated (Foster 1982). Much of the public thus welcomed the automobile as an alternative to relying on poorly managed mass-transit systems. One-third of the transit companies went bankrupt between 1916 and 1923, leaving many fewer miles of track and a declining level of service (Yago 1984).

Even if the transit companies had been more popular, they would have had a hard time competing. The farther one commuted, the greater the car's time advantage. In Kansas City in 1930, cars and trolleys moved at the same slow pace through downtown's rush-hour traffic. However, at two miles from the city center, cars had gained a five-minute advantage, which expanded to 15 minutes at seven miles. Along secondary trolley lines, the time differential was even greater (Interrante 1983). And even where it was cheaper and faster to use public transportation, mass transit had a hard time winning back car owners. Once people had put out the large sum of money it took to purchase an automobile, they felt committed to using it.

Although the Great Depression and World War II delayed the spread of car ownership to the more than 40 percent of American families without them in 1930, the automobile's central economic and cultural role was already set. For those working-class people who owned cars, as well as those who did not, a car was the great symbol of advancement that stood for a large share of "the American dream." Even when families experienced sharply declining incomes during the Great Depression, they sacrificed many things so they could hang on tenaciously to their cars (Lynd and Lynd 1937).

Once the car had captured such a central place in the economy and the culture, it was almost inevitable that motor vehicles would expand their dominance within the American transportation system. Each year, automobile companies spent millions of dollars on advertising to convince the public of the attractions of car travel. Along with its allies in the oil, trucking, and highway-construction industries, the automobile industry vigorously promoted its interests in Washington and in state capitals. WPA projects in the 1930s, for example, included a strong road-building component; 10 times as much WPA money was spent on street and highway projects as on mass transit (Foster 1982).

Other transportation options simply did not have the resources to compete for the attention of policymakers or the hearts of citizens. Even in cities where close to half the people did not own cars, most public officials were more concerned with making car travel easier than with improving mass transit. Planning commissions were dominated by commercial civic elites who were responsive to the needs of upper- and middle-class car owners rather than to mass-transit riders from the working class. They willingly allowed streetcar tracks to be ripped up, since cars were then left with more space and a smoother road, and street paving was simplified. The only cities that ended the 1930s with strong mass-transit systems were those, like New York, Boston, and Philadelphia, where particular political circumstances had produced a tradition of public mass-transit subsidies starting in the 1910s (Flink 1988).

In most places, financially troubled transit companies switched from streetcars to buses, which were less expensive to operate. But the decision inadvertently hastened the decline of ridership since buses proved to be less attractive and ultimately had less presence on the urban scene than the rail-based transit system had. By World War II urban bus ridership was equal to that of streetcars, but by the mid-1950s, even though there were six times more bus riders, the number of riders for both modes of travel was declining rapidly (Flink 1988).[1]

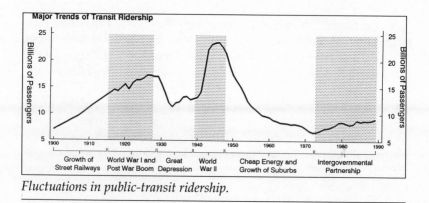

Fluctuations in public-transit ridership.

Interstate Highways and Motor-Vehicle Dominance

The establishment of the Interstate Highway System in 1956 not only solidified the overwhelming dominance of motor vehicles within the American transportation system but also symbolized the political power of motor-vehicle-related industries. The new legislation increased the federal share of highway funding from the 60 percent set in the 1944 Federal Aid Highway Act to 90 percent and established a specially earmarked Federal Highway Trust Fund. By ensuring that taxes on cars, gasoline, lubricants, and auto parts would go into this fund, the highway lobby guaranteed an ongoing, expanding revenue base for highways. The highway lobby had convinced government leaders that money spent on highways is a public investment, whereas that spent on public transportation is a costly subsidy (Yago 1984). Consequently, nearly all federal spending on land transportation went to highways.

After 1956, average yearly federal highway spending increased six times and was well over $5 billion by 1973. With this money, the United States built the most extensive highway system in the world (Dunn 1981).

The Interstate Highway System sped the decline of passenger railroads. It became much more convenient and cheaper for families to drive distances of several hundred miles rather than take a train. At the same time, airplanes were robbing the railroads of long-distance travelers. Even in a market where railroads should have been competitive—business trips of less than 300 miles—the railroads were squeezed out by cars and airplanes. Airplanes became the preferred mode for business travel. Trains were perceived as unreliable, inconvenient, and old-fashioned (Dunn 1981).

Railroads remained the most important carriers of freight, but the interstate highways helped their competitors in the trucking industry. Railroads already had declining profits and market share. Heavy industries like coal and steel, which depended on the rails, were either diminishing in importance or growing slowly, while service industries and producers of lightweight consumer goods who could best use trucks were growing. As industry and population moved away from older cities in the Northeast and Midwest, the trains saw profitable patterns of shipping disrupted. It was no longer possible to achieve the balanced two-way movement of commodities in which agricultural products from the South and West flowed to the industrial cities of the Northeast and the same boxcars re-turned carrying manu-factured goods. At the same time, the gov-ernment regulatory system weakened the railroads' ability to compete by retaining cumbersome and costly regulations that stifled competition and dated from an era when there had been a real-istic fear of the rail-roads' power (Dunn 1981).

As early as the 1940s, interstate highways changed urban development patterns.

The interstate high-ways had an especially profound impact on the shape of American cities. Motor vehicles had already prompted industry to spread out from the center city and workers to live farther from their workplaces. The urban interstate highways accentuated these trends and also made comprehensive urban transportation planning more difficult. The government's highway planners believed their task was to build a highway system rather than an integrated transportation system, so they did not coordinate their highway plans with existing or possible future mass-transit systems. Not only did this further disadvan-tage railroads and urban mass transit, but a tremendous opportunity was also lost to build a coordinated urban transportation system in which commuters and shippers could easily switch from one mode of transpor-tation to another.

Government highway planners were so focused on building an efficient system of moving motor vehicles that they were blind to the full impact of their roads on the cities they were supposedly serving. They constructed highways that bisected or destroyed neighborhoods, re-duced the cities' housing stock, eliminated their parks, and damaged their appearance (Flink 1988).

The Automobile under Attack

By the late 1950s, just when public approval of an automobile-based transportation system seemed absolute, critics began to mount a series of attacks. Problems caused by 60 years of automobiles were becoming more apparent. Community groups in several cities attacked specific highway plans as threats to the quality of urban life. In their first notable victory, in San Francisco, they stopped the completion of the Embarcadero freeway and in 1966 prompted the city to reject over $240 million in federal highway aid (Dunn 1981).

Other critics attacked the car itself. Los Angeles was the site of the first major dispute. Its large number of motor vehicles, combined with a mountain-ringed location, had made smog a visible and increasingly disturbing phenomenon. Some residents called for a curb on motor-vehicle emissions and helped pass the first California air-pollution law in 1960.

Automakers were not anxious to change their products to lessen Los Angeles's smog. As historian John Rae notes, "The overall response of the motor vehicle industry regrettably followed a pattern that applied to every major public issue affecting the industry during approximately the twenty years from 1955 to 1975. First, industry spokesmen denied the problem existed; they then conceded that it did exist but asserted that it had no solution; finally, they conceded that it could be solved but that the solutions would be very expensive, difficult to apply, and would require a long time to develop" (1984).

Air pollution received national attention in the 1960s, and, as a result, the Motor Vehicle Air Pollution and Control Act of 1965 set the first federal emissions standards. Five years later, the federal Clean Air Act further reduced emissions levels effective in 1975 and 1976 (although manufacturers were later granted a two-year extension).

At the same time that critics were questioning the health impact of automobiles, Ralph Nader and others attacked their safety. Based on Nader's criticisms, the Senate Government Operations Committee began holding hearings in 1965 that led to legislation setting safety standards for new cars effective with 1968 models.

The air-pollution and auto-safety controversies publicized two of the inherent problems with motor vehicles and also shook many Americans' confidence in the Big Three automakers. In both cases, these manufacturers were shown to be slow to act and less willing to embrace innovation than supposedly more technologically backward overseas competitors.

Oil Crises and Energy Efficiency

The Big Three automakers had become so complacent and resistant to change that when a crisis hit they were unprepared and again reacted slowly. The Arab oil embargo of 1973 reduced America's supply of oil dramatically and produced long lines and much higher prices at gas pumps. In response, Congress in 1975 required car manufacturers to increase the fuel efficiency of their products. At the time, the fleet average for new American-made cars was less than 14 miles per gallon (mpg), but the legislation required that each company reach a level for new cars of

27.5 mpg by 1985. At the same time, the Environmental Protection Agency was instructed to create a gas-mileage guide to aid consumers in comparing the fuel efficiency of different vehicles. The guide was required to be distributed in all dealers' showrooms and a sticker posted on the window of every new vehicle.

Fuel shortages from the oil crises.

Congress extended its efforts to increase automobile fuel economy when in 1978 it passed the so-called gas-guzzler tax. Manufacturers of new cars with low fuel-economy ratings were taxed on each car they sold. Cars had to meet a standard to avoid the tax, and that standard increased each year until it reached 27.5 mpg in 1985. Depending on the car's fuel efficiency, the tax could be anywhere from $500 to $3,850.

With fuel efficiency an important factor in consumers' car-buying decisions, foreign manufacturers with relatively small, fuel-efficient cars won an increasing share of the American market. By the end of the 1970s, many consumers and critics ridiculed the American automobile industry as a bloated dinosaur, and one of the Big Three, the Chrysler Corporation, was on the verge of bankruptcy.

Not surprisingly, the controversies of the 1960s and the oil crises of the 1970s advanced efforts to slow the rapid decline of urban mass transit and the railroads.

Gas lines during the 1979 oil crisis.

Even at the start of the 1960s, some members of President Kennedy's administration had wanted to use federal funds to support public transportation, but they met congressional resistance and succeeded only in securing modest loans for the nation's troubled commuter railroads. However, in 1964, the Urban Mass Transportation Act authorized capital grants for public-transit systems and stimulated cities to take over ownership of their mass-transit systems. At the same time, states began to subsidize their major mass-transit systems. But almost 90 percent of

| Figure 1 | **US Primary Energy Use and GNP** |

US energy consumption and gross national product, 1960-1989, indexed to 1973.

Note: 100 on the Energy Use Index scale compounds to 1973 energy use (74 quads) and GNP ($3 trillion).

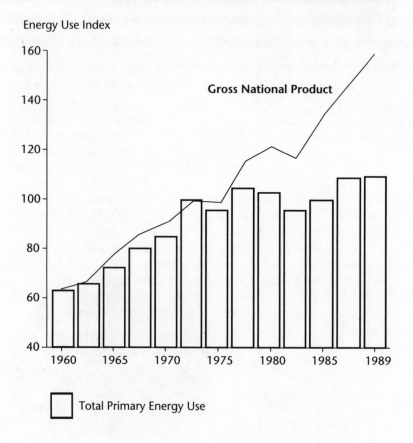

Sources: UCS estimates; Lawrence Berkeley Laboratory; Davis (ORNL) 1989.

such aid was concentrated in eight states, and most went to commuter railroads rather than subways, buses, or trolleys (Dunn 1981).

Two actions during the Nixon administration solidified the federal role in mass transit and dramatically increased government funding for it. In 1970, Congress passed the Urban Mass Transportation Assistance Act providing $10 billion over 12 years. Then, three years later, with the economic and environmental costs of a motor-vehicle-dominated transportation system more apparent, Congress authorized using about 10 percent of the highway trust fund for mass transit. Opposition to the concept of an earmarked trust fund had been mounting, so "the highway forces concluded that the best way to protect the trust fund was to give the transit lobby a piece of the action" (Dunn 1981). The federal government was soon providing significant funds for transit capital improvements as well as operating assistance. Major new transit systems or extensions opened in San Francisco, Atlanta, the District of Columbia, and elsewhere, and the national decline in transit ridership was halted.

The federal government also stepped in to shore up the nation's railroad system. By the late 1960s, many railroad companies, including the recently merged Penn Central, were either bankrupt or close to it. The government directed a reorganization of the many bankrupt lines in the Northeast and established a quasi-public corporation, Amtrak, to take over passenger rail service. Yet, despite receiving billions in public funds, Amtrak recaptured few intercity travelers outside of the Northeast Corridor. An old, unreliable rail infrastructure, the continued convenience of automobiles, and the growing popularity of air travel placed the passenger rail system at a disadvantage. Railroads remained a substantial shipper of freight but a relatively insignificant carrier of people (Davis et al. 1989).

Transit in Washington, DC.

When viewed as a whole, however, transportation policy was moving in a positive direction at the end of the 1970s. The link between GNP and energy use was broken as the US economy continued to grow while energy consumption leveled out (Figure 1). Cars, airplanes, trucks, and most other transportation vehicles were starting to use less energy per passenger or ton of freight. The various government actions, combined with changing consumer preferences, improved the energy efficiency of America's motor vehicles. From 1975 to 1986, the fuel economy of new cars increased from 16 to 28 mpg, while new light trucks increased from 14 to 22 mpg (TRB 1987). Overall, 2.5 million barrels of oil per day were saved, amounting to annual savings of $40 billion to consumers (McNutt and Greene 1989). The energy efficiencies of other transportation vehicles, and especially those that carried freight, improved in response to high oil prices following the oil crises.

Unfortunately, these improvements were outweighed by the dramatic increases in vehicle use. As more autos and trucks filled the roads and congestion worsened, more roads were built. From 1970 to 1987, the number of autos grew at an average annual rate of 2.4 percent and trucks increased by 6 percent, while financing for US highways increased by 15 percent a year (Davis et al. 1989; GAO 1990e).

Table 1
US Consumption of Petroleum by End-Use Sector, 1973-1990 (quads)

Year	Transportation	Percentage transportation of total	Residential and commercial	Industrial	Electric utilities	Total	Total in million bbl per day*
1973	17.83	51.2%	4.39	9.10	3.52	34.84	17.66
1974	17.40	52.0%	4.00	8.69	3.37	33.46	16.96
1975	17.61	53.8%	3.81	8.15	3.17	32.74	16.59
1976	18.51	52.6%	4.18	9.01	3.48	35.18	17.83
1977	19.24	51.8%	4.21	9.77	3.90	37.12	18.81
1978	20.04	52.8%	4.07	9.87	3.99	37.97	19.24
1979	19.83	53.4%	3.45	10.57	3.28	37.13	18.82
1980	19.01	55.6%	3.04	9.53	2.63	34.21	17.34
1981	18.81	58.9%	2.63	8.29	2.20	31.93	16.18
1982	18.42	60.9%	2.45	7.80	1.57	30.24	15.33
1983	18.59	61.9%	2.50	7.42	1.54	30.05	15.23
1984	19.28	62.1%	2.59	7.90	1.29	31.06	15.74
1985	19.54	63.2%	2.57	7.72	1.09	30.92	15.67
1986	20.23	62.8%	2.58	7.94	1.45	32.20	16.32
1987	20.80	63.3%	2.62	8.19	1.26	32.87	16.66
1988	21.51	63.0%	2.70	8.44	1.56	34.21	17.34
1989	21.69	63.2%	2.66	8.19	1.68	34.03	17.20
1990	21.55	63.9%	2.55	8.27	1.38	33.75	17.11

* Calculated from Total column. One million barrels per day of petroleum equals 1.973 quadrillion Btu per year.

Sources: UCS estimates; EIA, Monthly Energy Review, *February 1991.*

The Amnesia of the 1980s

During the 1980s, the memory of two oil crises faded, and by 1989 the price of transportation fuels was lower than a decade earlier. When adjusted for inflation, fuel costs were even lower than in 1960. The Reagan administration was so hostile to the concept of improved energy efficiency that it weakened those measures that were already in place. It downplayed distribution of EPA's gas-mileage guide and permitted the fuel economy of vehicles manufactured after 1986 to decline. Automobile manufacturers deemphasized fuel economy and instead promoted larger, more powerful cars.

The United States therefore continued to use record amounts of energy for transportation—well over twice as much oil than for any other sector (Table 1). From 1973 to 1989, petroleum used for transportation grew at an average rate of 1.3 percent annually, while all other sectors of the economy reduced their consumption during this period (Figure 2).

Figure 2 **Changes in Petroleum Use by All Sectors**

Annual growth trends in petroleum consumption, 1973-1989.

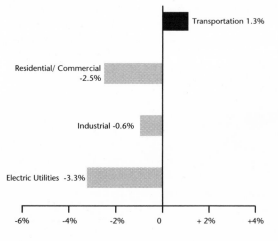

Annual % increase or decrease change in energy use

Source: EIA, Monthly Energy Review, *January 1990.*

The changes in transportation that had taken place between 1900 and 1990 had made Americans much more mobile, but had also placed them in a precarious situation in which their economy relied on foreign suppliers and their environment suffered from serious problems caused by burning such large quantities of petroleum. As the 1990s began, the transportation system faced economic and environmental disaster, but the nation's political leaders expressed little concern or even interest. Iraq's invasion of Kuwait in August 1990 showed the folly of having ignored transportation's growing energy use and ever greater oil imports during the 1980s. Perhaps this latest crisis will produce the permanent changes that are needed in the transportation system.

Notes

1. In a 1974 report to the Senate Subcommittee on Antitrust and Monopoly, Bradford Snell claimed that a General Motors-led conspiracy destroyed urban mass transit. He pointed out that GM, first on its own and then in partnership with Standard Oil of California, Firestone Tire, and others, had acquired control of transit firms in close to 50 cities in order to replace trolleys with buses. However, although these companies may have speeded the decline of trolley systems, the same result would have occurred regardless of the validity of the conspiracy argument. Transit-system managers wanted buses because they were less expensive to purchase and operate. "It did not take illegal conspiracies by giant corporations to induce private management to put profits before public service" (Dunn 1981).

2 Overview of the US Transportation Sector

As our history has revealed, transportation is inextricably linked to a host of national problems—energy, environmental, and economic. Before discussing solutions to these problems, let's explore how Americans travel, how goods are shipped, and how much energy and money are devoted to our transportation activities.

How Americans Travel

Most Americans choose to travel in private vehicles, mainly cars and light trucks or vans (LTVs). There were 187 million cars and LTVs on the road in 1989, or 1.5 cars for every working American. Over half of all households owned at least two vehicles (Davis et al. 1989). From 1970 to 1989, the number of vehicles on the road increased a staggering 73 percent (Figure 3). A substantial portion of the increase was in light trucks and vans; although there are still many fewer of these vehicles on the road than cars, their numbers are growing five times faster.

Americans not only like to travel in their own private vehicles, they often prefer to travel alone in them. The average occupancy of the American automobile is 1.7 passengers, and the number is even lower for commuters: only 1.15. The percentage of Americans who commute to work alone in their cars has been rising steadily and now stands at 85 percent.

Over three-quarters of all passenger travel is done in cars, and when LTVs are included all but 3 percent of total vehicle-miles of travel (VMT) is accounted for. (The few remaining vehicle-miles are accounted for by bicycles, mass transit, aircraft, and pedestrians.) As a result, VMT have risen steadily, at about 3 percent a year (Figure 4).

Another common measure of transportation demand is passenger miles of travel (PMT). Autos and light trucks account for 87 percent of

| Figure 3 | Increase in Number of Highway Vehicles |

Number of US cars and trucks, 1970-1989.

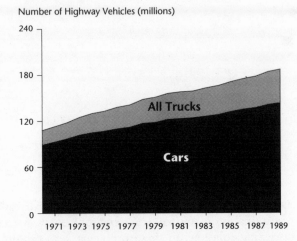

Number of Highway Vehicles (millions)

Source: Davis (ORNL) 1989.

| Figure 4 | Vehicle Miles Traveled in Cars and Trucks |

Vehicle miles of travel, by mode, 1935-1989.

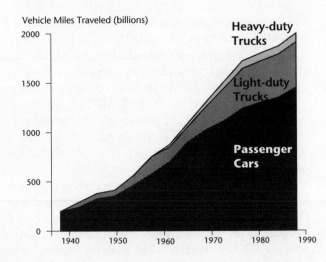

Vehicle Miles Traveled (billions)

Sources: UCS estimates; Rosenberg 1990.

PMT, and airplanes account for 11 percent. Indeed, air travel is the fastest-growing form of transportation in the United States, increasing twice as fast as motor-vehicle travel. At the bottom of the scale, mass transit, bicycling, and walking account for less than 1 percent each of all passenger miles (Davis et al. 1989). (See Table 2.)

Table 2
Measures of Domestic Passenger Travel (1987)

Transport Method	# Vehicles (millions)	Annual est. Miles/vehicle (thousands)	Vehicle-miles Traveled (billions)	Passenger-miles Traveled (billions)	Vehicle Fuel Efficiency (Miles per Gallon)
Automobile[a]	130.4	—	1,357	2,307	19.2
–household	119.8	9.7			
–fleet	10.6	18[e]			
Light Truck[b]	35.5[d]	6.9	245	467	13.5
Motorcycle	4.9	2.0	10	11	—
Transit Bus	0.6	3.3	2	43	0.3
Rail	0.8	1.3	1	24[f]	0.8
Air[c]	0.2	40	8	341	0.4[h]
Bicycle	86.0	1.4[g]	40[i]	40	[j]
Pedestrian	250.0	0.07	17	17	[j]

Notes:
a. Considers fleets of 4 or more vehicles. Average commute occupancy equals 1.15 passengers per vehicle.
b. Personal passenger trucks only.
c. Certificated route air carriers and general aviation; general aviation aircraft *only* for number of vehicles.
d. Calculated assuming 75% of all light trucks used as personal passenger vehicles, based on 1982 data that 73% of all light trucks do not carry freight.
e. Estimated by calculation, wide range in this category—18 to 27 thousand miles/vehicle.
f. Comprised of: Amtrak, 5.4 billion pass-mi; light and heavy rail , 11.6 billion pass-mi; commuter rail, 6.8 billion pass-mi.
g. Assumes 3 miles one way and 240 days per year.
h. Based on aircraft FE of 49 seat miles per gallon, divided by 125 seats/aircraft.
i. Calculated by 2.7 million bicycle commuters @ 1,400 miles annually plus 20 million recreation cyclists @ 1,600 miles annually.
j. Bicyclist uses an average of 35kcal per mile of food energy and pedestrian uses 100kcal per mile.

Sources: UCS estimates; Davis (ORNL) 1989; Ross 1989; League of American Wheelmen 1989.

How Goods Are Shipped

Virtually everything Americans purchase requires commercial transporting. Goods move via five principal means: truck, rail, water, pipeline, and air. Railroads and water vessels each haul more tons of freight over more miles than any other vehicles. Of the three trillion ton-miles moved between US cities in 1987 (a ton-mile, as the term suggests, is one ton moved one mile), rail and water vessels together accounted equally for 60 percent of the total, while trucks and pipelines represented the remaining 40 percent. Although air freight is growing rapidly, it still accounts for less than 1 percent of all shipments by weight (Figure 5).

Railroads primarily move coal, grain, and chemicals, while water vessels handle mainly petroleum and petroleum products, sand and gravel, and coal. Trucks haul a wide array of payloads, from gasoline to lumber to food products. Pipelines carry crude oil, coal slurry, and water, and airplanes move mail and other express freight.

Freight activity increased an average of 1.7 percent annually from 1972 to 1985 (Ross 1989). Trucking represents a significant portion of this increase, due in part to deregulation and changes in business practices. In 1980 the trucking industry was deregulated (along with the railroads),[1] resulting in expanded trucking service—a 66-percent increase in trucking companies after six years of deregulation (Thompson and Sek 1989, GAO 1989a). Moreover, trucking benefited from changes in the way business and industry handle inventory and production. The trend is now toward smaller inventories, delivered more frequently and in smaller lots. These "just-in-time" deliveries offer customers greater

Figure 5	**Tonnage Hauled Transporting Freight**

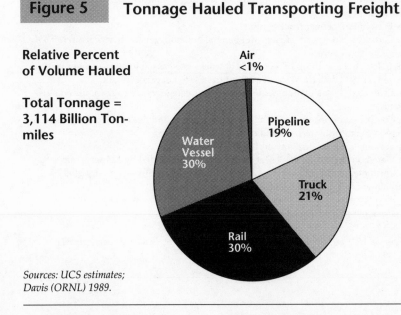

Relative Percent of Volume Hauled

Total Tonnage = 3,114 Billion Ton-miles

Air <1%

Pipeline 19%

Water Vessel 30%

Truck 21%

Rail 30%

Sources: UCS estimates;
Davis (ORNL) 1989.

flexibility, but at a cost of more traffic congestion, higher fuel consumption, and more pollution (Hillsman and Southworth 1990).

Of all freight modes, trucks have the greatest impact on the operating efficiency of the transportation system. Pipelines, ships, aircraft, and rail are isolated from the hub of most transport activities, which is primarily on the roads. Trucks, on the other hand, contend for what little precious space is available on roadways.

How Congestion Affects the Transportation Network

Congestion on our streets, highways, and in airports is bad and getting worse at an alarming rate. Not only does congestion cut transportation operating efficiency, it is also costly: overcrowded roads and airports waste time and energy, generate extra pollution, harm human health, and damage the economy. The Federal Highway Administration (FHWA) estimates that congestion wastes 1.4 billion gallons of fuel annually, 2 percent of the energy currently used for highway passenger transport, and the US Department of Transportation estimates that congestion costs each driver $375 annually in extra fuel and maintenance expenses (Lomax et al. 1989). According to an FHWA estimate, in just three years, between 1985 and 1988, traffic delays from road congestion increased by 57 percent (GAO 1989b). By 1987 nearly two-thirds of all interstate roads in urban areas were congested during peak travel times. And the skies are crowded too. The Federal Aviation Administration (FAA) currently considers 16 airports to be congested (operating at over 160 percent of capacity).

Congestion is extremely destructive to the environment. The inefficient operation it causes—reduced speed, frequent acceleration, stop-and-go movement, and longer trips—increases air pollution and greenhouse-gas emissions. For example, carbon dioxide emissions double when average speed drops from 30 to 10 mph, and hydrocarbon and carbon monoxide emissions triple at speeds of less than 35 mph compared with a constant speed of 55 mph (CEC 1990).

Traffic congestion is a health hazard. High carbon monoxide concentrations on crowded roads, for example, can restrict oxygen flow to the brain of a driver sitting in traffic, impairing driving performance (GAO 1989a). Exposure to ozone can cause chest tightness, coughing, headaches, and nausea as well as pulmonary disease, heart disease, and cancer. Aggressive behavior and physiological reactions have also been linked to exposure to congested traffic conditions (GAO 1989a).

Congestion also jeopardizes US economic vitality. Because it increases the number of accidents, it results in higher labor and vehicle operating costs, also triggering rises in insurance rates. As it slows transport of people and freight, congestion reduces overall productivity, thereby increasing the cost of doing business. By some estimates, crowding on our highways is responsible for a loss of $73 billion a year to the nation's economy, or 2 percent of GNP (Rowand 1989).

THE ROLE OF THE WORK COMMUTE. Although less than one-third of all local miles traveled are work-related, the worst congestion often occurs during commuting hours (Lowry 1988). The average commute is five miles, one way, at 30 miles per hour (Davis et al. 1989).[2] In 1983, 75 percent of commuters traveled alone to work in cars and light trucks and vans, 15 percent carpooled, and only 5 percent used public transit; the remainder bicycled, walked, or worked at home (Figure 6). But national figures for transit ridership can be deceiving because they dilute transit's actual effectiveness by averaging ridership over the entire nation rather than emphasizing transit's role in metropolitan areas, where it operates best. Cities carry from 25 percent (Denver) to 88 percent (New York City) of their commuters in mass transit, dramatically reducing the energy and environmental impacts of commuting (AASHTO 1988).

Many coastal metropolitan areas offer ferries or other water vessels for commutes between downtown and suburbs. Because they are not slowed by road congestion, ferries can have high operating efficiencies. And they offer passengers an attractive alternative to driving.

Figure 6	Auto Reliance and Commuting

Passenger-transport modes used for commuting, 1983.

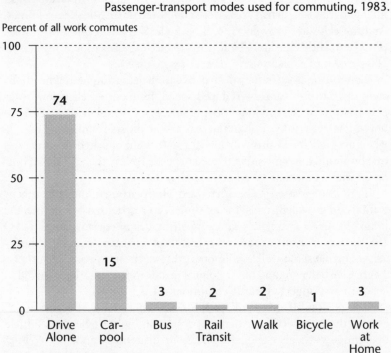

Percent of all work commutes

Source: Ferguson, Transportation Research Board, Paper No. 890769, January 1990.

THE ROLE OF HEAVY TRUCKS. While every vehicle on the road helps produce congestion, heavy-duty trucks contribute more than their share. They account for only 12 percent of total highway traffic in urban areas, but increasingly cause significant delays. Part of the reason is that trucks have gotten bigger and heavier since deregulation, and many roads have not been upgraded to handle them. So while the number of highway accidents involving passenger cars declined over the past decade, the number involving heavy trucks increased (DOT 1987a, GAO 1989a).

But trucking is also a victim of traffic congestion. According to the FHWA, economic losses of commercial shipments due to congestion range from $19 to $23 billion a year, not including many incidental costs to industry (GAO 1989a).

How Much Energy Is Used for Transportation

Transportation consumes roughly 13 million barrels of oil a day. This is nearly three-quarters of US petroleum use and two-fifths of all the energy used in the United States each year (Figure 7). About two-thirds of the energy that transportation consumes is used directly, as fuel burned in vehicles, and one-third is used indirectly, building and maintaining roads and vehicles and producing the fuel itself (EIA 1990a, Casler and Hannon 1989).

Unlike other sectors of the economy, which depend on a variety of fuels, transportation runs almost exclusively—over 97 percent—on oil (Figure 8) (Davis et al. 1989). Since 1975, the United States has consumed more oil for transportation (both directly and indirectly) than it produces. In 1990 the ratio was 7.5 million barrels a day produced domestically versus 12.2 million barrels a day used for transportation (Figure 9).[3] This shortfall offers one explanation for the US's quick militarization of the Middle East when oil imports were involved.

DIRECT ENERGY USE. Energy used directly for transportation is often analyzed according to where vehicles travel (highway or nonhighway) and what they carry (passengers or payload). By the first measure, highway travel accounts for 74 percent of transportation energy use, nonhighway transport (air, water, rail, and pipeline) accounts for 20 percent, and 6 percent is split between off-highway (heavy-duty construction and farm vehicles) and military operations. By the second measure, passenger transportation accounts for 62 percent of direct transportation energy use, freight accounts for 35 percent, and 3 percent is used for military operations (Davis et al. 1989). By either measure, cars consume the lion's share of energy (Figure 10).

While cars and light trucks each use more energy than aircraft, the growing demand for commercial air travel has led to ever greater jet-fuel consumption. Even with a doubling of aircraft energy efficiency since 1970, energy use by commercial air carriers has grown 2 percent annually (Greene 1989). Today, passenger air travel accounts for an estimated 8

Figure 7	**Petroleum and Energy Used by All US Sectors**

Comparison of total petroleum and energy consumption in 1989.

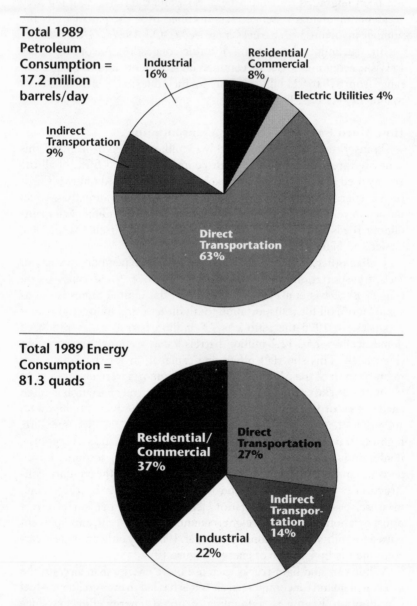

Total 1989 Petroleum Consumption = 17.2 million barrels/day

Industrial 16%

Residential/ Commercial 8%

Electric Utilities 4%

Indirect Transportation 9%

Direct Transportation 63%

Total 1989 Energy Consumption = 81.3 quads

Residential/ Commercial 37%

Direct Transportation 27%

Indirect Transportation 14%

Industrial 22%

Sources: UCS estimates; EIA, Monthly Energy Review, *January 1990; Casler and Hannon,* Journal of Environmental Economics and Management, *Vol. 17, 1989.*

Figure 8	Transportation Sector Petroleum Dependence

Relative use of various fuels for each sector of the US economy, 1989.

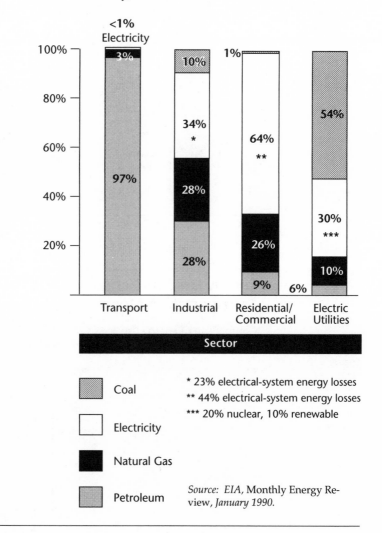

* 23% electrical-system energy losses
** 44% electrical-system energy losses
*** 20% nuclear, 10% renewable

Source: EIA, Monthly Energy Review, *January 1990.*

percent of total transportation fuel use—a 38-percent increase in just five years (Davis et al. 1989, Greene 1989). (See Table 3.)

Of the energy consumed to move freight, the majority is used by trucks. Although they carry only 20 percent of the nation's payload, trucks burn 59 percent of the energy devoted to moving freight (Davis et al. 1989). Water vessels use 14 percent, pipelines 10 percent, and farm

Figure 9	## Domestic Transportation Oil Shortfall

US oil production and transportation consumption, 1973-1990.

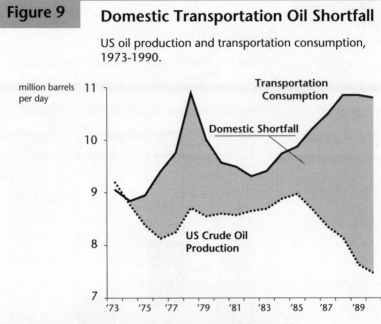

Source: UCS estimates; EIA, Monthly Energy Review, *February 1991.*

Figure 10	## Energy Used by Various Transportation Modes

Comparison of energy use across modes, and relative share of vehicle energy use within modes, 1987.

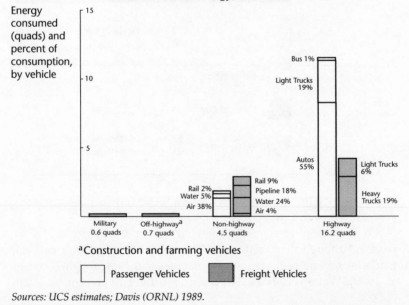

aConstruction and farming vehicles

☐ Passenger Vehicles   ■ Freight Vehicles

Sources: UCS estimates; Davis (ORNL) 1989.

Table 3
Transportation Energy Use by Mode (1987)

Mode & Vehicle	Load[a]	Energy (Quads)	Usage (mbpd)[b]	Percentage of Total
HIGHWAY		16.2	7,658	73.6
Automobiles	p	8.8	4,186	40.3
Motorcycles	p	c	12	0.1
Buses		0.2	74	0.7
Transit	p	0.07	35	0.3
Intercity	p	0.02	10	c
School	p	0.06	29	0.3
Trucks		7.2	3,386	32.6
Light-duty[d]	p/f	4.1	1,904	18.3
Other trucks	f	3.1	1,482	14.3
OFF-HIGHWAY[e]		0.7	314	3.0
Construction	f	0.2	99	1.0
Farming	f	0.5	215	2.0
NON-HIGHWAY		4.5	2,121	20.4
Air	p/f	1.9[f]	895	8.7
Genl. Aviation[g]		0.1	66	0.6
Dom. carrier		1.6	739	7.2
Intl. carrier		0.2[h]	90	0.9
Water		1.3	626	6.0
Domestic Trade	f	0.4	175	1.7
Foreign Trade	f	0.7	342	3.3
Rec. Boats	p	0.2	109	1.0
Pipeline		0.8	366	3.5
Natural Gas	f	0.6	266	2.6
Crude Oil	f	0.09	43	0.4
Oil Products	f	0.07	32	0.3
Coal Slurry	f	c	2	c
Water	f	0.05	23	0.2
Rail		0.5	234	2.2
Freight[i]	f	0.4	197	1.9
Transit	p	0.04	19	0.2
Commuter Train	p	0.02	11	c
Intercity	p	0.02	7	c
MILITARY OPERATION		0.6	306	2.9
Total[j]		**22.0**	**10,399**	**100.0**

Notes:

a. Load considers what the vehicle carries: p=passenger, f=freight.

b. Energy use in thousands of barrels per day of crude oil equivalents based on Btu content of a barrel of crude oil.

c. Negligible amount.

d. Two-axle, four-tire trucks. Note that personal passenger light-duty trucks account for an estimated 2.6 quads; the remainder is used for hauling freight.

e. This considers heavy-duty vehicles. 1985 data.

f. Passenger air travel accounts for an estimated 1.7 quads.

g. All aircraft in the US civil air fleet except those operated under FAR parts 121 and 127 (i.e., air carriers larger than 30 seats and/or a payload capacity of more than 7,500 pounds). General aviation includes air taxis, commuter air carriers, and air travel clubs.

h. This figure represents an estimate of the energy purchased in the US for international air carrier consumption.

i. Includes Class 1,2, and 3 railroads.

j. Totals may not include all possible uses of fuels for transportation (e.g., snowmobiles).

Sources: Davis (ORNL) 1989; Ross, Annual Review of Energy, *1989.*

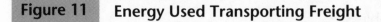

Figure 11   Energy Used Transporting Freight

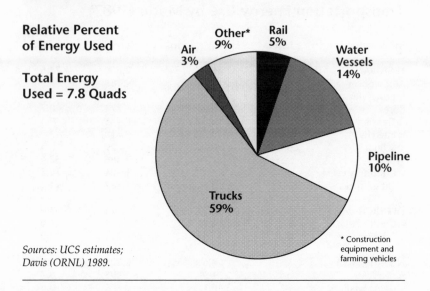

Relative Percent of Energy Used

Total Energy Used = 7.8 Quads

Other* 9%

Rail 5%

Air 3%

Water Vessels 14%

Pipeline 10%

Trucks 59%

Sources: UCS estimates; Davis (ORNL) 1989.

* Construction equipment and farming vehicles

and construction equipment 9 percent. Rail, although it moves one-third of US freight, accounts for a scant 5 percent of energy consumption. Airplanes use the remaining 3 percent (Figure 11). From 1972 to 1985, energy used for freight transportation increased at a rate of only 0.5 percent per year due to improvements in energy efficiency.

The two principal factors that determine direct transportation energy use are vehicle energy intensity and the number of vehicles in use (see How Americans Travel, above). Energy intensity is a measure of the amount of energy required to carry a payload (passenger or freight) one mile.[4] It is determined largely by the particular vehicle's design and to a lesser extent by how well it is maintained and operated. Generally, cars and light trucks are the most energy-intensive forms of passenger travel, and alternatives such as vanpools and rail transit are the least energy-intensive. Heavy trucks are the most energy-intensive freight hauler, using more than four times as much energy to move a ton of freight over a mile as both rail and water vessels. Pipelines are difficult to compare to other modes because pipeline energy intensities vary widely depending on what the pipeline is carrying (Table 4).

Since 1970, the energy intensities of nearly all transportation vehicles have decreased as a result of greater operating efficiency. Aircraft lead the way with the largest efficiency gains. Transit buses and rail are the only modes whose energy intensities increased during this period—i.e., their efficiencies went down—but this was due more to decreases in ridership rather than to inefficient vehicle design (Figure 12).

Table 4
US Passenger and Domestic Intercity Freight Energy Intensities (1989)

Transport Mode		Average vehicle occupancy	Btu per vehicle-mile	Btu per passenger-mile[a]
PASSENGER				
Automobile	All travel	1.7	6,530	3,841
	Commute	1.15	8,333[b]	7,246
	Carpool	2.2	8,333[b]	3,788
	Solo Commute	1	8,333[b]	8,333
Motorcycle	All travel	1.1	2,496	2,269
Personal Truck/Van	All travel	1.9	9,048	4,762
	Commute	1.15	9,615[c]	8,361
	Vanpool	10.9	9,615[c]	882
	Solo Commute	1	9,615[c]	9,615
Transit Rail	All travel	22.8	80,550	3,534
	Commute	50.0[d]	89,500[e]	1,790
Commuter Rail	All travel	36.1	113,228	3,138
	Commute	65.0[d]	125,809[e]	1,935
Intercity Rail (Amtrak)	All travel	20.5	52,107	2,537
	Commute	50.0[d]	57,318[e]	1,146
Transit Bus	All travel	10.2	38,557	3,761
	Commute	20.0[d]	42,413[e]	2,121
Intercity Bus	All travel	21.5	20,176	939
Air[f]	All travel	61.6	430,648	6,991
	Commute	100[d]	473,712[e]	4,737
Bicycle	All travel	1	140	140
Walk	All travel	—	300	300
FREIGHT			(Btu/ton-mile)	
Truck			1,898	
Water Vessel			402	
Pipeline[g]			270-2,765	
Train			443	
Aircraft			n/a	

Notes:
a. Btu per passenger-mile were calculated by dividing Btu per vehicle-mile by the average vehicle occupancy rate.
b. Assumes an average passenger car fuel efficiency of 15 mpg rather than 19 mpg during commute periods due to decreased efficiency from slower speeds and increased idling.
c. Assumes passenger van/light truck efficiency of 13 mpg during commute periods.
d. Assumes that load factors during commutes are approximately double average load factors.
e. Assumes that fuel efficiency decreases 10 percent due to heavier loads and increased idling time.
f. Commercial airlines only (1988 data).
g. Very wide range of pipeline energy intensity: 270 Btu/ton-mile for crude oil to 2,765 Btu/ton-mile for coal slurry.

Sources: UCS estimates; Davis (ORNL) 1989; Komanoff 1990; and National Academy of Science 1991.

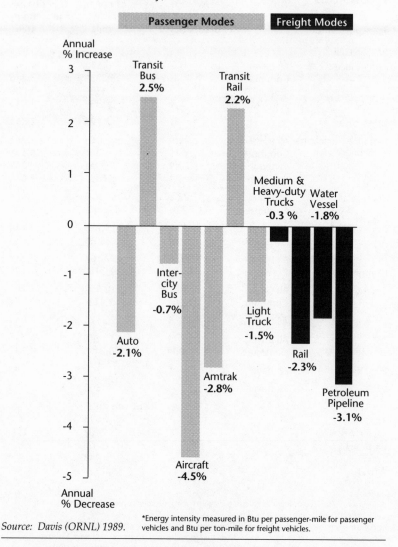

| Figure 12 | **Trends in Vehicle Energy Intensity*** |

Annual percent change in vehicle energy intensity, 1970-1987.

Source: Davis (ORNL) 1989.

*Energy intensity measured in Btu per passenger-mile for passenger vehicles and Btu per ton-mile for freight vehicles.

The number of vehicles on the road and how they are operated also affect direct transportation energy use. As the number of vehicles increases (to the point where the infrastructure is congested), efficiency of operation drops; this commonly occurs during the work commute. Stop-and-go traffic and speeds under 30 mph reduce both road and vehicle efficiency, using more energy. Consequently, the work commute, which accounts for at most 15 percent of total travel time,

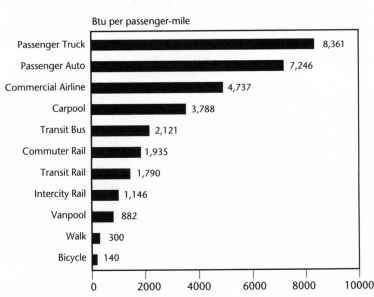

Figure 13 **Energy Use by Vehicle for Commuting**

Relative energy intensity of passenger commute vehicles, 1987.

Btu per passenger-mile

Vehicle	Btu per passenger-mile
Passenger Truck	8,361
Passenger Auto	7,246
Commercial Airline	4,737
Carpool	3,788
Transit Bus	2,121
Commuter Rail	1,935
Transit Rail	1,790
Intercity Rail	1,146
Vanpool	882
Walk	300
Bicycle	140

Source: UCS (see Table 4 for sources and assumptions).

consumes a full one-third of the energy used for passenger travel.[5] The average commuter driving a car or truck uses twice as much energy as she would if carpooling and four times as much energy as she would if riding mass transit. Vanpools, bicycles, and walking are by far the most energy-efficient means of commuting (Figure 13).

INDIRECT ENERGY USE. The transportation sector consumes energy indirectly—producing fuels, building and maintaining infrastructure, manufacturing and repairing vehicles, and carrying on related support activities. One-third of total transportation energy (14 percent of all US energy) is consumed in these activities.

Extracting and refining crude oil to make transportation fuels uses significant amounts of energy. Additional energy is expended distributing fuels throughout the market. For every barrel of oil used directly for transportation, about a quarter of a barrel is required to produce, refine, and distribute that oil.[6]

Building and maintaining roads and other transportation infrastructure is another substantial indirect energy expenditure,[7] as is motor-vehicle manufacturing and repair.[8] Other transportation activities, such as aircraft manufacture and parts supply, and water, pipeline, and rail transport also use energy indirectly.[9]

How We Pay for the Transportation System

Transportation activities consume nearly 20 percent of GNP, more than $700 billion a year (Casler and Hannon 1989, Davis et al. 1989).[10] Of this amount, less is spent on local mass transit than any other transportation activity. The disparity is particularly noticeable between road and transit expenditures: new road construction receives 14 times more than new transit construction, and road repair and maintenance receives 28 times more than transit maintenance.

Where do the funds to build and maintain roads come from? Consumers pay user fees, including taxes on gasoline and other fuels, into the Highway Trust Fund (see box). Receipts from the fund covered about half of the money spent on road construction and maintenance in 1985; the remainder was paid for by state and local governments.

How these funds are spent is determined by Congress, which reauthorizes the trust fund every three to five years. An estimated $200 billion will be spent for surface transportation over the rest of the decade. As in the past, far more will be slated for roads than for mass transit.

Similarly, fuel taxes are levied on aviation fuels, and a 10-percent ticket tax is collected each time an airline ticket is purchased. These revenues go into the Aviation Trust Fund, which is reauthorized by Congress every other year.

It is clear that the costs of building, maintaining, and supporting our auto-based transportation network cannot be met by current federal taxes alone. The abundant subsidies for roads—over and above fuel-tax revenues—not only prove this but also dispel the myth that automobiles "pay their own way" while transit requires taxpayer subsidization (ATA 1988). All transportation services, highways and mass-transit systems alike, require subsidies.

The highest subsidies go to highways and heavy-rail systems, which are generally the most expensive options in terms of capital costs. Busways, high-occupancy-vehicle facilities, and light-rail systems are usually more affordable. Light rail and highways can be very expensive to operate, however; operating-and-maintenance (O&M) costs for highways have increased dramatically over the past three decades (Markow et al. 1990).

FUEL COSTS AND AUTO TAXATION. Americans pay less for transportation fuels and vehicle taxes than consumers in other developed countries. Elsewhere, gasoline taxes of 100 to 350 percent are levied, compared to the current US tax of 35 percent (Figure 14). Moreover, unlike the United States, other countries use most of their higher tax receipts for general revenue rather than for further highway expenditures.

The prices of various petroleum products refined for the transportation sector—gasoline, jet fuel, diesel fuel, and railroad diesel—have fluctuated dramatically over the past decade. Price indexes for gasoline and jet fuel depicted in Figure 15 mirror the price trends for other

The Highway Trust Fund

Starting in 1916, the US Treasury furnished grants to the states to help pay for building roads to deliver mail. Forty years later the Highway Trust Fund was created. The fund is an accounting system under the jurisdiction of the Treasury that uses revenues from highway taxes to reimburse state governments for the federal share of money spent on improving the federal highway system.* Congress appropriates amounts that the Federal Highway Administration can spend on the federal highway program each year and sets formulas for apportioning money to the states.

The user fees that support the Highway Trust Fund include:

- a 9.1-cent-per-gallon tax on gasoline and special fuels used in highway vehicles (except gasohol, which is currently taxed at 3 cents per gallon);**
- a 15.1-cent-per-gallon tax on diesel fuel and other special fuels for highway vehicles;***
- a graduated tax on tires over 40 pounds;
- a 12-percent fee at retail price on new trucks and trailers over 33,000 and 26,000 pounds gross vehicle weight, respectively;
- a heavy-vehicle use tax imposed on trucks over 55,000 pounds (gross weight).

From 1956 to 1989, the fund collected about $220 billion, $205 billion of which was allotted to the states as of June 1989. The annual allotment to the states in 1989 was $14 billion. Mass transit has received only $50 billion of these federal funds since the Urban Mass Transportation Administration (UMTA) program began.

The 1956 Revenue Act set an expiration date of 1971, but the fund has been extended several times since. Under present law highway-user taxes dedicated to the fund and expenditures from the fund are scheduled to expire on September 30, 1993. The outlook for the future of the fund is uncertain.

* The IRS maintains a separate Highway Trust Fund account even though highway-user tax revenues are deposited along with all other receipts in the US Treasury.

** The 1982 Surface Transportation Assistance Act allowed one cent of the gasoline tax to be dedicated to mass-transit use only. The Budget Reconciliation Bill of 1990 increased the gasoline tax by 5 cents a gallon (half of the increase goes to transportation and half to budget-deficit reduction).

*** Since 1986, the additional one-tenth of a cent on both diesel and gasoline is used for an Underground Storage Tank Trust Fund to clean up leaking underground fuel tanks and is administered by EPA.

Sources: General Accounting Office, Transportation Infrastructure: Federal Efforts to Improve Mobility, *December 1989, and* The Federal Highway Trust Fund, *by the Road Information Program. In* Transportation Research Quarterly, *Vol. 44, No. 1, January 1990.*

Figure 14 Gasoline Prices by Country

Relative share of gasoline taxes to total price, 1988.

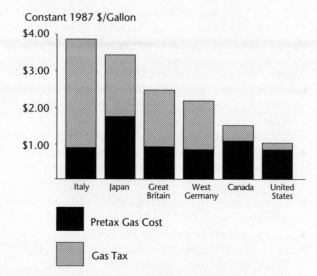

Constant 1987 $/Gallon

Sources: UCS estimates; EIA, International Energy Outlook, *1988; OECD,* Energy Policies and Programmes of IEA Countries: 1988 Review, 1989.

Figure 15 Fluctuating Prices of Transportation Fuels

Fuel prices, excluding taxes, 1978-1990 (estimated), indexed to 1978.

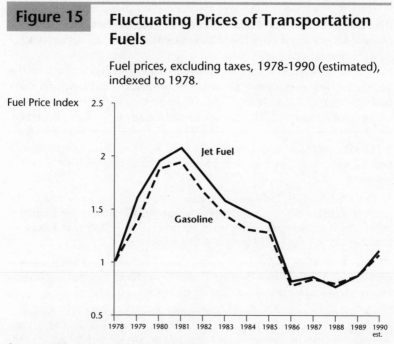

Sources: UCS estimates; Davis (ORNL) 1989.

transportation fuels. The general downward trend for petroleum fuels was reversed (at least temporarily) during the occupation and ensuing war with Iraq. However, Saudi Arabia was able to make up the lost Kuwaiti production during the war, creating a glut in the market once the war was over and restoring cheap gasoline prices.

HIDDEN COSTS OF TRANSPORTATION. The major hidden energy and environmental costs attributed to transportation can be evaluated in monetary terms. These include health-care costs and crop losses attributed to air pollution, costs to militarize the Middle East to protect oil imports, lost economic productivity due to traffic congestion, cleanup costs of oil spills, costs to mitigate greenhouse-gas emissions, and deaths and injuries from traffic accidents. Together the external costs that can be readily valued range from $130 billion to $285 billion a year—as much as $2.50 per gallon of gasoline, or $0.15 per mile driven.[11] Needless to say, none of these "side effect" costs associated with our transportation sector is accounted for in today's price of oil or cost of driving.

Americans pay gasoline (and other fuel) taxes of about $0.34 per gallon, on average. However, these taxes cannot even cover the estimated costs of repairing our crumbling roads and bridges, let alone the hidden social costs of transportation. By some estimates, $95 billion a year would be required to cover all of our infrastructure repair and maintenance costs, the equivalent of a tax of about $0.80 per gallon or $0.05 a mile charged to all motor vehicles.

ALLOCATING HIGHWAY COSTS BETWEEN USERS. If equity were the goal, each vehicle would be charged based on its share of use and the damage it inflicts on the transportation network. However, cars and light trucks are charged at a much higher rate than are heavy trucks and buses. Currently, gasoline taxes on cars and light trucks pay for 72 percent of the cost of repairing and maintaining roads, while heavy trucks cover most of the remaining 28 percent. Yet, on a typical highway, cars and light trucks account for only 45 percent of highway costs, while heavy- and medium-duty trucks account for 53 percent, and buses for 2 percent (Fwa et al. 1990).

Heavy trucks have a disproportionate impact on highway costs compared with other vehicles—up to 100 times greater than the impact of passenger cars (Kitamura et al. 1990a). Moreover, the move to heavier and larger trucks will have even higher system costs.

Future Transportation Trends

ENERGY CONSUMPTION. Direct consumption of petroleum for transportation increased by an average 2.6 percent per year between 1983 and 1989, and today stands at nearly 11 million barrels of oil a day (Figure 16) (EIA 1990a). The Energy Information Administration (EIA) predicts that consumption will rise even faster between 1990 and 2000, from 3.5 to 9 percent annually (EIA 1988). That forecast will prove conservative,

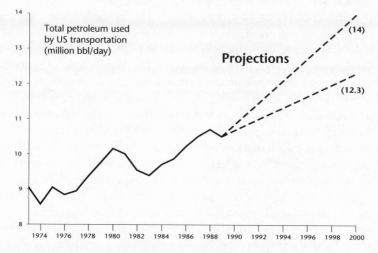

Figure 16   **US Transportation Petroleum Use**

Trends in transportation oil consumption, 1973–2000 (projection).

Sources: UCS estimates; EIA, Annual Energy Review 1988, *May 1989;*
EIA, International Energy Outlook 1989—Projections to 2000, *May 1988.*

however, if the present growth trend continues. Under the current growth scenario, by the year 2000 we would be using 14 million barrels of petroleum a day—a 32-percent leap from 1989 levels—and emitting two billion tons of CO_2 a year, compared with 1.7 billion tons emitted in 1989.

The EIA also predicts that almost all future energy growth will be in petroleum use. Electricity, natural gas, and other alternative fuels *taken together* are expected to comprise less than 1 percent of this projected growth (EIA 1988). While the Clean Air Act Amendments of 1990 will require gasoline reformulations (and therefore replace some oil with alcohols and ethers), natural gas, electricity, and other alternative fuels are not expected to penetrate the market at a significant level until after 2000.

Even as US oil demand continues to rise, domestic oil production will fall. This means that transportation in the United States will be fueled by an increasing proportion of imported oil. By 2000, the average barrel of crude will be 40 percent domestic and 60 percent imported, so that the 14 million barrels a day we will be using for transportation will exceed domestic production levels by 65 percent (Figure 17) (EIA 1988). Even if production incentives keep US production at the current 7 million barrels a day, domestic production will meet only one-half of our transportation oil demands.

More troubling in terms of national security, the US is importing an increasing amount of oil from politically unstable sources, including the Persian Gulf countries and Nigeria (EIA 1990a).[12] These countries

Figure 17 Trends in Oil Use by the Transportation Sector

Relative share of oil used for transportation compared to total US oil use from domestic and imported sources (projected to year 2000).

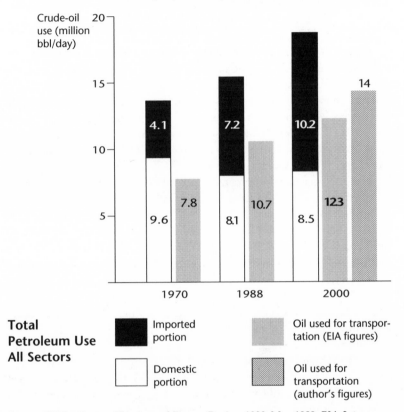

Sources: UCS estimates; EIA, Annual Energy Review 1988, May 1989; EIA, International Energy Outlook 1989—Projections to 2000, *May 1988.*

accounted for one-third of all US oil imports in 1989—up 11 percent from a year earlier (EIA 1990a, EIA 1989).[13]

In August 1990 Iraq invaded Kuwait, triggering the third US oil crisis in less than two decades. By the end of August, the price of crude oil had doubled and gasoline prices had jumped 20 percent. A month after the invasion, the US was planning to spend $33 million a day through Fiscal Year 1991 for a military buildup in the Persian Gulf to protect our future oil interests. Another way of putting it is that the buildup cost the equivalent of an average 40 cents per gallon of imported gasoline.[14] The war with Iraq was costly both in monetary and social terms, and it represents a significant hidden cost of depending on Arab OPEC imports. Furthermore, the cost will be a continuing one, since even if future wars are avoided, the US is expected to maintain a constant military presence in the Middle East.

Yet another aspect of our increasing dependence on foreign oil is the growing trade deficit. According to Department of Commerce calculations, imported oil accounted for 50 percent of the nation's $108-billion trade deficit in 1990. Oil imports now represent a substantially greater portion of the trade deficit than they did just two years ago (roughly 30 percent in 1988 and 40 percent in 1989).

FACTORS AFFECTING FUTURE TRANSPORTATION. As we have seen, despite national security risks and the substantial and growing chunk of the trade deficit attributed to oil imports, oil consumption for transportation is on the rise. In fact, if business-as-usual trends continue, the Department of Energy projects that 70 percent of the oil used in the US will be imported by 2010 (DOE 1991). Several factors will generate the increases:

■ **Americans will drive more than ever, especially in light trucks, vans, and jeeps.** Average light-duty VMT (cars plus light trucks) are expected to increase 43 percent by 2000 (OTA 1989a). A much larger proportion of these miles will be driven in light trucks and vans. According to Automotive News, by 1999 LTVs will dominate the road (Vander Schaaf 1989). This prediction is supported by current trends: light-truck VMT grew at five times the rate of autos between 1970 and 1985, largely because light trucks were used as passenger vehicles rather than freight haulers (Plotkin 1989). This trend is particularly troubling because today's light trucks are 25 percent less fuel efficient than cars, and emit 25 percent more carbon dioxide and 25-35 percent more hydrocarbons, nitrogen oxides, and carbon monoxide (EPA 1989).

But national average projections understate the much greater increases in vehicle use in some cities. Houston and Phoenix, for example, are projected to experience a 4-percent annual VMT growth, while San Diego and Atlanta could experience annual increases of 11 percent (OTA 1989a, Hawthorne 1989). The Department of Energy estimates that by 2010 autos and light trucks alone will account for nearly three trillion vehicle-miles of travel, up from their current 1.7 trillion VMT (Westbrook and Patterson 1989).

■ **The proportion of urban driving will increase, leading to even more congestion on roads.** In 1987 urban travel accounted for 63 percent of all driving; DOE estimates that by 2010 this share will increase to 72 percent (Westbrook and Patterson 1989).[15] Peak-period travel under congested conditions, which accounted for 39 percent of highway travel in 1980, will increase to 62 percent by 2005 (Reno 1988). As urban driving outpaces road capacity in the next century, congestion may increase up to 10-fold.

What these figures mean is that by 2005 the average commuter from one suburb of a metropolitan area to another could spend up to five times as long in traffic as in 1990. This could mean moving at five miles per hour over a 10-mile trip—a two-hour commute. Not only time but fuel would be wasted; the FHWA projects that by 2005, 7.3 billion gallons of fuel will be wasted each year—7 percent of projected oil use for highway passenger transport (GAO 1989a).[16]

■ **Suburban sprawl will continue, further increasing commuting distances and congestion.** Between 1980 and 1986, about 85 percent of the population growth in the United States occurred in metropolitan areas. Three-quarters of this growth occurred in suburbs (OTA 1989a). According to the FHWA, this rate and pattern of growth—much of it totally or substantially unplanned—is expected to continue (DOT 1988a). Such unplanned growth will move jobs farther from homes, increasing commuting distances and congestion.

In the past, the response to unbridled development was to build more roads. However, many local governmental agencies are predicting that not enough highways can be built to accommodate projected growth over the next 30 years. Thus congestion nationwide could increase catastrophically, by up to 1,000 percent in certain areas (Figure 18).

■ **Passenger and freight air travel will boom.** The Federal Aviation Administration forecasts a 63-percent increase in domestic passenger travel by the year 2000. Air-freight transport is expected to increase at an even greater rate. Because of the rapid growth in air traffic, DOE projects that aviation fuel use will more than double, from 1987's 970,000 barrels a day to two million barrels of jet fuel a day by 2010 (Greene 1989). The FAA

Figure 18 **Projected Increases in Nationwide Congestion**

Estimated growth in congestion on all US roads, 1985-2005.

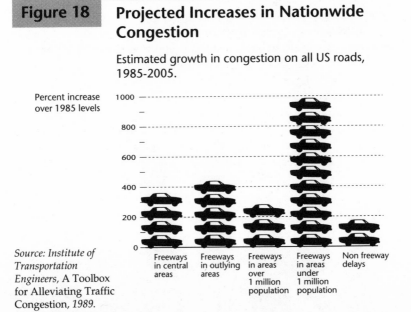

Source: Institute of Transportation Engineers, A Toolbox for Alleviating Traffic Congestion, *1989.*

predicts that airport congestion will triple by 2020, with 42 additional airports operating over capacity if no new airports are built (Owen 1988).[17]

■ **An increasing proportion of freight will be hauled in a less efficient manner.** Manufacturers in many industries are switching to "just-in-time" deliveries to enhance business flexibility by providing inventory more frequently and in smaller lots. This kind of transport relies on aircraft and trucks, which are much more fuel-intensive than rail and water vessels. Thus over the next decade the energy required for freight transportation will increase more than it would have with older methods of transport (Hillsman and Southworth 1990). Additionally, where trucks (especially larger, heavier twin and triple trailers) are used instead of railroads and ships, pollutant emissions and traffic congestion will increase.

Conclusion

The challenge facing Americans is to balance our demands for travel with the availability of energy and our ability to keep our bridges, roads, and airports in good repair. The transportation network cannot expand without regard for financial and physical limits, nor can future growth be allowed to put undue stress on the environment.

The answers to US transportation problems do not lie in expanded construction programs. More than new highways and airports, innovative alternatives are needed. Given the projected increases in miles traveled by personal cars and trucks, heavy trucks, and airplanes, it would be a mistake simply to accept projected demand and attempt to satisfy it. Doing so will force a high price on the nation in increased smog, acid rain, greenhouse-gas emissions, traffic congestion, a rising trade deficit, reduced economic competitiveness, and greater security risks. To avert these consequences, policymakers can apply a range of alternative transportation strategies aimed at modifying anticipated demand. In the long run, this will prove more efficient and cost-effective.

The United States could learn about cost-effective transportation strategies from Europe and Japan, where the high cost of driving has spurred the development of alternatives to the automobile such as mass transit, bicycling, and walking. The next chapter examines the policies that gave rise to these alternatives.

Notes

1.   The Motor Carrier Act of 1980 (P.L. 96-296) led to trucking deregulation, and the Staggers Rail Act of 1980 (P.L. 96-448) led to railroad deregulation.

2.   Figures are for 1983.

3.   Throughout this chapter, EIA 1989 data are used for direct transportation energy use and domestic crude-oil production, and Casler and Hannon 1989 is used for indirect transportation energy consumption, unless otherwise cited.

4.   For passenger modes the measure of energy intensity commonly used is Btu per passenger-mile, and for freight the measure typically is Btu per ton-mile.

5.   Commute travel time is calculated by multiplying five hours of rush hour a day by five days a week, and dividing by 168 hours a week (24 hours a day times seven days a week). Commute oil use is calculated based on an estimated 2.2 million barrels per day of fuel used for daily commuting, divided by energy used for all passenger transportation methods—6.2 million barrels per day.

6.   In 1985, an estimated 64.7 quads of energy was produced in the United States, of which 21.2 quads was petroleum (EIA 1989). The transportation sector uses an estimated two-thirds of this oil directly, or 13.3 quads. Since producing, refining, and distributing domestic petroleum adds another 26 percent to total use, this sector used about 3.4 quads of energy (petroleum) indirectly in 1985. Scaling this figure to 1989 levels, transportation indirectly used on the order of 3.8 quads to produce and distribute petroleum fuel.

7.   In 1985, an estimated 4.8 quads was used for new transportation construction and 1.7 quads was used for maintenance and repairs. In order to estimate the indirect energy used for transportation infrastructure construction and repair, commodity output values were obtained from the US Department of Commerce. Based on 1977 outputs, 5.8 percent of all new construction expenditures was used for new highways and streets and 0.4 percent was used for new local transit facilities, while 9 percent of total repairs and maintenance was spent on highways and streets and 0.3 percent funded local transit facilities (Wendling 1990).

8.   Motor-vehicle manufacturing used three quads of energy indirectly in 1985 and vehicle repair used approximately one quad of energy.

9.   These activities and their SIC (Standard Industrial Classification) codes include aircraft and repair (6000), transportation equipment (6100), railroads (6501), local transport (6502), motor-freight transport (6503), water transport (6504), air transport (6505), pipeline transport (6506), and transportation services (6507). According to Casler and Hannon, 1989, these subsectors used 711, 406, 275, 157, 712, 668, 580, 416, and 31 quads of indirect energy, respectively, in 1985.

10.   Motor-vehicle manufacture and repair constitute the largest expenditures—$187 billion and $94 billion, respectively. Outlays for roads amount to $32 billion for both new construction and repairs, while local transit construction and repairs amount to $2 billion. The cost of petroleum to fuel the sector is estimated at $48 billion. Other transportation costs: air transport, $110 billion; railroads, $38 billion; motor freight, $86 billion; water transport, $43 billion; pipelines, $7 billion. An estimated $55 billion is spent on assorted transportation services and equipment.

11. These external costs assume the following hidden social costs for transportation: $4-93 billion a year in health-care costs attributed to air pollution from motor vehicles; $3-8 billion a year for crop losses due to air pollution; $73 billion a year in lost productivity and $2 billion a year as wasted fuel due to traffic congestion; $20-40 billion annually not compensated by insurance companies as a result of traffic accidents; $15-54 million daily to militarize the Persian Gulf to secure oil imports; $12 billion a year to mitigate the effects of greenhouse-gas emissions; and $2 billion annually for cleanup on each major oil spill (the valuation of actual environmental damage is too difficult to estimate).

Pollution-related health-care costs, economic productivity lost due to congestion, and traffic injuries and fatalities cost society, on average, as much as $0.80, $0.60, and $0.30 per gallon (or $0.05, $0.04, and $0.02 per mile), respectively. Militarizing the Persian Gulf region to protect oil imports costs on the order of $0.40 a gallon ($0.02 per mile), while full-scale war in this region cost the US and its allies half a billion dollars a day, which would dwarf the current price of fuel if it were included in the market price. Greenhouse-gas emissions and oil spills, while important, account for less of the total social costs, an estimated $0.07 per gallon each. (Average oil use and vehicle fleet fuel-economy values were used to convert total costs to "per gallon" and "per mile" figures.)

12. The Persian Gulf countries include Iran, Iraq, Kuwait, Qatar, the United Arab Emirates, and Saudi Arabia. The US did not import any oil from Iran in 1988 and 1989. Average 1990 oil imports from Iraq, Kuwait, and Qatar were 600,000 barrels a day, but no oil was imported from Iraq and Kuwait during the fourth quarter of 1990.

13. Calculated from Energy Information Administration figures.

14. This is based on 2.1 million barrels per day of Arab OPEC oil imports.

15. For regulatory purposes, manufacturers currently calculate composite vehicle fuel efficiency based on an EPA formula using a figure of 55 percent for urban driving; however, the urban share has not been at this level since 1972.

16. This assumes that the 1987 energy use for highway passenger transport of 5.4 million barrels per day (bpd) increases at a rate of 1 percent per year, to 6.5 million bpd in 2005 (using the EIA projected annual increase from 1990 to 2000).

17. The FAA considers an airport congested if it operates on average at more than 160 percent of its capacity.

3 International Transportation

Transportation dilemmas are not ours alone. The growing appetite for energy to provide increased mobility is found the world over. A brief look at transportation abroad—especially at examples of innovative strategies—can help shape US policy for the future.

Transportation systems vary widely. Geography, infrastructure, land-use patterns, travel habits, crime rates, and cultural attitudes all affect transportation patterns. Americans, for example, use their automobiles far more than citizens of other developed countries. But this may not be a reflection of greater affluence; rather, it is more likely due to geography, the lack of coordination between land-use and transportation policies in the United States, and the low taxes on automobiles in the United States (Pucher 1988).

Most developed countries other than the United States depend heavily on public transportation, bicycles, and walking for urban passenger transport. The Swiss and British use public transit for nearly 20 percent of all trips; the Dutch and the Danish use bicycles for 20-30 percent of their trips; Swedes and West Germans prefer to walk, making about a third of all urban trips on foot (Table 5) (Pucher 1988, MCPD 1989). Superior public transit, of course, and better opportunities for walking and bicycling account to some degree for these preferences. But more advanced land-use and transportation planning in these countries makes alternatives to the automobile possible.

Steep tax rates may be another reason citizens of many other countries rely less on automobiles. The average US sales tax on a new midsize car in 1982 was 5 percent, while in other countries it was 25-50 percent (Pucher 1988). And taxes contribute to the much higher cost of petroleum outside the United States. American consumers thus pay four to seven times less to buy and operate their cars than consumers in other nations (Table 6). Moreover, unlike the United States, other countries

Table 5
Modal Split of Urban Passenger Transport, by Country (as Percent of Total Trips)

Country	Auto	Public Transport	Bicycle	Walking	Motorcycle & Moped	Others
			Mode			
United States (1978)	82.3	3.4	0.7	10.7	0.5	2.4
Canada (1980)	74.0	15.0	——————— 11.0 ———————			
West Germany (1978)	47.6	11.4	9.6	30.3	0.9	1.1
Switzerland (1980)	38.2	19.8	9.8	29.0	1.3	1.9
France (1978)	47.0	11.0	5.0	30.0	6.0	1.0
Sweden (1978)	36.0	11.0	10.0	39.0	2.0	2.0
Netherlands (1984)	45.2	4.8	9.4	18.4	1.3	1.0
Italy (1981)	30.6	26.0	——————— 43.4 ———————			
Austria (1987)	38.5	12.8	8.5	31.2	3.7	5.3
Great Britain (1978)	45.0	19.0	4.0	29.0	2.0	1.0
Denmark (1981)	42.0	14.0	20.0	21.0	...	3.0

Source: Pucher, APA Journal, *Autumn 1988.*

use most of their higher tax receipts for general revenue rather than for further highway expenditures.

Modes of Transportation in Europe

BICYCLES AND PEDESTRIANS. The northern European countries provide extensive, coordinated bikeway networks in both urban and rural areas, allowing bicycles to compete with autos for efficient mobility. The Netherlands, Belgium, Denmark, and West Germany build bikeways with right-of-ways that are separate from auto traffic (Pucher 1988). And pedestrian zones in most European cities are coordinated into overall urban development, providing extensive areas in which auto traffic is prohibited. It appears that when bicyclists and pedestrians are safe, as they are in much of Europe, people use these transport modes.

Bicycles also provide important access to public transit throughout Japan and Northern Europe. In the Netherlands the bicycle is a common link to mass transit; 36 percent of Dutch railway passengers and 20 percent of regional bus passengers bicycled to transit in 1981. In a number of West German and Japanese suburbs, bicycles accounted for roughly half of all public-transit access (Replogle 1988). In addition to safer access, these countries encourage bicycle use by providing secure parking facilities at transit stations.

By comparison, the United States has not developed the link between bicycles and public transit. Auto links to transit—"Park & Ride"—are

Table 6
Taxes on Auto Ownership and Use, by Country

Country	Avg. retail gasoline price/gallon (1987)*	Gasoline tax percentage (1987)	Sales tax as % of price for new, medium-sized car (1982)**	Average annual taxation on car (1982)**
United States	0.95	35	5	119
Canada	1.40	56	n.a.	n.a.
West Germany	2.31	138	14	566
Switzerland	2.57	170	8	587
France	3.07	317	33	730
Sweden	2.50	133	41	450
Netherlands	3.03	245	47	825
Belgium	2.61	178	25	606
Italy	3.75	285	22	n.a.
Austria	2.84	150	52	525
Great Britain	2.38	178	25	652
Denmark	3.75	355	186	758

Note: Effective tax rates are shown here both for gasoline and for car purchases. Such rates express tax payments as a percentage of pretax price.
* In 1987 US dollars. ** In 1982 US dollars.

Source: Pucher, APA Journal, *Autumn 1988.*

much more popular in America. But these are much more energy and space intensive and result in more pollution and traffic congestion than bike-and-ride and walk-and-ride connections.

TRAINS. For over a century, rail transit has been an integral part of the geography of Europe, navigating through the hearts of its cities. Rail is especially well suited to a constellation of towns that form relatively high-density clusters separated by only one to three hours' travel time. Some 100 million people live in such a constellation in the large triangle between Paris, London, and the Rhine area. Here rail can serve both passengers and freight better than airplanes and trucks.

European rail is not only better tailored to cater to the area's needs, it is also more efficiently financed than America's. One reason is Europe's long history of continuing rail subsidization. Because maintenance and modernization have received steady funding over the years, European rail systems have averted deterioration. By maintaining their railroads, European countries have benefited from lower annual subsidies than the United States has paid. Switzerland's high-quality transit service, for example, enjoys high ridership with less than one-sixth the per-passenger subsidy of the United States (Pucher 1988).

Moreover, Europe's trains keep pace with new technology. The latest result is the proposed 18,750-mile, high-speed (125-190 mph) network of connecting rail lines to be completed by 2015 (Bouley 1989). The advantage of expanding rail service in Europe is that the infrastructure already exists throughout much of the continent, particularly in the cities. Coordination is the key—all the lines being built are well integrated into the existing network for rapid point-to-point service.

Europe's rail system, developed step by step over many decades, is clearly superior to America's. Trains there provide the fastest service to the most places at the best price, unlike US trains. In fairness, America's greater distances lend themselves better to air travel. But shorter-distance air travel is hardly affordable for most Americans. And trips of less than 750 miles can be costly in terms of delays due to air-traffic congestion. It would be wise for the US to consider a serious commitment to improve its rail system through continued support of Amtrak and investments in a high-speed rail network.

AUTOMOBILES. Europeans have shown a continuing interest in innovative automobiles. In Switzerland, personal electric commuter vehicles (EVs) are catching on as an alternative form of urban transport. A two-seater EV sells for about $16,000 (not including taxes) (NAS 1989). Currently there are about 200 of these EVs on the road. They travel at speeds of 35 mph, accelerate from 0-35 mph in 25 seconds, and have an operating range of 50 miles between electric charges (Blum 1990). For limited urban mobility, these vehicles operate at a lower social cost (less pollution and energy use) than do large, gas-guzzling automobiles.

In order to make EVs more compatible with long-distance commutes, the Swiss government's Agency for Decentralized Energy has established special parking spaces at rail stations that can recharge EVs while owners ride mass transit to work (NAS 1989). At the end of the day, the EVs are ready to travel another 50 miles. Because electricity is generated at some of these central parking locations by solar photovoltaic power, these vehicles can operate completely pollution-free.

The French government is conducting a joint research program with French auto manufacturers on a "green" car. The $200-million program aims to reduce pollution from conventional car engines, study different configurations such as two-stroke engines and gas turbines, research state-of-the-art chemical batteries, and experiment with fuel alternatives including natural gas, hydrogen, electricity, and oxygen.

European Transportation Policies

European advances are not just technology-based; they are also regulatory in nature. In 1988, the Swedish parliament adopted a new transportation-policy act, one important feature of which is that new system user fees are based on explicit valuations of external social costs. Some of these social costs include air pollution, noise, congestion, accidents, road maintenance, travel time, and traffic surveillance. Including these externalities aids in the transportation policymaking process. For

Table 7
Social Marginal Costs of Road Traffic in Sweden (1987)

(US dollars per 100 vehicle-miles; 1987 dollars)	Transport Mode					
	Private Car[1]		Truck		Bus	
Transportation Activity	Rural	Urban	Rural	Urban	Rural	Urban
Road Maintenance[2]	$0.2	$0.2	$7.7	$5.6	$6.7	$4.9
Traffic Surveillance	$0.3	$0.3	$0.3	$0.3	$0.3	$0.3
Congestion (average)	$0.2	$4.3	$1.3	$13.0	$0.5	$13.0
Accidents	$2.7	$9.2	$3.6	$10.9	$3.9	$35.7
Health & Environment	$1.6	$7.0	$6.6	$16.4	$5.6	$39.0

Notes:
1. The social marginal costs are shown for a private car with no catalytic converter (the "costs" for health and environment are $0.2 and $1.2 per 100 miles, respectively, for a car with a catalytic converter).
2. Road maintenance costs are average values for trucks (22.5 ton) and buses (16 ton) and are mean values for different tire and axle combinations.

Source: Hansson, The Swedish Approach to Multi-modal Transportation Planning, *1990.*

fiscal year 1989-90 the government assessed users $3.5 billion to cover the social costs of road vehicles (Hansson 1990).

Specifically, the Swedish government assesses road-user charges—gasoline taxes and distance-based taxes—based on the social marginal costs (i.e., the cost to society of one more vehicle) for use of urban and rural roads (Table 7). In 1989 the responsibility for these costs of urban traffic rested most heavily on trucks and private cars without emission controls. Applying these Swedish valuations of social costs, the US highway fleet causes an estimated $235 billion in damage to our environment, health, and roads as a result of congestion and accidents. Cars and light trucks account for 85 percent of these costs, heavy-duty trucks for 13 percent, and buses for 2 percent.

Europeans are also basing many proposed changes in transportation policy on their concern about global climate change. In the Netherlands the official global-warming policy places heavy emphasis on the transportation sector and has set out to:

■ improve the public transport system (infrastructure, operation, and pricing)

■ target high-speed rail as an alternative to air transport

■ introduce "automobile-kilometer-reduction plans" for business and other institutions

■ improve bicycle facilities (separate lanes/bike paths and bike-parking facilities near railway stations)

Table 8
Petroleum Used for Transportation, by Country (1986)

Country	Transport as a % of Total	Total Transport Petroleum Use (million gallons)	Gasoline (million gallons)	Percentage Gasoline of All Transport Use
United States	67.1%	133,478	89,408	67%
Canada	56.5%	10,988	7,434	68%
France	45.8%	10,587	5,677	54%
Italy	45.6%	8,392	3,533	42%
Sweden	41.3%	2,004	1,215	61%
Great Britain	59.3%	11,288	6,610	59%
West Germany	39.0%	12,927	7,532	58%
Japan	37.0%	16,942	8,468	50%

Sources: OECD, Energy Statistics 1985-1986; *Davis (ORNL) 1989.*

■ introduce a "road-pricing" system to enable introduction of variable toll rates according to time of day and week
■ shift fixed automobile costs (vehicle registration and usage fee) to variable costs (fuel, parking, tolls)
■ reduce tax breaks for auto commuters
■ use zoning regulations to coordinate building locations with public transit infrastructure.
The Dutch government estimates that annual expenditures for all of these transportation programs will be roughly $350 million in 1994 (in then-current dollars) (Metz 1990).

Conclusion
Americans use far more transportation energy than any other country—on the order of 10 times more than Japan, Western Europe, and Canada. Our transportation sector accounts for two-thirds of our petroleum consumption, while most other industrialized countries dedicate less than half their petroleum use to transportation (Table 8) (OECD 1988b).

One result of our inordinately high use of petroleum is that the US transportation sector alone emits more carbon dioxide than many other countries emit in total (Figure 19). In the next chapter, these carbon dioxide and other transportation emissions are evaluated.

Figure 19   Carbon Emissions from Fossil Fuels, by Region

Comparison of carbon emissions in selected regions worldwide to US transportation carbon emissions, 1985.

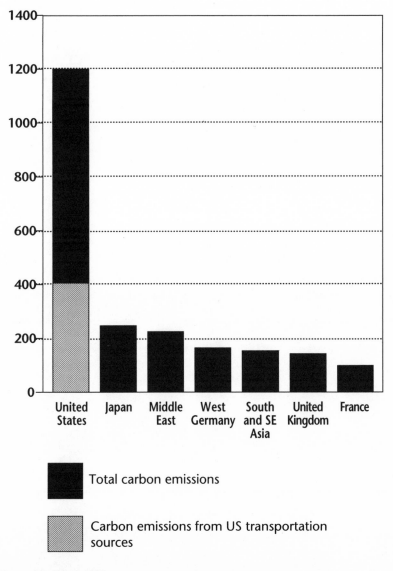

Million tons of carbon per year

Total carbon emissions

Carbon emissions from US transportation sources

Source: MacKenzie 1989.

4 Greenhouse Gases and Other Air Pollutants

The US Senate Committee on Environment and Public Works, following much testimony on the Clean Air Act, reported that "most experts agree that if we do not change our pattern of polluting the atmosphere, many of us, our children, and our grandchildren will experience devastating climate changes of a magnitude and at a rate that will preclude natural evolutionary responses" (Senate 1989). Greenhouse-gas emissions and other air pollutants from transportation play a major role in this prediction.

The greenhouse effect occurs when gases in the atmosphere—carbon dioxide (CO_2) and others—trap heat and keep the Earth warm. Without this naturally occurring atmospheric blanket, the Earth would be some 35 degrees Centigrade colder, making life impossible. However, it is widely believed that human activities are adding to the concentration of greenhouse gases, amplifying the greenhouse effect and causing the Earth's temperature to rise beyond its natural level.

Climatologists project that increased emissions of greenhouse gases will lead to changes in precipitation, ocean currents, and seasonal weather patterns. Storm patterns could be altered and soil moisture reduced, resulting in agricultural dislocations and economic hardship. Coastlines could be eroded by rising sea levels, valuable wetlands destroyed, and water resources contaminated by saltwater intrusion. These changes could lead to the extinction of animal and plant species (Senate 1989).

The six principal man-made gases that are known contributors to the greenhouse effect are carbon dioxide, chlorofluorocarbons (CFCs), methane (CH_4), nitrous oxide (N_2O), carbon monoxide (CO), and ozone (O_3). Carbon dioxide is the principal greenhouse gas, contributing half of the effect of all man-made greenhouse gases (Figure 20) (Rind 1989).

Figure 20	Human Contributions to the Greenhouse Effect

Relative share of man-made greenhouse emissions, 1988.

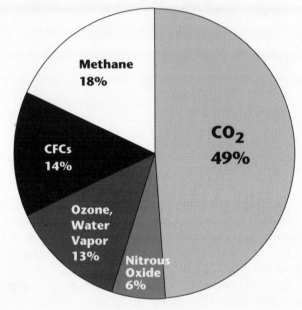

Source: EPA, "The Greenhouse Effect: How It Can Change Our Lives," EPA Journal, Vol. 15, No. 1, Jan./Feb. 1989.

In addition, many of the same pollutants that contribute to the greenhouse effect are also principal causes of smog, acid·rain, depletion of the ozone layer, and other air-pollution problems. Complex chemical reactions transform emissions of hydrocarbon (HC), nitrogen oxides (NO_x), and carbon monoxide from sources that burn fossil fuels into a whitish haze (smog), a yellowish-brown cloud (principally NO_x), and acid rain (nitric and sulfuric acids).

Our transportation system is responsible both directly for emissions from vehicle tailpipes and indirectly for emissions associated with fuel extraction, refining and distribution, infrastructure construction, and vehicle manufacturing. Emissions due to direct combustion of transportation fuels are the focus of the discussion below (Figure 21). Where available, indirect emissions are presented.

Carbon Dioxide

Although CO_2 does not have as much heat-trapping ability as the other greenhouse gases, more of it is emitted into the atmosphere than

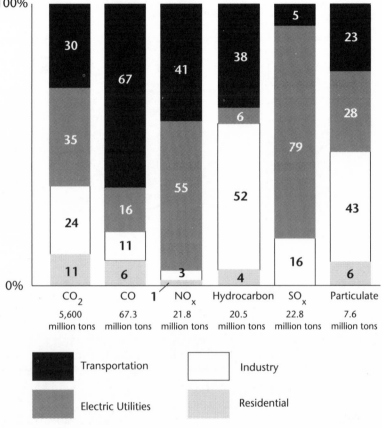

Figure 21 Air Pollution by Source

Proportion of US air emissions from each economic sector, 1988.

Relative share of emissions by sector

CO$_2$	CO	NO$_x$	Hydrocarbon	SO$_x$	Particulate
5,600 million tons	67.3 million tons	21.8 million tons	20.5 million tons	22.8 million tons	7.6 million tons

■ Transportation   □ Industry

▓ Electric Utilities   ▒ Residential

Sources: UCS estimates; EPA 1990.

any other greenhouse gas. Like all other CO$_2$ emissions, those attributable to transportation are increasing—17 percent between 1982 and 1987 (Figure 22). Moreover, business-as-usual trends indicate that these emissions will continue to climb unless effective transportation and land-use policies are implemented.

Based only on the direct energy used by all US transportation sources, this sector emitted about 1.7 billion tons of carbon dioxide in 1988 (Table 9). By 2000, CO$_2$ emissions from this sector are expected to increase to 1.9-2.2 billion tons annually.

Automobiles and trucks are the two largest sources of CO$_2$ emissions. Cars and trucks together were responsible for 20 percent of total US

Figure 22   CO₂ Emissions from US Transportation Activities

Trends in carbon dioxide emissions from the transportation sector, projected to year 2000.

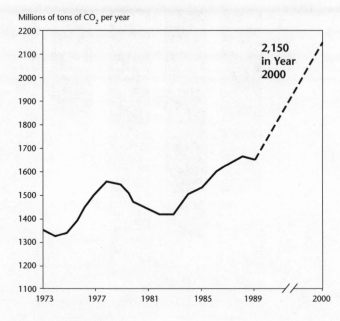

Sources: UCS estimates; MacKenzie 1989.

emissions in 1988 (OTA 1989a). Airplanes, ships, pipelines, and railroads contributed lesser amounts.[1] Emissions result not only from direct end-use combustion but also from fuel extraction, processing, refining, and distribution. These ancillary sources are estimated to account for an additional 14 percent of CO_2 emissions above direct emissions (DeLuchi et al. 1989a, OTA 1990).[2]

Chlorofluorocarbons (CFCs)

CFCs are man-made chemicals available in assorted forms—solvents, foams, refrigerants, aerosols, and air-conditioning coolants. These chemicals are the most potent of the greenhouse gases; each molecule of CFC-12 has 20,000 times more capability to retain infrared radiation than does a molecule of carbon dioxide (OECD 1989). CFCs are responsible for two distinct but closely related global environmental problems: destruction of the upper ozone layer, which shields the earth against harmful ultraviolet radiation, and global climate change.

Automobile air-conditioning units, which use mainly CFC-12, account for about a quarter of CFC use in the United States (Senate 1989,

Table 9
Transportation Sector Carbon Dioxide Emissions (1988)

Refined Product Used By Transportation	Fuel Used (million barrels per day)	Energy (quads)	CO₂ Emission Factor (lb/gallon)	Million Tons CO₂/yr
Motor gasoline	7.15	13.74	19.7	1,080
Distillate fuel oil (Diesel)	1.65	3.53	21.6*	270
Jet fuel	1.45	2.98	19.7	220
Residual fuel oil	0.33	0.75	23.4*	60
Aviation gasoline	0.03	0.05	17.7	6
Liquefied petroleum gases	0.03	0.04	13.0*	3
Lubricants	0.08	0.17	n/a	n/a
TOTAL	10.71	21.26		1,640+

*Estimated using approximation of molecular weight of fuel.

Sources: UCS estimates; EIA, Annual Energy Review 1988, *May 1989.*

Doniger 1990).[3] The entire charge of CFC-12 in an auto's air conditioner is released over the vehicle's lifetime—50 percent escapes during servicing, 30 percent through routine leakage, and the remaining 20 percent escapes during vehicle scrappage.

Two other CFCs are often used in vehicle manufacturing, CFC-11 and CFC-113. CFC-11 is used as a blowing agent to produce foam products such as seats, and CFC-113 is used as a solvent for degreasing parts and cleaning electronic components and fuel injectors. Like CFC-12, these CFCs have formidable heat-trapping qualities. General Motors is working on developing processes that will either recover and recycle or eliminate these CFC emissions altogether during vehicle manufacturing (Postma 1990).

As early as 1978, the US started reducing its CFC production and consumption (which now accounts for about 700 million pounds a year—one-third of the world total in 1989) by banning the use of CFCs in aerosol cans (OECD 1989). As of January 1989, the 1987 Montreal Protocol on Substances that Deplete the Ozone Layer had been signed by 50 nations, including the United States. The protocol required industrialized nations to limit CFC consumption in 1989, to reduce CFC use 50 percent by 1998, and to limit halogenated hydrocarbon use starting in 1992.[4]

In June 1990, environmental ministers from 93 nations (including the US) agreed at a landmark meeting to phase out the production and use of CFCs by the end of the century. The accord is thought to have strengthened the Montreal Protocol. In addition, a new fund was created to help poor nations change their technology to one based on chlorine-free compounds.

Methane

Methane is another potent greenhouse gas, trapping heat 25 times as effectively as carbon dioxide (OECD 1989). Principal transportation sources of methane include natural-gas pipelines as well as releases during the production and processing of petroleum fuels. Over half (57 percent) of the natural-gas emissions in the United States in 1989 were a result of producing petroleum for the transportation sector (DeLuchi et al. 1989a).[5]

However, transportation activities are responsible for more methane emissions indirectly than directly. Carbon monoxide has been found to increase methane concentrations (EPA 1987). Since the transportation sector accounts for the majority of US CO emissions, this sector is largely responsible for the buildup of methane concentration. While increases in CO concentrations on the order of 5 percent per year have been measured in the US and 1-2 percent per year in the USSR, global changes in CO concentrations are difficult to measure accurately, given the spatial and temporal variability of CO (EPA 1987).

Methane emissions are not regulated by the federal government; instead methane is considered part of total hydrocarbon emissions. The Clean Air Act makes the distinction between nonmethane hydrocarbons (also referred to as reactive hydrocarbons) and total hydrocarbons, which include methane. Methane was not regulated in the past because it was considered inert and nonreactive.

Carbon Monoxide

Carbon monoxide, a gas formed as a by-product during the incomplete combustion of all fossil fuels, is an air pollutant in its own right and is also implicated in the formation of smog. CO is not itself a greenhouse gas, although it does contribute to methane buildup and therefore indirectly contributes to greenhouse-gas emissions (EPA 1987).[6] Exposure to this odorless and colorless gas can cause headaches and place additional stress on anyone exposed—drivers, passengers, pedestrians—who has heart disease.

The transportation sector is the primary source of CO emissions. Cars alone can account for up to 80 percent of ambient CO emissions in local hotspots where cars sit and idle (such as in traffic congestion); the transportation sector nationwide accounts for two-thirds of US CO emissions (GAO 1989a, EPA 1990).[7] Electric utilities and industrial processes that burn fossil fuels make up most of the remaining CO emissions nationwide (Figure 21).

In 1988, 44 metropolitan areas in the United States failed to meet the federal CO air-quality standard (EPA 1990). The health-based CO standard specifies upper limits of 9 parts per million (ppm) CO and 35 ppm CO for the one-hour and eight-hour averages that are not to be exceeded more than once a year (EPA 1990). Furthermore, despite recent improvements, air quality is expected to worsen by the mid-1990s because of growing congestion, an increase in the number of vehicles, an increase in vehicle miles traveled, and slower vehicle turnover (Gushee and Sieg-Ross 1988, Hawthorne 1988). The increase in VMT alone will likely cancel out any improvements in air quality that result from better emission controls. In fact, CO emissions are projected to increase by up to 30 percent in the next two decades (Senate 1989).

Oxides of Nitrogen and Nitrous Oxide

Two oxides of nitrogen—nitrogen dioxide (NO_2) and nitric oxide (NO)—are formed in a combustion engine when air is used for burning fuel. Because air is 79 percent nitrogen, some of the nitrogen in the air oxidizes along with the fuel, forming oxides of nitrogen (NO_x). Over 90 percent of these emissions are in the form of NO.

Oxides of nitrogen are one of the six principal pollutants (known as "criteria" pollutants) regulated under the Clean Air Act. NO_2 is characterized by the yellowish-brown cloud that looms over many city skylines, while NO is colorless. Nitrogen oxides can irritate the lungs, cause bronchitis and pneumonia, and lower resistance to respiratory infections. These pollutants also lead to the formation of smog, and are chemical precursors to a known greenhouse gas—ozone. In 1988 over 40 percent of US emissions of NO_x came from the transportation sector (EPA 1990). Moreover, these emissions are responsible for acid rain, which is thought to be destroying forests and acidifying water resources.

Significant reductions in NO_x emissions from cars and light trucks have been achieved since 1970. Even with further controls, however, the benefits of greater reductions are likely to be canceled out by the steady increase in US vehicle miles traveled. Thus, even with a tightening of vehicle tailpipe standards, NO_x emissions are projected to increase by up to 30 percent in the next two decades (Senate 1989).

Nitrous oxide (N_2O), on the other hand, is a known greenhouse gas that comes directly from vehicle exhaust. N_2O emissions are a function of the chemical composition of the fuel as well as the type and age of the vehicle's catalytic converter (DeLuchi et al. 1989a). Nitrous oxide traps heat 250 times more efficiently than does carbon dioxide. Emissions of N_2O from US vehicles in 1985 were less than 2 percent of CO_2-equivalent emissions (DeLuchi et al. 1989a). Automobiles are thus minor contributors of N_2O emissions.

Hydrocarbons

Hydrocarbons (HCs) are a broad class of pollutants made up of hundreds of specific compounds containing the elements carbon and hydrogen. The simplest HC, methane, does not readily react with NO_x to form smog. All other nonmethane HCs (NMHC) react with NO_x to form smog and are often referred to as volatile organic compounds (VOCs) or reactive organic gases (ROGs).

Hydrocarbons are emitted from anthropogenic sources such as auto and truck exhaust, evaporation of gasoline and solvents, and petroleum refining. In some regions, biogenic sources such as vegetation also emit HCs in the summertime.

Highway vehicles alone contribute an estimated 45 percent of total reactive HC emissions nationwide (OTA 1989a). Air, rail, and marine transportation vehicles account for another 6 percent, while the petroleum industry accounts for 5 percent of US HC emissions. In 1988 the transportation sector was responsible for some seven million tons of reactive HCs (EPA 1990).

HCs are emitted from transportation sources two ways: from the tailpipes of cars and trucks in the exhaust formed when gasoline is burned, and when gasoline evaporates from vehicle fuel tanks and gas-station pumps. Roughly 70 percent of these HC emissions comes from tailpipe exhaust, and the remaining 30 percent is released through evaporation (Platte 1990). Evaporative emissions are a function of a fuel's vapor pressure—the lower the vapor pressure (measured as Reid Vapor Pressure, or RVP), the lower the evaporative HC emissions.

Just as improvements in nitrogen oxide emissions will likely be canceled out by an increase in vehicle miles traveled, so will improvements in hydrocarbon emissions. In fact, hydrocarbon emissions are projected to increase by up to 30 percent by 2010 (Senate 1989).

Ozone

The white haze hanging over our dirtiest cities is tropospheric ozone, or smog.[8] This greenhouse gas is not emitted directly into the air; rather, it is formed when ozone precursors, mainly nonmethane hydrocarbons (NMHC) and oxides of nitrogen, react in the presence of heat and sunlight. Exposure to ozone can produce shortness of breath and, over time, permanent lung damage. Ozone may be harmful at levels even lower than the current federal air standard. In addition, ozone can damage crops and reduce their yields.

The primary source of smog is auto exhaust. In 1985, the US transportation sector accounted for nearly one-half of all hydrocarbon and nitrogen oxide emissions (OTA 1989a). As HC and NO_x emissions from motor vehicles increase, so does smog. As smog increases, it will exacerbate global warming, in a continuing cycle. The process works like this: (1) pollutants combine with heat and sunlight to make smog; (2) smog contributes to global warming; (3) more heat means more smog.

More than 100 of our cities are choking on smog (Weisskopf 1990). And roughly half of all Americans live in areas that exceed the ozone standard at least once a year (EPA 1990). In 1988, 317 urban and rural areas in the US earned "non-attainment" classification for ozone because they could not meet federal clean air standards (OTA 1989a).

Sulfur Oxides (SO$_x$)

Emissions of sulfur oxides are the result of oxidization of the available sulfur in a fuel.[9] Sulfur oxides are a health hazard and are important contributors to acid rain. These emissions, however, are primarily linked to power plants that generate electricity with coal.

In 1988, the transportation sector accounted for about one million tons of SO$_x$—only 5 percent of total SO$_x$ emissions in the US (EPA 1990). These emissions could increase significantly, however, if high-sulfur coal is used to produce alternative transportation fuels such as methanol or electricity for electric vehicles in the future.

Total Suspended Particulates (TSP)

Total suspended particulates—or particulate matter—comprise another category of criteria air pollutants. It includes emissions of dust, soot, smoke, and other suspended matter. Particulates are respiratory irritants, and they may be implicated in acid-rain formation.

In 1988, the transportation sector accounted for almost two million tons of TSP—23 percent of the nation's particulate emissions (EPA 1990). Diesel fuels emit more particulates than any other conventional transportation fuel, so the bulk of transportation particulates comes from diesel trucks. Electric trains are responsible for indirect emissions of particulates from power plants that generate electricity. Fuel oil and coal generation have relatively high TSP emissions, whereas natural gas emits relatively little TSP, and non-biomass renewable resources generate no TSP.

Health Costs Attributed to Air Pollution

The annual cost to human health and the environment from vehicle pollution has been estimated at between $4 and $93 billion. In addition to morbidity, as many as 120,000 deaths each year can be linked to air pollution (Cannon 1990). Vehicle pollution is also responsible for extensive environmental deterioration, including damage to agriculture and wildlife, corrosion and soiling of buildings, degradation of visibility, and contamination of water by leaking underground fuel-storage tanks.

In-Use Transportation Emissions

Both EPA and the California Air Resources Board are authorized to establish emission standards for mobile sources and certify emission rates of new vehicles through laboratory procedures. However, in-use (actual) emission rates are consistently higher than laboratory-certified levels as a result of improper vehicle maintenance, varying fuel quality, varying driving habits and conditions, and deterioration of catalysts in the catalytic converter. The computation of in-use emission rates is done by EPA for most transportation vehicles. These models account for many variables that affect emissions including ambient temperature; altitude; vehicle speed; percentage of VMT associated with cold start, hot start, and stable conditions; fuel type; and on-board emission-control technologies.

To illustrate how in-use emissions can be significantly higher than certified EPA emission standards, gasoline-fueled cars emit 2.6 grams per mile (g/mi) of hydrocarbon (from exhaust and running losses), over 20 g/mi of carbon monoxide, and 1.6 g/mi of NO_x (Platte 1990).[10] These actual emissions are six times higher than certified levels of hydrocarbon emissions and CO, and twice as high as certified NO_x emissions.

Emissions per passenger mile by transport mode are calculated for ease in comparing the pollution levels of different transportation vehicles (Table 10). Bicycling and walking are the cleanest forms of transportation; they contribute no pollution. In terms of CO_2, vanpools have the lowest emissions followed by carpools, along with most electrified mass-transit modes. In terms of reactive hydrocarbon (NMHC) and CO emissions, electric rail transit has the lowest emissions, followed by airplanes and buses. Carpools and vanpools emit the least NO_x, SO_x, and particulates. Cars and light trucks have the highest emission levels per passenger mile for all principal pollutants. In fact, a single-occupancy car emits twice as much NO_x, three times as much CO_2, 10 times as much hydrocarbon, and 17 times as much CO as mass transit.

Clean Air Act Amendments of 1990

The Clean Air Act was amended by Congress and signed into law in 1990. Title Two of the act focuses on controlling mobile source (car and truck) emissions.

The major vehicle provisions include: more stringent tailpipe standards for cars and trucks; reformulated-gasoline requirements; an oxygenated-fuels program for carbon monoxide nonattainment areas; a California clean-car pilot program; and a clean-fuels program for vehicle fleets in 22 of the worst air-pollution areas.

The new law establishes tighter tailpipe emissions standards for hydrocarbons, carbon monoxide, and nitrogen oxides. The Tier I standards are to be phased in beginning with vehicles produced in model year 1994. By the end of 1999, EPA will determine the need, cost, and feasibility of additional Tier II standards for vehicles produced in model year 2004 and later. The new law also extends the useful-life requirements for passenger-car emission controls from 5 years/50,000 miles to 10 years/100,000 miles. In addition, for the first time EPA will establish a tailpipe standard for carbon monoxide under cold-temperature conditions. Vehicle emissions resulting from gasoline evaporation during

Table 10
Comparison of Emissions Between Various Passenger-Transport Modes*

Transport Mode	CO_2 (kg/pass-mi)	NMHC[1]	CO	NO_x	TSP	SO_2[2]
		⊢——— (in grams/passenger-mile)———⊣				
TRUCK (gasoline):						
–Single occupancy	0.70	3.20	27.46	2.05	0.01	0.23
–Average occupancy	0.37	1.68	14.45	1.08	0.01	0.12
CAR:						
–Single occupancy	0.51	2.57	20.36	1.61	0.04	0.07
–Average occupancy	0.31	1.51	11.98	0.95	0.03	0.04
VEHICLE RIDESHARE:						
–3 person carpool	0.33	0.86	6.79	0.54	0.01	0.05
–4 person carpool	0.22	0.64	5.09	0.40	0.01	0.03
–9 person vanpool	0.07	0.36	3.05	0.23	<0.01	0.03
BUS (diesel):						
–Transit	0.29	0.25	1.21	1.82	0.17	n/a
RAIL:						
–Amtrak/intercity						
diesel	0.20	0.12	0.6	0.9	0.08	0.51
electric	0.12	neg	0.05	1.1	0.08	2.07
–Commuter (diesel)	0.24	1.04	1.44	4.10	0.28	0.63
–Transit (electric)	0.17	neg	0.06	1.48	0.11	2.89
AIRCRAFT[3]	0.53	0.05	0.52	1.08	n/a	0.08
BICYCLE	0	0	0	0	0	0
WALK	0	0	0	0	0	0

Notes:

* Emission factors (convert from emissions in vehicle-miles to emissions in passenger-miles using occupancy factors from Table 2):

    Diesel: 1.68×10^{-4} lb CO_2/Btu

    Gasoline: 1.71×10^{-4} lb CO_2/Btu

    Jet fuel: 1.66×10^{-4} lb CO_2/Btu

    Electricity: 1.04×10^{-4} lb CO_2/Btu-equivalent; neg NMHC; 0.04 lb CO/MBtu; 0.92 lb NO_x/MBtu; 1.8 lb SO_2/MBtu; 0.067 lb TSP/MBtu (Average 1987 power plant emission in U.S.).

    Heavy-duty diesel engines: 2.51g NMHC/veh-mi; 12.3g CO/veh-mi; 18.5g NO_x/veh-mi; 1.7g TSP/veh-mi.

    Single passenger auto: 2.57g NMHC/veh-mi; 20.36g CO/veh-mi; 1.61g NO_x/veh-mi; 0.04g TSP/veh-mi.

    Single passenger light truck: 3.2g NMHC/veh-mi; 27.5g CO/veh-mi; 2.1g NO_x/veh-mi; 0.01g TSP/veh-mi.

1. NMHC—Nonmethane hydrocarbons or reactive organic compounds, 9 RVP.

2 . SO_2 emissions calculated based on 0.03 weight percent sulfur in gasoline fuel.

3. Assumes a PW4050-powered 767-200 flying 288 statute miles (250 nautical miles) seating 65% of its 240-passenger capacity. (Note: emissions per passenger-mile change proportionately with passenger occupancy—e.g., if this aircraft was only 25% full, emission factors would increase by a factor of 2.6.)

Sources: Davis (ORNL) 1989; EIA, May 1989; author's calculations; EPA Mobile4 model and personal communications with Lois Platte (EPA Ann Arbor Laboratory); personal communications with Walt Stevenson (EPA Research Triangle Park, NC); personal communications with Frank Pane, United Technologies-Pratt and Whitney, East Hartford, CT.

refueling will be controlled; and EPA must issue regulations to improve the systems that control evaporative emissions when vehicles are in operation and parked.

Reformulated (cleaner) gasoline will be required in the nine smoggiest US cities beginning in 1995. Within one year of the act's enactment, EPA must promulgate regulations for reformulated gasoline to be used in gasoline-fueled vehicles. The goal of fuel reformulations is to reduce volatile-hydrocarbon emissions and toxic air pollutants, while considering fuel cost, health, environmental, and energy-related impacts.

Fuel quality will also be controlled in 41 carbon monoxide nonattainment areas during the four winter months, when pollution levels are at their highest. This program is scheduled to begin November 1, 1992, and will require fuel with a 2.7 percent oxygen content.[11]

Two "clean fuels" programs are specified in the Clean Air Act Amendments. "Clean fuels" include compressed natural gas, ethanol, methanol, liquefied petroleum gas, electricity, reformulated gasoline, and possibly other fuels. The first program is a California clean-car pilot program. The act establishes emission standards and allows the auto and fuel industries to determine whether to meet the standards by vehicle controls, new fuels, or a combination of both. The program will be phased in beginning in 1996 with 150,000 cars and light-duty trucks. By 1999 the program will expand to cover 300,000 cars per year. More stringent standards (Phase II) will begin in 2001. States with ozone nonattainment areas may elect to "opt-in" to the California program.

The second clean-fuels program requires the 22 areas with the worst air quality to limit the mobile-source emissions from centrally fueled fleets of 10 vehicles or more. This program will be phased in beginning in 1998.[12] Credits will be issued for fleet programs that go beyond EPA requirements.

For cars sold within their boundaries, states are allowed to adopt California's more stringent tailpipe standards. This option is being considered by New York as well as other states.

The tighter tailpipe standards required under the Clean Air Act Amendments are expected to reduce motor-vehicle emission levels by about 15 percent in the near term. However, by 2005, when most improvements have been realized, emissions are expected to rise. By 2010, on-road hydrocarbon, NO_x, and CO emissions are expected to be 30-40 percent greater than in 1989 due to increases in VMT levels (Figure 23).

Conclusion

Greenhouse warming and air pollution are both inextricably linked to the burning of petroleum. As greater quantities of fossil fuels are consumed by the transportation sector, in line with DOE projections, air quality will most likely get worse. And deteriorating air quality is linked with increasing greenhouse-gas emissions.

To counter these energy and emission trends, we will need break-throughs in vehicle fuel efficiency, widespread use of clean alternative transportation fuels, and significant shifts in transportation demands. These strategies are discussed in the following chapters.

Figure 23   On-Road Emissions

Trends in air pollution from cars and trucks, projected to 2009. (Assumes 4% growth in vehicle miles traveled.)

Percent of 1989 Emissions

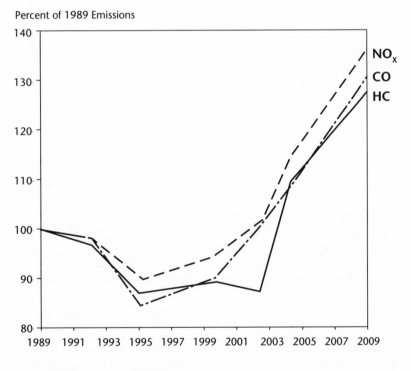

Sources: UCS estimates; Walsh 1990.

Notes

1. According to Congressional Research Service calculations, airplanes contributed 210 million tons of CO_2, ships 101 million tons, pipelines 81 million tons, and railroads 53 million tons in 1988.

2. Of the estimated 14 percent, flaring accounts for about 1 percent, while production, processing, refining, and transmission account for 13 percent of secondary CO_2 emissions.

3. Automobile air-conditioning uses about 175 million pounds of CFC-12 annually.

4. In response to the protocol, a new Title VI was added to the federal Clean Air Act, known as "Stratospheric Ozone Protection," which includes phaseout schedules for CFCs, halons, carbon tetrachlorides and methyl chloroform.

5. Calculated based on 9.5 quads of domestic oil used for US transportation, multiplied by 8 standard cubic feet per million Btu oil. The methane emission factor was 0.02 quad natural gas per quad oil produced for US consumption divided by the net heating value of natural gas (21,300 Btu/lb.), divided by the density of natural gas (8 lb. per standard cubic foot).

6. Note that CO reacts readily with the hydroxyl radical OH in the atmosphere. OH is also the mechanism for removing methane; thus the more CO there is, the less OH is available for methane removal.

7. Total US carbon monoxide emissions in 1988 were about five million tons.

8. Tropospheric ozone (smog) in the lower atmosphere should not be confused with ozone in the upper atmosphere, which forms the protective layer against harmful ultraviolet radiation bombarding Earth. The latter is beneficial and in danger of being destroyed by CFCs and other halogens, while smog is detrimental to health and welfare and a known greenhouse gas.

9. The sulfur content of gasoline is about 0.03 percent by weight, and sulfur oxide emissions per gallon of gasoline are 0.8 grams per gallon. Assuming an average automobile-fleet fuel economy of 19.2 mpg, average fleet emissions of SO_x are estimated at 0.04 grams per mile. Emissions from diesel fueled vehicles are higher.

10. EPA Mobile4 estimates are based on "average" gasoline cars (calendar year 1990).

11. EPA may delay the start of the oxygenated-fuels program by two years if the domestic supply and distribution capacity is determined to be "insufficient."

12. The implementation of this program is delayed to 2001 if vehicles meeting these standards are not being sold in California by 1998.

5 Alternative Transportation Fuels

The US transportation sector has relied on petroleum for virtually all of its energy needs for decades. But as the social and environmental costs of using petroleum mount, the nation may choose to replace conventional fuels with alternative fuels. As the Department of Energy notes, "The most promising technological opportunities for further reductions in oil consumption rest in the development of alternative fuel systems" (DOE 1986).

Energy sources other than conventional gasoline can fuel this nation. There are many alternatives, derived from a wide array of natural resources. Switching to one or more of these alternative fuels can do more than reduce our oil consumption—it can also reduce greenhouse-gas and other air emissions and ameliorate a host of other problems.

Several important criteria should be considered in evaluating alternative fuels. After a brief discussion of these criteria, an evaluation of each fuel follows.

Cost and Availability

One major hindrance to the introduction of alternative fuels is the low price of oil. The difference in cost between conventional and alternative fuels is a formidable market barrier for new fuels.[1] However, when the external costs of petroleum fuels are considered—social and environmental costs such as air pollution, acid rain, oil spills, global warming, national security, and others—the price differential shrinks. Table 11 summarizes efforts to project the costs of alternative transportation fuels as compared to gasoline.[2]

Another obstacle to alternative fuels is the coordination required between vehicle and fuel manufacturers. So far, neither has been willing to act first—either to market the alternative fuels for new vehicles or to

Table 11
Projected Alternative Transportation Fuel Prices and Full-Cycle Supply Costs[a]

Alternative Fuel	Fuel Price Only[b] ($1988/gal-eq)	Current Full-cycle Supply Cost[c] ($1988/gal-eq)	Future Full Cycle Supply Cost[c] ($2000/gal-eq)
Gasoline	0.60	0.70	1.00
Reformulated gasoline	0.82	0.97-1.07[d]	1.25
CNG	0.54	0.99	1.15[e]
Methanol	0.86	1.16-2.13[f]	1.29[g]
Ethanol[h]	1.75	1.88	1.04-2.07
LPG	0.97	n/a	n/a
Electricity	1.56-3.57[i]	2.59-3.90[j]	n/a
Hydrogen	n/a	3.10-11.75[k]	1.68-2.35[l]

Notes:
a. Fuel prices are wholesale costs and net of taxes unless otherwise noted. Full-cycle supply costs include fuel production, distribution, marketing, and vehicle retrofit.
b. Price calculation is in equivalent gallons of gasoline and does not include vehicle retrofit, fuel distribution, or marketing.
c. Full-cycle costs include fuel production, distribution, and marketing plus vehicle retrofit.
d. Arco estimate; consumer cost net of taxes.
e. Synthetic natural gas made from coal.
f. Low end of price range assumes natural gas feedstock; high end of price range assumes wood feedstock.
g. Assumes woody-biomass feedstock.
h. All ethanol price estimates assume corn feedstock, except lower range for future supply costs which use woody-biomass feedstock.
i. Low end of price range assumes off-peak electricity from the grid; high end of price range assumes residential, peak-demand electricity.
j. Estimate in 1985$ for current technological capability; if all technology is optimized, cost can range from $0.04 to $0.41 per eq-gallon (DeLuchi 1989).
k. DeLuchi estimate for solar hydrogen.
l. Photovoltaic-derived hydrogen with optimized technology (Ogden and Williams 1989).

Sources: California Energy Commission, AB234 Report, 1989; DeLuchi et al., "Electric Vehicles," 1989; Sweeney 1990; Ogden and Williams 1989; DeLuchi, "Hydrogen Vehicles," 1989; and Brower 1990.

manufacture the vehicles that will use the new fuels—unless there is a guarantee of profits to be made or public policy dictates otherwise.

Consumer convenience is yet another factor affecting the availability of alternative fuels. With gasoline we can refuel almost anytime and anywhere. Limited fuel availability is a substantial drawback to consumers. Studies indicate that owners of alternative-fueled vehicles are as concerned about fuel availability as they are about vehicle performance (Sperling et al. 1989a).

Today some new fuels are market-ready but have no market niche; others look promising but require further development. Given the imperfections in market competition and pricing, however, public poli-

Criteria for Evaluating Alternative Fuels

■ Costs to consumers must be competitive with the market price for gasoline, and the fuel must be readily available.

■ The natural resources from which each fuel is produced must be available from secure sources in quantities adequate to serve transportation's long-term needs.

■ The fuel's properties must not present unacceptable public risks, and it must be easily transportable and safely storable.

■ Greenhouse-gas and other emissions into the air should be minimal, and other environmental impacts should be acceptable.

■ The necessary modifications to engines, service stations, etc., in order to use the fuel must be technologically and financially feasible.

■ Government regulatory barriers must be removed so that the most promising alternative fuel(s) can compete effectively in the market.

cies may be required to bring these fuels to market. Achieving widespread use of alternative fuels in the US is likely to be a longer-term strategy.

Hardware Modifications

For an alternative fuel to be marketable and gain consumer acceptance, both vehicles and fuel infrastructure may first need to be redesigned. Such modifications must be technologically feasible and cost effective. Alternative fuels can be used in a vehicle's engine in a variety of configurations: dual-fuel, flexible-fuel, or dedicated-fuel systems. All three are being used now to some extent around the world. Dual-fuel compressed natural gas (CNG) cars, trucks, and buses are common in northern Italy. Flexible-fuel vehicles have not been used on a large scale in any country. Dedicated-LPG fuel systems are used extensively in the taxis of Japan, Korea, and Thailand (DOE 1988b).

■ Dual-fuel systems allow the vehicle's engine to operate on either an alternative fuel or a conventional fuel such as gasoline. These systems typically enable the engine to operate on a gaseous fuel and a liquid fuel, one at a time. A simple switch accomplishes the changeover. In most cases, dual-fuel vehicles are somewhat heavier and have less trunk space than conventional vehicles because they require more fuel and hardware.

■ Flexible-fuel systems allow the engine to operate on a variable mixture of two or more different fuels, provided all fuels are in the same physical state—for example, when all are liquids such as gasoline and methanol.

■ Dedicated-fuel systems operate only on a single fuel. These systems usually are less costly and operate more efficiently than dual-fuel and flexible-fuel systems.

Resource Base and Secure Supply

Most transportation fuels can be made from more than one resource; some of these resources are renewable and some are not. Propane and reformulated gasoline, for example, are made from fossil fuels—exhaustible resources—while ethanol and hydrogen are more likely to be derived from renewable resources. Moreover, not all fuels are available domestically in ample quantities; some must be imported from politically unstable areas. The security of our long-term transportation needs depends on being able to manufacture fuels domestically from renewable resource bases.

Fuel Properties and Safety Concerns

Each fuel is characterized by a unique set of properties, including physical state; heating value, or energy content; octane rating; density; and safety concerns (see Table 12). The physical state of a fuel—solid, liquid, or gaseous—is important because existing engine technologies are not designed to burn fuels in other than a liquid form.

The heating value, or energy content, of a fuel represents the amount of heat generated during combustion in a vehicle's engine. Typically it is measured in terms of the *net* heating value, with a high value being desirable. This is one of the most important properties of a fuel, because a relatively high energy content—such as that of gasoline—means that less fuel must be stored on board. A fuel's properties also affect engine efficiency; the octane number is an indication of maximum thermal efficiency for spark-ignition engines.

Fuel density is a measure of the weight of a fuel per unit of volume. Along with energy content, it determines the storage volume and weight of the fuel, which in turn affect the vehicle's operating range (the more fuel a vehicle can carry, the greater its range).

Fuels must also be examined from a safety perspective. A fuel should not present unacceptable public risks at any point, from initial resource extraction to end use. However, no one fuel is inherently safer than all others in every respect; all have the potential to be used safely if the necessary precautions are taken. Reducing the risks associated with some fuels may require design modifications to both vehicles and infrastructure.

Some of the properties that determine whether the fuel is safe for wide-scale use are ignitability, explosiveness, and flammability.[3] For obvious reasons, high autoignition temperatures are preferable, as are high flashpoints and narrow flammability limits. Measures of a fuel's toxicity include exposure limits for inhalation, ingestion, skin absorption, and contact over time.

Table 12
Properties of Selected Transportation Fuels

				FUELS				
Properties	Gasoline	Diesel No. 2	LPG (HD-5)	CNG	Methanol	Ethanol	Hydrogen	Electricity (EVS)
Constituents	Mixture of Hydrocarbons $(C_4\text{-}C_{10})$	Mixture of Hydro-carbons	95% propane 5% butanes	60-98% methane; rest ethane & other parafins, CO_2, H_2, He, N_2	CH_3OH Methyl Alcohol	C_2H_5OH Ethyl Alcohol	Elemental Hydrogen gas, H_2	Energy generated from both fossil and non-fossil fuels
Physical State	liquid	liquid	gas	gas	liquid	liquid	gas	current
Boiling Range (°F @ 1atm)	80 to 420	320 to 720	-44 to 31	-259[a]	149	173	-423	n/a
Density (lb/ft³)	43 to 49	49 to 55	31[b]	8[c]	49.2	49.2	0.9-gas 4.4-liquid 169-metal	156-180
(lb/gal)	5.8 to 6.5	6.5 to 7.3	4.1[b]	1.07[c]	6.6	6.6	0.12-gas 0.58-liquid 23-metal	n/a
Net Energy Content Btu/lb	18,700-19,100	18,900	19,800	21,300[a]	8,600	11,500	51,800-gas 51,800-liquid 780-metal	60-140[d]
Btu/gal	112,000-121,000	123,000-128,000	82,000	22,800[a]	56,560	75,670	5,300-gas 30,100-liquid 17,600-metal	
Autoignition Temperature (°F)	450-900	400-500	920-1,020	1,350	878	795	1085	n/a
Flashpoint (°F)	-45	125 (min)	-100 to -150	-300	52	70	-420	n/a
Octane Number Range (R+M) 2	87 to 93	n/a	104[e]	120[e]	99	100	n/a	n/a
Flammability Limits (volume % in air)[f]	L=1.4 H=7.6	L=0.7 H=5.0	L=2.4 H=9.6	L=5.3 H=14	L=6.7 H=36	L=4.3 H=19	L=4 H=74	n/a
Sulfur Content (wt %)	0.02-0.045	0.2-0.25	neg[g]	neg[g]	none	none	none	fossil base: variable; non-fossil: none
Human Exposure Limit for Fuel (ppm)[h]	500	n/a	n/a	nontoxic	200	1,000	nontoxic	n/a

See notes on following page

Notes:
n/a = not applicable.
a. Pure methane. Other minor constituents (ethane, propane, etc.) boil at higher temperatures.
b. At 80° F with respect to water at 60° F.
c. 100% methane @ 80° F and 2,400 psi with respect to water at 60° F.
d. Energy content range for electricity considers the range from lead-acid batteries at 40 watt-hr/kg. to Lithium-metal sulfide batteries at 90 watt-hr/kg.
e. Octane ratings above 100 are correlated with given concentration of tetraethyl lead in 150-octane.
f. L=lower; H= higher
g. Natural sulfur content is very low, though measurable.
h. Toxicity ratings given for air contaminants; the lower the number, the more toxic the contaminant.

Sources: DOE, Assessment of Costs and Benefits of Flexible and Alternative Fuel Use in the U.S. Transportation Sector, *January 1988; Ogden and Williams, October 1989; DeLuchi, "Hydrogen Vehicles" 1989; CRC* Handbook of Chemistry and Physics, *1976; UCS calculations.*

Greenhouse-Gas and Other Emissions

Fuel combustion is implicated in many forms of atmospheric pollution, such as smog, acid rain, and the emission of greenhouse gases. Pollution from burning the fuel itself accounts for its "primary emissions," while secondary emissions are released when a fuel is extracted, manufactured, distributed, and stored. Together the fuel's primary and secondary emissions characterize its full-cycle emissions. The less severe the environmental impacts of these full-cycle emissions, the more desirable an alternative fuel becomes, with the goal being a fuel that is much less polluting than gasoline.

Emissions of greenhouse gases and other air pollutants, water pollutants, and solid wastes are discussed in this section. CO_2-equivalent emissions from alternative fuels are quantified and other air emissions are presented in Table 13 (DeLuchi et al. 1988a).

Existing Government Policies

The government plays a crucial role in reducing uncertainty in both consumers' and industry's choice of an alternative fuel. Once the government targets a specific fuel for market offering, it must provide continued support for its choice, backed by a steady stream of incentives and subsidies. Studies show that it is only at this high level of government commitment that a new market niche can be established (Sperling et al. 1989a).

However, the government can be very inefficient when it prematurely backs new fuels and promotes policies that are either inconsistent or short-lived. Over the years, many alternative-fuel policies, both economic and regulatory, have been enacted only to be relaxed or rescinded. These actions interfere with competitive market forces. In 1988, for example, Congress passed the Alternative Motor Fuels Act, which requires the federal government to acquire methanol, ethanol, and natural-gas vehicles; to study the use of alcohol and natural gas in heavy-duty trucks and buses; and offer manufacturers of alcohol and natural-gas

Table 13
Comparison of Emissions from Alternative Fuels to Gasoline/Diesel

Fuel Type	Fuel Source	Green-house Impact[a] (billion tons/Yr)	CO$_2$	NO$_x$	NMHC	CO	SO$_x$	Toxics
				Increase or Decrease in Emissions[b]				
Gasoline and Diesel	Crude Oil	1.336	baseline	baseline	baseline	baseline	baseline	baseline
Reformulated Gasoline	Crude Oil	n/a	more	slightly less	slightly less	slightly less	much less	n/a
Methanol	Natural Gas	1.293	-3%	slightly less	slightly less	slightly less	less	less total, but more formaldehyde
Methanol	Coal	2.639	98%	slightly less	slightly less	slightly less	more	
Ethanol	Corn, Sugar Cane, Other Crops	0.868	-35% to 0%	less	less	same	less	less
Ethanol	Lignocellulose plants (fast-growing trees, shrubs, and grasses)	0	-100%	less	less	same	less	less
Compressed Natural Gas (CNG)	Natural Gas	1.081	-19%	slightly more	less	much less	less	less
Liquefied Petroleum Gas (LPG)	Crude Oil	n/a	n/a	more	same	less	less	less
Electric Vehicles[c]	New coal sources	1.683	23%	more	more	more	much more	more
Electric Vehicles	Nonfossil fuels	0	-100%	much less	much less	much less	much less	less
Hydrogen	Nonfossil fuels (electrolysis of water)	0	-100%	less	none	none	none	less
	Hydrides from coal	2.677	100%	more	more	more	much more	more

See notes on following page

Notes:
a. In CO_2-equivalent emissions; CH_4 and NO_2 emissions from power plants converted to equivalent CO_2 mass emissions by factors of 11.6 and 175, respectively. Does not include emissions of chlorofluorocarbons or changes in the distribution and concentration of tropospheric ozone, resulting from emissions of vehicular nitrogen oxides and reactive hydrocarbons.
b. Change in all emissions emitted per mile, relative to petroleum, and NO_x= nitogen oxides; CO_2 = carbon dioxide; NMHC= reactive hydrocarbon; CO=carbon monoxide; SO_x = sulfur oxides; and toxics= certain compounds such as formaldehyde and benzene.
c. If electricity is generated using the current power-generating mix, then no impact on CO_2 emissions. If additional capacity were required, the use of coal-fired plants would result in a moderate increase of CO_2, and the use of natural-gas-fired plants in a moderate decrease.

Sources: DeLuchi, Sperling, and Johnson "Transportation Fuels and the Greenhouse Effect," *1989; DOE 1988a.*

---

automobiles credits toward meeting their fleet-wide fuel-economy standards (House 1988). Yet alternative fuels such as hydrogen, fuel cells, and electricity may be even cleaner burning than alcohol and natural-gas vehicles, and most alternative-fueled cars today are less energy efficient than conventional vehicles; thus the Alternative Motor Fuels Act could hinder both long-term improvements in air quality and increases in the overall efficiency of the vehicle fleet.

In order to allow promising alternative fuels to compete, government policies like this act that give special treatment to select fuels (such as ethanol tax credits) should be carefully reviewed. Otherwise the new fuel or fuels of choice may be blocked by market barriers even though they meet all the necessary criteria.

Compressed Natural Gas

ADVANTAGES	DISADVANTAGES
+ Nontoxic and noncorrosive	- Cumbersome fuel tank
+ Global and US natural-gas supplies more plentiful than those of oil	- Nonrenewable resource
+ Very high thermal efficiency	- Cheaper fuel could lead to increased energy demand overall
+ Reduced engine maintenance	- More frequent refueling and longer refueling time
+ High autoignition temperature and narrow flammability range	- Low flashpoint
+ Noncarcinogenic	- Possible increase in NO_x emissions
+ Low CO and reactive-hydrocarbon emissions	- Modify refueling stations with compressors
+ No threat to land or water pollution from spillage	- Requires new supply strategies— natural-gas transmission companies operate separately from today's oil companies
+ Well suited to larger, heavier fleet vehicles	
+ Lowest projected full-cycle cost of any alternative fuel	

Natural Gas (Compressed and Liquefied)

COST AND AVAILABILITY. Converting an existing vehicle to run on dual-capacity CNG costs between $1,200 and $3,500 for vehicle hardware (CEC 1989), or 34 cents per gallon of gasoline-equivalent (Sweeney

1990). According to the Department of Energy, it may be more economical to produce dedicated-CNG vehicles than to convert old vehicles. In any case, CNG vehicles are expected to cost more than conventional ones because pressurized-CNG tanks are more expensive than gasoline tanks (DOE 1989a). Even with these added hardware costs, CNG still has the lowest projected cost of any alternative fuel, according to some estimates—99 cents per gallon of gasoline-equivalent (Sweeney 1990).[4] In fleet applications where CNG can be purchased in large quantities the price could be even lower. According to the California Energy Commission, CNG costs only about half as much as methanol, its nearest cost competitor (CEC 1989).

Market availability, however, could be a problem because those who currently supply gasoline (oil companies) are not the same as those who supply natural gas (pipeline-transmission and CNG distribution companies). Thus switching to natural gas could drastically change the structure of the transportation fuels industry. This uncertainty has hindered oil companies and pipeline-transmission companies from joining together to advocate CNG as strongly as have suppliers of other alternative fuels such as methanol and ethanol. Nonetheless, CNG refueling stations are springing up in some cities, and public utilities as well as some major oil companies are marketing CNG for transportation. In San Francisco, for example, Pacific Gas & Electric will have seven CNG refueling stations open to the public by the end of 1990 (Egan 1990b).

HARDWARE MODIFICATIONS. Conventional gasoline engines require only minor modifications to run on natural gas in a dedicated mode. CNG is typically stored on board the vehicle in a pressure cylinder three to four feet long and 28 inches wide (Egan 1990b). Despite the cylinder's size, dedicated-CNG vehicles can be designed so that no trunk space is forfeited; some trunk space is always forfeited with a dual-fuel configuration (CEC 1989).

Today most natural-gas vehicles are dual fuel and are converted from stock vehicles using certified conversion kits. The hardware includes a storage tank, pressure regulator, mixing device, and various fuel lines and valves. Ideally, retrofitting would include changes to intake and exhaust ports and increased compression ratios. Dual-fuel capability requires hardware that can weigh an additional 400 pounds and occupy 190 gallons of storage space (DeLuchi et al. 1987).

Fuel-injected as well as non-fuel-injected engines can be converted to natural gas. In fact, converted fuel-injected engines can compensate for the lower volumetric efficiency of natural gas (and the resulting 10-15 percent less power than a gasoline engine). In terms of vehicle maintenance, CNG prolongs the life of engines, spark plugs, and lubricating oil; a 500,000-mile engine life is not atypical.

Engines are not the only things that need modifying. Refueling stations must also get new equipment. The cost to incorporate compression equipment may be $50,000 to $250,000 per station (DOE 1989a).

And in order to handle significantly increased demand for CNG, the current pipeline distribution network may require expansion.

Since modifying an existing vehicle means having a dual-fuel system that reduces storage capacity and lowers fuel efficiency, CNG may be better suited to large, heavy-duty vehicles such as buses and trucks that are put to limited, high-mileage use—fleet vehicles and/or dedicated-fuel vehicles. Indeed, these "niche" markets can serve to demonstrate the virtues of CNG.

RESOURCE BASE AND SUPPLY. Natural gas is comprised of up to 98 percent methane, the simplest hydrocarbon compound, one atom of carbon and four of hydrogen (CH_4). The remainder is ethane, other simple hydrocarbons, and inert gases. Once produced, natural gas must be processed to remove impurities and bring it up to regulated sales specifications.

Although natural gas is not common in the US transportation sector today, it is standard in all other sectors and has extensive transportation applications in other countries. For instance, natural gas supplies over half the energy used in American homes and 35 percent of the energy to the US industrial sector (EIA 1989). But there are only about 30,000 CNG vehicles operating in the United States (DOE 1988b).

According to the Department of Energy, proven US natural-gas reserves amount to 187 trillion cubic feet (33 billion barrels of crude-oil equivalent). Undiscovered, recoverable natural-gas resources in the US are estimated at 755 trillion cubic feet (EIA 1989). And the known reserves of natural gas far exceed those of oil worldwide. Gas utilities have estimated that each natural-gas vehicle demands an average 80,000 cubic feet of natural gas a year (CEC 1989). Thus if all US motor vehicles had run on CNG in 1987, less than 2 percent of the recoverable domestic natural-gas reserves would have been consumed. Notwithstanding domestic supply, which accounts for 93 percent of US usage, most US imports of natural gas come from Canada (EIA 1989). While future supplies of natural gas are expected to be adequate for any foreseeable increase in demand, pipeline distribution capacity will require expansion.

In addition to naturally occurring gas reserves, methane can also be produced from biomass by both existing technology and by more innovative microbial methods not yet in commercial use. Biomass is a renewable resource and very ample in supply. One source estimates that readily available biomass resources could generate 85 percent of US natural-gas demand (OECD 1986). This projection may be largely overstated, however, because the 20-25 quads of biomass feedstock required cannot be generated in any sustainable form by agriculture or fast-rotation forestry.

FUEL PROPERTIES AND SAFETY CONCERNS. Natural gas can be stored cryogenically as a liquid (liquefied natural gas, or LNG) at temperatures below -259 degrees F (-162 degrees C). Natural gas is also stored at ambient (room) temperature as compressed natural gas (CNG) at very high pressures ranging from 2,400 to 3,000 pounds per square inch (psi). CNG is more common than LNG in the transportation sector. Because even under pressure CNG's density is much lower than that of gasoline, a pound of it occupies about five times the space of a pound of gasoline. This means that with current vehicle designs and storage capabilities, the driving distance for CNG vehicles ranges from 80 to 200 miles between refueling.

Though less dense than gasoline, CNG has a 10-percent higher net energy content per unit weight than gasoline. But, as mentioned above, because of lower volumetric efficiencies, CNG-fueled engines have about 10-15 percent less engine power than equivalent-size gasoline engines (DOE 1988a).[5]

CNG storage entails two kinds of safety risks: an explosion of the tank or an explosion resulting from chemical reaction of the fuel with air. Based on CNG's low expansion-energy potential, the risk of a tank explosion is minimal compared to the risk of explosion due to CNG contact with air after leakage or tank rupture, especially in confined spaces. But CNG tanks appear to be well made and have survived remarkable durability tests in extensive worldwide applications without leakage or rupture. In fact, there has never been a fire in a natural-gas vehicle.

Overall, CNG is considered less hazardous than gasoline. It needs more energy to ignite, ignites at a higher absolute temperature, and requires higher concentrations in air to burn than gasoline. Moreover, CNG flames burn at a colder temperature and radiate less heat than gasoline flames. When leaked in open air, CNG quickly disperses because it is lighter than air. On the downside, CNG has a low flashpoint, meaning that it can burn or explode at fairly low temperatures. It is nontoxic, noncarcinogenic, and noncaustic—considerably more benign than gasoline or methanol (DeLuchi et al. 1988a). However, CNG can be an asphyxiant, and contact with LNG can cause frostbite.

GREENHOUSE-GAS AND OTHER EMISSIONS. CNG produces emissions with an impact comparable to or less than those from gasoline. Carbon monoxide emissions of CNG fuels are much lower because of the nearly complete mixing that occurs with gaseous fuels.[6] Total hydrocarbon emissions from CNG engines are about the same as those from gasoline engines, while reactive-hydrocarbon emissions (nonmethane hydrocarbons) are lower. Emissions of nitrogen oxides (NO_x) may be higher because CNG vehicles do not have emission-control systems equivalent to those running on gasoline today. With comparable systems, NO_x emissions would be about the same as from gasoline engines. Development of electronically controlled CNG fuel systems could bring NO_x emissions below those of gasoline (DOE 1988a).

Switching to CNG may result in moderate reductions in greenhouse-gas emissions—19 percent lower than conventional fuels (DeLuchi et al. 1989a). This estimated reduction in emissions takes into account that the use of natural gas both as CNG and as a feedstock for methanol or electric vehicles could increase methane emissions during fuel combustion and by venting from pipelines, storage facilities, and production operations.

Since it is released as a gas when leaked, CNG cannot be "spilled." Therefore it does not pose a threat to either water or land.

EXISTING REGULATIONS. Natural-gas utilities are and have been heavily regulated; state utility commissions typically regulate the price and contract terms in natural-gas transactions. Widespread use of CNG has been hampered because service stations that want to install natural-gas facilities are treated as regulated utilities. As natural-gas deregulation continues, however, CNG may become a viable alternative to gasoline.

But other policies currently limit the use of CNG. For example, whether necessary or not, CNG vehicles are currently restricted from using some bridges, tunnels, and parking spaces because of safety concerns (DOE 1988a).

To promote this fuel, the following measures are needed: further demonstration of the potential for natural-gas passenger vehicles; continued deregulation of natural gas; incentives for purchasing CNG vehicles; and investments in gas distribution facilities. A steadily increasing price of oil, of course, would speed the whole process.

The Urban Mass Transportation Administration (UMTA) has committed $35 million to help transit authorities acquire CNG and other alternative-fuel buses (Lippman 1990). And new coalitions, such as public utilities and natural-gas producers advocating the use of CNG, are fighting for continued government R&D funding for CNG.

Propane

ADVANTAGES	DISADVANTAGES
+ Lower CO emissions	- Limited supplies
+ No threat to land or water pollution from spillage	- Nonrenewable, fossil-fuel resource
	- Cumbersome fuel tank
+ Very narrow flammability-limit range	- More frequent refueling than gasoline
	- No significant reduction in carbon dioxide emissions
+ Currently very low price	
+ Inexpensive hardware modifications	- NO_x emissions could increase
	- High coefficient of expansion could cause tank rupture
+ Well suited to larger, heavier fleet vehicles	- Heavier than air, so poses a safety hazard in the event of leakage
	- Very low flashpoint

Liquefied Petroleum Gas (Propane)

COST AND AVAILABILITY. LPG, a fossil-fuel derivative, is a by-product of oil production and refining, and is also produced during natural-gas processing. LPG is currently competitively priced because it is a fossil-fuel derivative. Thus as the prices of crude oil and natural gas fluctuate, so does the price of propane. The California Energy Commission projects that in 1993 the wholesale price of LPG will be only 42 cents per gallon of gasoline-equivalent (in 1988 dollars) (CEC 1989). In addition, the cost is a relatively low $500 to $1,000 to modify gasoline engines for dual-fuel use with LPG (DOE 1988a).

LPG fuel-system technology is demonstrated, especially for dual-fuel systems. The Environmental Protection Agency anticipates that LPG could play a marginal role in alternative-fuel fleet vehicles, such as heavy-duty trucks and transit buses where supply permits. But LPG is not expected to play a significant role in fueling passenger cars because of its restricted supply and limited environmental benefits.

HARDWARE MODIFICATIONS. As noted, LPG vehicles are most commonly dual-fuel conversions of gasoline vehicles and act as secondary fuel systems. LPG vehicle owners can use whichever fuel is cheaper. Dedicated-LPG vehicles, common in Japanese, Korean, and European taxis, operate better than dual-fuel systems (DOE 1988b).

For use in a vehicle, LPG is commonly stored as a liquid in a pressurized tank at 70 to 150 psi. Storage tanks in dual-fuel applications take up twice as much room as gasoline tanks and add up to 200 pounds to the weight of the vehicle. Dedicated-LPG vehicles, however, do not suffer size restrictions; thus smaller vehicles, like forklifts, can use LPG.

Supply-infrastructure modifications for LPG fueling are relatively minimal. An LPG distribution network is in place and capable of being enlarged. Aboveground LPG storage tanks are generally less expensive to install than underground gasoline storage tanks.

RESOURCE BASE AND SUPPLY. About 30 percent of US LPG is refined from crude oil, and 70 percent is extracted from natural gas (CEC 1989).

LPG currently supplies less than 1 percent of US transportation energy, fueling an estimated 350,000 trucks, farm vehicles, school buses, and other fleet vehicles (Davis et al. 1989). LPG is used more for space heating and as a chemical feedstock than it is for transportation. In 1988, 98 percent of the daily US production of 1.7 million barrels of LPG was used for residential, commercial, and industrial purposes (EIA 1989). The potential sources of additional LPG for transportation by 1995 include one billion gallons a year from Canadian surpluses and an estimated 10 billion gallons annually from the Middle East and Indonesia (CEC 1989).

FUEL PROPERTIES AND SAFETY CONCERNS. LPG consists of about 95 percent propane and 5 percent butanes that liquefy at temperatures ranging from -44 degrees F (-42 degrees C) to +31 degrees F (-1 degree C). It can be kept liquid at room temperature when stored at a pressure of 150 psi. LPG is heavier than gasoline and occupies 32 percent more on-board space per unit weight than gasoline. Propane's heating value per unit mass is 8 percent higher than that of gasoline, however.

One safety advantage of LPG is its high autoignition temperature. Another is its narrow range of flammability, second only to gasoline's. On the other hand, the flashpoint of LPG is very low—it can burn or explode at low temperatures—which is undesirable in terms of safety.

Although LPG is stored as a liquid, it is a gas both when burned and leaked. Thus the safety concerns are similar to those for CNG regarding leakage and rupture.

When LPG vehicles are exposed to strong sunlight, pressures in the fuel tank can increase to hazardous levels. For this reason, pure LPG is more commonly used in cooler climates to avoid overpressuring and explosions, and is usually not used in warmer climates.

At very low ambient temperatures (below 0 degrees F, -18 degrees C), LPG fuel pressure is sometimes insufficient for adequate vehicle operation. Thus LPG has a narrower temperature operating range than other alternative fuels.

Another safety concern with LPG is its high coefficient of expansion as fuel temperature increases. Frequent cooling and warming cycles can rupture the tank and cause spillage. To avoid this, LPG tanks should not be filled to more than 80 percent of their theoretical capacity (OECD 1986). Furthermore, because LPG vapor is heavier than air, leaks can cause the vapor to accumulate near the ground under still airflow conditions. This presents a safety risk, especially during bulk transfer in the event of an accidental release around a combustion source.

GREENHOUSE-GAS AND OTHER EMISSIONS. When LPG is made from natural gas, the CO_2-equivalent emissions may be slightly lower than those from gasoline. When LPG is made from crude oil, however, CO_2-equivalent emissions may increase slightly. Depending on the air-fuel ratio, CO emissions are usually lower than those from gasoline because of the complete mixing capability of gaseous fuels. Hydrocarbon emissions from LPG vehicles are about the same or slightly higher than those for gasoline, and less reactive, depending on the emission-control system in place. NO_x emissions are most likely to be increased because LPG fuel systems do not interact with current three-way catalyst emission-control systems (DOE 1988a).

Because, like CNG, liquefied petroleum gas is a gaseous vapor at ambient temperatures, it does not pollute water in the event of a release. Likewise, "spillage" evaporates upon release, so pollution on land is not an issue.

EXISTING REGULATIONS. LPG vehicles are restricted from using many bridges, tunnels, and enclosed parking garages because this fuel poses risks of fire and/or explosion if it is leaked in confined spaces. While both LPG and CNG vehicles may be subject to similar regulations, the risks are more serious for LPG because it is much heavier than air and therefore does not readily disperse.

Methanol

ADVANTAGES	DISADVANTAGES
+ Higher engine power rating	- Higher ignition requirements, could
+ Few engine modifications required	be difficult to start in cold weather
for dual-fuel capability	- Large fuel tank required for same
+ Good antiknock fuel	driving distance
+ Possibly lower NO_x emissions	- More frequent refueling stops
+ Hydrocarbon emissions thought to	- Highly corrosive to metal, rubber, and
be less photochemically reactive	plastic components
	- Highly toxic
	- Soluble in groundwater; could lead to
	water contamination
	- Formaldehyde by-product is a
	suspected carcinogen
	- Nonrenewable resources may be
	required, uses imported natural-gas
	and oil feedstocks
	- High emissions when made from coal
	- Increases greenhouse-gas emissions
	significantly
	- Wide-ranging flammability limits
	- Volatile
	- Conducts electricity
	- Very high capital cost to produce
	- Predominantly an imported fuel if
	large volumes are required

Methanol

COST AND AVAILABILITY. Domestically produced methanol—commonly known as wood alcohol—is an alcohol-based fuel that costs about $1.16 per gallon of gasoline-equivalent when derived from natural gas (in 1988 dollars) (Sweeney 1990, DeLuchi et al. 1988a). However, when derived from wood fiber it can cost up to $2.13 per gallon of gasoline-equivalent. Imported methanol is expected to be cheaper, about $1.05 per gallon of gasoline-equivalent (Sweeney 1990).[7] Thus domestically produced methanol is unlikely to be cost-effective compared with imported methanol. In any case, domestic CNG will probably cost less than even the cheapest imported methanol fuel. In early 1990, methanol was only somewhat more expensive than premium unleaded gasoline because it was purchased from chemical manufacturers, which had excess capacity. The price is expected to rise sharply if future demand triggers capital outlays for new production facilities.

The cheapest source of methanol today requires natural-gas feedstocks, a commercially available technology. Other feedstocks, notably coal and wood, have not yet been demonstrated on a commercial scale, although in the next decade coal will probably become economic. Methanol can also be produced from biomass, but this is significantly more expensive today. Even though methanol is commercially available, production plants are expected to cost $1 billion each to build, according to the EPA. Thus methanol suppliers are likely to require government backing and guaranteed markets before making this fuel widely available.

HARDWARE MODIFICATIONS. Methanol is commonly used as a flexible fuel in engines that can use more than one fuel at a time, because it can be mixed with gasoline and even ethanol in a vehicle's engine without major modifications. There are no switches for the driver to flick in a flexible-fuel vehicle. Sensors monitor the fuel mixture, and an on-board computer controls a redesigned fuel injector for optimal fuel combustion.

Nevertheless, some hardware changes are required for the most efficient use of methanol. Since it has about half the energy of gasoline, a methanol-fueled vehicle will need a larger fuel tank to achieve a gasoline-size operating range. In addition, pure methanol corrodes certain metals; the fuel tank and fuel-delivery system must be made from corrosion-resistant materials such as stainless steel. Substitutions have to be made for zinc, lead, aluminum, and magnesium used in parts, as well as certain rubbers and plastics. And because methanol conducts electricity, parts that carry voltage require insulation. Overall, more frequent maintenance is necessary for methanol vehicles than for gasoline vehicles.

RESOURCE BASE AND SUPPLY. Methanol and other alcohol fuels (such as ethanol; see below) are a distinct set of fuels called oxygenates, in which oxygen is added to these hydrocarbon-based fuels to provide more complete combustion. Today most methanol (71 percent) is made from natural gas (although it can also be made from coal, oil, organic wastes, crops, and wood products) by a process called steam reforming, or by partially oxidizing hydrocarbon gases. Other current feedstocks of methanol include heavy hydrocarbons (17 percent), light-hydrocarbon gases (8 percent), and coal (4 percent) (DOE 1988a). In the future, methanol could be economically produced by gasification of coal and biomass.

Methanol currently supplies 280 million gallons of the transportation sector's annual energy demand—only 0.09 percent in 1986 (DOE 1988a). Most of this is used as fuel additives and for manufacturing methyl tertiary butyl ether (MTBE; see section on this additive below) rather than as pure (or neat) methanol. In order to fuel all of today's automobiles, about nine million barrels per day (bpd) of methanol would be required. However, maximum domestic methanol production, even 20 years from now, is estimated at five million bpd. Thus foreign methanol would be required if the US transportation sector were to be converted to this fuel; worldwide methanol production would have to increase 13-fold to satisfy potential US demand by 2000 (Difiglio 1989). Even fuel blends of only 10-percent methanol would require current domestic methanol production to expand tenfold to fuel the automobile fleet alone (Segal 1988).

In the event that the world market for methanol grows substantially larger, the US would require natural-gas feedstocks from the USSR, OPEC countries like Iran and Qatar, and possibly Norway and Mexico (DOE 1988c). But if the methanol market remains relatively small, US arctic gas, which is expensive to produce, may well be tapped.

FUEL PROPERTIES AND SAFETY CONCERNS. Methanol improves vehicle performance by providing about 5-20 percent more power per unit volume than gasoline. In addition, methanol has good antiknock properties, which permit higher compression ratios, resulting in thermal efficiency 10-20 percent better than gasoline (DOE 1988a).

On the negative side, methanol has a much lower energy density than gasoline—about 50 percent less heat content. A gallon of methanol will deliver only a 14-mile driving range as compared to an average 28 miles on a gallon of gasoline. Methanol can form flammable mixtures in the vapor space of vehicle fuel tanks, causing explosions due to its low autoignition temperature and wide flammability limits.[8] Moreover, the flashpoint of methanol is in the middle range compared to other fuels—another disadvantage.

Methanol is toxic, volatile, and burns with an invisible flame. It is less toxic than gasoline in low concentrations, but more toxic in high concentrations (DeLuchi et al. 1988a). Thus exposure to large spills could threaten safety. Prolonged skin contact with pure methanol is dangerous (even more so than with gasoline), and contact with methanol blends is even worse. Ingestion is extremely hazardous, and since methanol is odorless, colorless, tasteless, and an alcohol, accidental ingestion is more likely than with gasoline. (Olfactory additives could be used to deter accidental ingestion, however.)

GREENHOUSE-GAS AND OTHER EMISSIONS. Manufacturing methanol using only natural gas as the feedstock would result in approximately the same greenhouse-gas emissions as those from gasoline. Manufacturing methanol from coal would increase CO_2-equivalent emissions by 98 percent over current gasoline emissions (DeLuchi et al. 1989a). Emissions data for methanol are highly uncertain because emissions will depend on future control technologies (DeLuchi et al. 1988a). Based on current controls, CO, reactive hydrocarbons, and NO_x emissions may be reduced slightly compared with gasoline-vehicle emissions (DOE 1988a). Methanol is less volatile than gasoline, having less than half the evaporative pressure; this would result in fewer emissions (i.e., less evaporation) from the fuel tank and while refueling (from refueling hoses).

From an emission-reduction perspective, methanol is especially attractive for substitution in diesel engines. Methanol diesels typically emit half the NO_x of their diesel counterparts, have virtually no particulate emissions, and emit about the same levels of CO and hydrocarbons (DOE 1988a).

Burning methanol does produce significantly higher levels of formaldehyde, a suspected carcinogen, than does burning gasoline. Pure
methanol fuel produces four to eight times more aldehyde emissions
(including formaldehyde) than gasoline does (OECD 1988a). Formaldehyde emissions from cars are a health concern; since methanol exhaust is
more toxic than gasoline exhaust, improved emission-control systems
would be required.

Methanol is completely soluble in water and thus could cause serious
contamination of water supplies in the event of a spill.

EXISTING REGULATIONS. Alcohol fuels have benefited from federal
policies in the past. The 1980 Energy Security Act contained extensive
alcohol-fuel provisions, including over $1 billion in authorizations for
loan-guaranteed funding. During the Reagan administration, part of the
Energy Security Act's funding was rescinded, but the government loan
guarantees, and some $10 million in annual R&D funding, has been
maintained for alcohol-based fuel blends (both ethanol and methanol)
(Segal 1988).

The Alternative Motor Fuels Act of 1988 requires that the federal
government purchase methanol, ethanol, and natural-gas vehicles and
offers fuel-economy credits to manufacturers who sell these vehicles.
This act removes a barrier for certain alternative fuels (including ethanol,
methanol, and natural gas) but not others.

In California an Advisory Board on Air Quality and Fuels was
established in 1989 with the express purpose of reporting to the California legislature on "the impacts and feasibility of methanol-fueled vehicle
production and methanol available mandates" (CEC 1989). It appears
that California has selected methanol as its preferred alternative fuel; the
California Energy Commission (CEC) has displayed an organized commitment to methanol and is an influential advocate of the fuel (Sperling
and DeLuchi 1989b). The expressed goal of the CEC is to have half of
California's state-agency vehicles using methanol by the year 2000
(DOE 1988a). Other methanol mandates and incentives are expected to
follow.

Also in California, the South Coast Air Quality Management District
adopted an Air Quality Management Plan in 1988 that could phase out
petroleum in southern California in favor of alternative fuels (SCAG
1989b). If southern California government agencies follow the state's
lead by adopting policies that promote a shift to methanol in an effort to
improve air quality, other, even cleaner-burning alternative fuels could
be damaged competitively.

Ethanol

ADVANTAGES	DISADVANTAGES
+ Few engine modifications required	- Can require large volume of crops and
+ Good antiknock fuel	energy to produce
+ Renewable resource	- Current distillation methods are very
+ Can reduce greenhouse-gas	energy intensive
emissions depending on crop-	- Large fuel tank required
growing requirements	- More frequent refueling
+ Cellulose conversion could be cost-	- Limited supplies for dedicated use
competitive in future	when made from crops such as corn
+ Hydrocarbon emissions thought to	- Fertilizer could pose a problem to
be less photochemically reactive	groundwater when made from
+ Low toxicity	commercial crops
+ Currently enjoys a federal tax	- High flashpoint and wide flammability
subsidy	limits could form flammable mixtures
+ Domestic resource base	in vehicle fuel tank
	- Degrades some elastomers and metals
	- May be impractical to distribute by
	nationwide pipeline system
	- Hard to start vehicle in cold
	temperatures
	- Corrosive
	- Currently expensive

Ethanol

COST AND AVAILABILITY. Ethanol, sometimes referred to as grain alcohol or ethyl alcohol, is another alcohol-based, oxygenated fuel. Today, it is produced either by fermenting sugars extracted from biomass materials like corn and sugarcane or made synthetically by the catalytic hydration of ethylene. Producing ethanol from these crops uses large amounts of energy for planting, fertilizing, cultivating, and harvesting; this currently makes it an expensive fuel. Estimates of the cost to produce, distribute, and market ethanol from corn range from $1.75 to $2.07 per gallon of gasoline-equivalent (Sweeney 1990, Ogden and Williams 1989, CEC 1989).[9] Because this price is too high to compete with gasoline, commercial viability will depend on government subsidies, mandates, and incentives. Of course, technological breakthroughs could dramatically lower costs and make ethanol competitive.

In 1989 gasohol (gasoline blended with 10 percent ethanol), competitively priced with gasoline, accounted for 8 percent of all motor fuel sold in the US (GAO 1990b). Corn-based ethanol will continue to be used as a blending agent with gasoline in the near term (Sperling 1989c). Widespread availability of pure ethanol fuel in the future depends on continued improvements in the conversion process of woody-biomass feedstocks. By 2000, woody-biomass ethanol could be priced more competitively at $1.04 per gallon of gasoline-equivalent (in 1988 dollars) (Brower 1990).[10]

Perhaps the world's most ambitious ethanol program, and one from which the United States might learn, is Brazil's. The Brazilians, who have been producing ethanol from sugarcane since the 1930s, have had a roller-coaster experience attempting to commercialize this fuel. Following the 1973 oil crisis, the government buttressed price subsidies for ethanol fuels by calling for increased numbers of ethanol-fueled vehicles. This program, called the National Alcohol Program, was implemented in two phases. The first phase focused on increasing the percentage of ethanol in gasohol to 20 percent by 1979, and the second provided consumer and manufacturer incentives intended to increase sales of dedicated-ethanol vehicles to one-half of total sales by 1985 (DOE 1988b). A third phase, proposing to increase ethanol production to 3.7 billion gallons by 1987, has remained on hold because of the drop in world oil prices from 1986 through early 1990 (DOE 1988b). At one point in the mid-1980s, ethanol-vehicle sales reached 73 percent of all sales, only to collapse abruptly to 9 percent. Again, in 1988 ethanol-vehicle sales hit 90 percent but a year later were down to only 50 percent.

Brazil's experience is a useful one from a government-policy perspective. The government's trepidation—its concern that new fuel supplies could not keep pace with vehicle demand and that fuel subsidies were getting out of hand—seems to have caused consumers to lose faith and has made the transition to ethanol extremely volatile. The lesson for us would appear to be, first, that availability of alternative fuels is inevitably linked to government intervention, but that, second, government backing for alternative fuels must be well thought out and consistent.

Unlike Brazil, the US never experienced a growth in dedicated-ethanol vehicles. Although gasohol gained in popularity during the 1970s oil crises, today it remains popular only in the Midwest, where ethanol is produced from corn. One US company (Archer Daniels Midland) supplies the bulk of all ethanol, and this producer has influenced Congress to extend a federal ethanol tax subsidy for over a decade.

HARDWARE MODIFICATIONS. Ethanol blends such as gasohol can be burned in today's engines as flexible fuels without modifications because gasohol vehicles use similar technology to gasoline vehicles. Flexible-fuel ethanol vehicles (whose engines can burn more than one fuel at a time) cost about $300 more than gasoline vehicles (at low production volumes) (DOE 1988a). Burning pure ethanol fuel, however, requires modifications because ethanol is corrosive and degrades some metals and elastomers commonly used in gasoline systems. In addition, ethanol vehicles require about 30 percent more fuel-storage capacity to achieve the same operating range as gasoline vehicles.

Ethanol fuels are not practical for nationwide distribution because they cannot be transported easily by existing gasoline pipelines. Ethanol requires special handling because it attracts water, which affects vehicle performance when introduced into the fuel system. Thus ethanol fuels are generally transported by truck or rail rather than by pipeline.

RESOURCE BASE AND SUPPLY. In 1988, about 800 million gallons of ethanol were sold in the United States (the motor-fuel equivalent of about 23 million barrels of crude oil), nearly all of it domestically produced. It was used to make over eight billion gallons of gasohol, enough to fuel 7 percent of US automobiles. Ninety-five percent of US ethanol was made from corn, and it used 5 percent of the domestic corn crop (DOE 1988a, GAO 1990b).

However, crop feedstocks, including sugar beets and sorghum as well as corn, are of limited use if the goal is to fuel all US vehicles with gasohol because they can supply only two to three billion gallons of ethanol a year in the next decade. Even at only the current 10-percent blending level for gasohol, the US would have to use about 40 percent of its harvest (corn and other crops) for ethanol production to fuel highway vehicles alone (Segal 1988).

In the future, it may be cost-effective to make ethanol from woody lignocellulose and herbaceous crops (such as trees, shrubs, and grasses) and waste biomass. One process under development to convert woody crops into ethanol consists of fermentation, hydrolysis, and enzymatic reactions. Another process not yet commercially available uses a method of alcohol extraction employing permeable, selective plastic membranes. Future ethanol supplies from these sources are estimated to range from 100 to 300 billion gallons a year (Lynd 1989). These ethanol (and other biofuel) supplies could replace 30-90 percent of US motor-vehicle gasoline and diesel consumption, assuming current demand levels (Brower 1990).

FUEL PROPERTIES AND SAFETY CONCERNS. Pure ethanol improves vehicle performance, giving up to 20 percent better thermal efficiency than gasoline and up to 10 percent more engine power per unit volume of fuel burned (DOE 1988a). Unfortunately, ethanol's low energy density translates into an operating range only two-thirds that of a gasoline-powered vehicle for the same volume of fuel. This means, of course, 30 percent more refueling stops are required without a larger ethanol fuel tank.

From a safety standpoint, pure ethanol is more likely than gasoline to form flammable mixtures in the vapor space of a vehicle's fuel tank because of its high flashpoint and wide flammability limits (DOE 1988a). Ethanol is a safety risk because of its very low autoignition temperature. Since most ignition sources come from outside the fuel tank, however, flame arresters in the tank's filler tube, or simply blending in gasoline components that raise the fuel's autoignition temperature, could reduce this safety concern.

GREENHOUSE-GAS AND OTHER EMISSIONS. Ethanol made from woody biomass could reduce greenhouse-gas emissions by 100 percent, since young plants absorb carbon dioxide as they grow and the conversion process requires little energy. However, the combustion of ethanol made from corn results in little to no reduction in greenhouse-gas emissions compared with burning gasoline, because of the substantial amounts of petroleum used for fertilizer, harvesting, and other activities (OTA 1990). If ethanol is produced from fast-growing woody crops, a small increase in net CO_2 emissions may result because of soil oxidation.

Aside from carbon dioxide, ethanol vehicles are thought to produce fewer emissions than gasoline vehicles when equipped with similar emission-control devices. In fact, emission-control catalysts should work more efficiently since ethanol burns at a lower temperature than gasoline. CO emissions should be equivalent or slightly lower, hydrocarbons could be less photochemically reactive, and NO_x should be appreciably lower, since ethanol combusts at lower temperatures (DOE 1988a).

Because ethanol is less volatile than many other fuels (one-fifth the evaporative pressure of gasoline), it is less likely to seep into the air, where it could be ignited. Burning ethanol also produces acetaldehyde, which is toxic in concentrations above 200 ppm. Additional tailpipe controls may be required to reduce these emissions. Ethanol fuel itself is not as toxic on skin contact as gasoline and methanol, however.

When ethanol is produced from food crops, fertilizer and pesticide runoff can endanger water supplies. Since biomass does not require the cultivation that food crops do, water pollution is less likely to be a problem. Nevertheless, care should be taken to use the least intensive cultivation methods when growing woody biomass so that water supplies are safe from runoff and contamination.

EXISTING REGULATIONS. Ethanol produced from biomass is supported through federal tax exemption under the Energy Tax Act of 1978 and the Energy Security Act of 1980. The former enacted a federal excise-tax exemption for fuels containing 10 percent or more alcohol when produced from domestic farm products; the exemption was extended until 1992 by the Windfall Profit Tax Act, further promoting the competitiveness of alcohol fuels.[11] The exemption amounts to a six-cent-per-gallon federal tax break on ethanol in gasohol; since gasohol is 10 percent ethanol, the equivalent tax subsidy for ethanol itself is 60 cents per gallon of pure ethanol, or 90 cents per gallon of gasoline-equivalent (DOE 1988a). Moreover, 23 states also provide tax incentives on ethanol blends and/or direct payments to ethanol producers (GAO 1990b).

Given these massive federal and state subsidies, gasohol has found a market niche in states where indigenous resources exist. Illinois, Ohio, Kentucky, Indiana, and Tennessee consumed over half of all the gasohol in the US (Davis et al. 1989). Ethanol-blended fuels (and other oxygenates) are also required during the winter months in Denver, Albuquerque, Phoenix, and Las Vegas in order to reduce carbon monoxide emission levels (GAO 1990b). Such regulations have helped create and sustain markets for ethanol fuel.

Reformulated Gasoline

ADVANTAGES	DISADVANTAGES
+ No hardware modifications required to vehicle or refueling station	- Nonrenewable resource
	- Uses imported oil feedstocks
	- Highly toxic
+ Distribution system in place	- Leakage contaminates water resources
+ Lower reactive-hydrocarbon and SO_x emissions	
	- Oil spills threaten species on land and in water
+ Narrow flammability limits	
+ Not appreciably more expensive than current gasoline blends	- Low flashpoint, thus explosive
	- Very low autoignition temperature, thus small leaks into air can readily cause fires
	- High capital cost to retrofit refineries
	- Asphyxiant at high temperatures
	- Little effect on new cars

Reformulated Gasoline

COST AND AVAILABILITY. Instead of moving away from gasoline altogether in the search for cleaner-burning fuels, several major oil companies have altered the chemistry of gasoline. Reformulated gasolines seem, so far, to be quite cost-competitive with gasoline. In late 1989, regular unleaded gasoline was selling for five cents per gallon more than certain reformulated blends. Manufacturers may be internalizing some of the cost of making reformulated gasoline in order to make it competitive. According to the Atlantic Richfield Company (ARCO), reformulated gasoline actually costs one to two cents per gallon more to make than regular leaded gasoline (GAO 1990a). If supply is expanded, however, consumers could pay up to an extra 25 cents per gallon for reformulated gasoline because of the high capital costs of retrofiting refineries (Egan 1990a).

Only limited amounts of reformulated gasoline are available in the near term. The production of larger amounts in more effective formulations would require substantial changes to existing refineries, taking several years (GAO 1990a).

HARDWARE MODIFICATIONS. Neither vehicles nor distribution facilities require hardware modifications for reformulated gasoline. As noted above, however, petroleum refineries do require costly retrofiting to produce the fuel. ARCO, for example, estimates this investment at $2 billion over the next five years (GAO 1990a). An estimated $20- to $30-billion capital investment would be required to reformulate all gasoline (GAO 1990a).

RESOURCE BASE AND SUPPLY. Reformulated gasoline is made from petroleum, the same as today's gasoline, with crude oil as its principal resource base. There is no standard specification for the fuel. Sold by several oil companies under a variety of trade names, each is a different product. Declining domestic crude-oil production in recent years makes the US more dependent on foreign oil to satisfy future supplies of reformulated gasoline. Since gasoline reformulations are likely to result in the production of lower volumes of gasoline per barrel of crude oil, an increase in the supply of crude oil would be required to maintain the current volume of gasoline demanded, increasing US oil imports (GAO 1990a). The average oil well in the US currently produces about 13 barrels per day (bpd) of oil, down from 18 bpd in 1970; in the Middle East, the average well produces more than 2,500 bpd. All of North America possesses only 4 percent of global proven oil reserves, and if these reserves are consumed at today's production rates, they will last only a decade. Persian Gulf countries, on the other hand, possess 65 percent of proven world reserves, which will last over a century even if no more oil is discovered (MacKenzie 1990).

FUEL PROPERTIES AND SAFETY CONCERNS. Reformulated gasolines are thought to burn cleaner than today's gasoline. Depending on the manufacturer's specifications, reformulated gasoline may have a lower Reid Vapor Pressure (8 RVP compared with the current 9 RVP) because of the removal of butane, making it less likely to evaporate. Likewise, benzene content may be reduced from 2 to 1 percent, heavier aromatics and olefin compounds (smog precursors) may be cut by one-third, and the fuel may have a higher octane rating than unleaded gasoline.

Safety concerns are the same as for gasoline. While reformulated gasoline (as well as traditional gasoline) has narrow flammability limits— desirable in terms of safety—very small leaks can cause fires. Both reformulated and traditional gasoline have a low flashpoint and a very low autoignition temperature, both of which may cause safety risks (DOE 1988a). Since gasoline vapors are heavier than air, they can linger in the open air, concentrating at the source of release and resulting in flammable mixtures. In addition, as a vapor at high temperatures this fuel, like gasoline, is an asphyxiant.

GREENHOUSE-GAS AND OTHER EMISSIONS. Reformulated gasoline is assumed to have slightly greater levels of greenhouse-gas emissions than the 1.3 billion tons of CO_2 a year emitted from the use of standard gasoline (DeLuchi et al. 1989a). The primary aim of reformulated gasoline is to reduce the reactivity of the 130 different hydrocarbons in a vehicle's exhaust to address urban smog problems. Current blends reduce reactive hydrocarbon emissions, lower evaporative emissions of hydrocarbons (which seep out of fuel tanks), halve emissions of benzene (a known carcinogen), and reduce sulfur emissions (as sulfur oxides) by 80 percent.

Reformulated gasoline is estimated to reduce CO emissions by 10 percent and NO_x emissions by 6 percent compared with regular leaded gasoline (Environment 1989). According to EPA, reformulated gasoline may achieve total automotive-emission reductions of 30 percent (GAO 1990a). Nevertheless, like gasoline, reformulated gasoline and its vapors are highly toxic. In fact, preliminary tests have found that reformulated gasoline could emit increased amounts of 1,3-butadiene (a suspected carcinogen).

Like gasoline, reformulated gasoline contaminates water when leaked or spilled. Both fuels form a thin film on the surface of water and can travel over and pollute large areas. As evidenced by the many recent oil spills in our nation's navigable waters, there is also a substantial ecological risk associated with transporting the crude-oil feedstock for these gasoline fuels.

EXISTING REGULATIONS. Federal legislators beset with public demands for clean air passed the 1990 Clean Air Act Amendments. One of several requirements is the sale of reformulated gasoline in the nine smoggiest US cities beginning in 1995.

In an effort to steer policymakers, oil companies are marketing reformulated gasolines in areas with the worst pollution problems. Oil companies are attempting to meet new state and federal standards and defend their market share of petroleum-based fuels against increasing competition from methanol, ethanol, and natural gas. Thus reformulating gasoline started as something of a voluntary standard, and manufacturers are, no doubt, pleased that final federal legislation included reformulated gasoline as the premier clean alternative fuel.

In October 1989, the three major domestic auto companies and 14 petroleum companies joined forces to research motor-fuel composition and vehicle emissions. The program's goal is to assess the air-quality improvements achievable with reformulated gasoline, methanol, and ethanol additives. The first phase of the program will test 26 gasoline formulations and two methanol fuels; 10 percent ethanol with reformulated gasoline; and the effects of adding ethers—MTBE and ETBE—to gasoline (GAO 1990a). Phase two will test the best of the new gasoline formulations identified in the first phase in prototype vehicles.

The federal government and several states recently issued rules to phase in lower fuel-vapor pressures. By 1992, the EPA will require no more than 9 psi in northern states and 7.8 psi in warmer southern states to reduce emissions due to evaporation in warm weather. These regulations are also supporting the widespread use of reformulated gasolines.

Oxygenated Additives — MTBE and ETBE

ADVANTAGES	DISADVANTAGES
+ No engine modifications required	- Nonrenewable resource base (MTBE)
+ Pipeline distribution system in place for oxygenated blended fuels	- Vapors are highly toxic
	- Asphyxiant at high temperatures
+ Lower carbon monoxide emissions	- Leakage contaminates water
+ Conventional engines burn these fuels more efficiently	resources
	- Relatively expensive, depends on tax credits to remain competitive

Oxygenated Fuel Additives (MTBE and ETBE)

COST AND AVAILABILITY. Methyl tertiary butyl ether (MTBE) and ethyl tertiary butyl ether (ETBE) are oxygenates; blending gasoline with either one adds oxygen to the fuel and can cause more thorough combustion in certain vehicle engines. This can reduce carbon monoxide emissions. MTBE costs about 60 cents a gallon to produce and is in plentiful supply. ETBE is a newly developed gasoline additive that costs up to 80 cents a gallon (Weiss 1990). Today, gasoline with MTBE is available at the pump for essentially the same price as unblended gasoline, whereas ETBE gasoline blends are not yet commercially available. Oxygenated fuels are already available in areas where their sale is mandated or other government incentives influence their availability.

HARDWARE MODIFICATIONS. Engines burning MTBE and ETBE oxygenates do not require hardware modifications. Unlike ethanol blends, MTBE and ETBE are blended with gasoline at the refinery and distributed by pipeline. Thus neither MTBE nor ETBE fuels require modifications to the fuel-distribution system.

RESOURCE BASE AND SUPPLY. MTBE is most commonly produced by converting butane to isobutylene, which is then combined with methanol. About 35 percent of the methanol produced in the US—over 300 million gallons in 1987—is used as a feedstock to make MTBE (Segal 1988). MTBE is blended at low levels with gasoline (about 1 percent) to make 1.2 billion gallons of oxygenated automotive fuel annually, approximately 1 percent of the gasoline sold in the United States (DOE 1988a). In 1987, MTBE accounted for 35 percent of all oxygenated-fuel sales; ethanol accounted for the remaining 65 percent (Segal 1988).

ETBE is an ether produced from a reaction of ethanol with isobutylene. ETBE-blended gasoline may be a better solution for carbon monoxide problems than gasohol because it requires only half as much ethanol as gasohol. ETBE blends are just beginning to establish a market niche for themselves and are not yet commercially available.

FUEL PROPERTIES AND SAFETY CONCERNS. Oxygenated fuels are very similar to gasoline. Thus their vapors are toxic, and at high temperatures these fuels, like gasoline, are asphyxiants. Oxygenated fuels must be handled carefully; they have the same safety risks as gasoline, including water and land pollution from spills.

GREENHOUSE-GAS AND OTHER EMISSIONS. Oxygenated fuels do not reduce greenhouse-gas emissions. The oxygen content in these fuels does, however, reduce other pollutant levels. Especially in older vehicles, fuels oxygenated with MTBE and ETBE can reduce CO emissions up to 30 percent by making the air/fuel ratios leaner. However, oxygenated fuels can result in higher evaporative-hydrocarbon emissions and slightly increased NO_x emissions.

Experts have testified before Congress in favor of an optimal oxygen content in gasoline of between 2 and 3.7 percent by weight (Senate 1989). An oxygen content of less than 2 percent does not reduce CO emissions significantly, while levels over 3.7 percent may affect fuel characteristics and negatively affect storage stability and volatility.

EXISTING REGULATIONS. Several regions have required the use of oxygenated fuels to combat their seasonal problems with carbon monoxide emissions. In 1987 Colorado made the use of oxygenated fuels mandatory during winter months in Denver and other front-range cities polluted by carbon monoxide. During the first two months of 1988, fuels sold in these areas had to contain 1.5 percent oxygen by weight. Since then, the requirement has gone up to 2 percent oxygen from November through February (Segal 1988). Phoenix, Albuquerque, and Las Vegas also require the use of high-oxygenated additives (such as MTBE) in the winter months to combat carbon monoxide pollution. Such regional regulations help promote the use of MTBE and ETBE. In fact, the 1990 Clean Air Act Amendments require that oxygenated fuels contain at least 2.7 percent oxygen and be sold in CO "non-attainment" areas by 1992.

While gasoline frequently contains only 1 to 2 percent MTBE, EPA regulations allow MTBE to be blended up to 15 percent in gasoline, and higher blends are becoming more common.

Electricity for Electric Vehicles

ADVANTAGES	DISADVANTAGES
+ No pollution from vehicle's tailpipe	- High full-cycle emissions if generated from coal and oil
+ Renewable if not generated from fossil fuels	- Current battery capacity limits driving distances
+ Low full-cycle emissions if generated from renewables	- Vehicle speed limited to under 60 mph in current prototypes
+ EVs are efficient and quiet	- Manufacture and disposal of certain batteries cause water and solid-waste pollution
+ Supply infrastructure in place (electric grid)	
+ Suitable for certain fleet applications	- Currently very expensive to operate EVs
	- Further RD&D commitments required

Electricity (Electric Vehicles)

COST AND AVAILABILITY. The Department of Energy estimates the operating cost of today's electric vehicle (EV) to be about twice that of a gasoline vehicle (DOE 1988a). Other estimates put full-cycle costs of

EVs (including fuel costs for power plants and other indirect energy costs) in the range of 25 to 36 cents per mile, compared with 28 cents per mile for gasoline vehicles (DeLuchi et al. 1989b). The low end of this cost range assumes that several optimal conditions exist: high vehicle efficiency, high battery energy density, low-cost off-peak power, low initial battery cost, long battery-cycle life, long EV life, and low maintenance cost. At the high end, EVs would be cost-competitive only if gasoline costs rise to three to four dollars a gallon. It is impossible to predict whether the low or high cost predictions will come to pass; much depends on the outcome of further R&D, the future price of oil, and the outcome of conflicts in the Middle East.

Clearly, EVs are not yet a viable replacement for all types of highway vehicles. At this point they are probably best suited for fleet operations or as the second car in a household where daily traveling distances are limited and high power is not required. As development progresses, EVs may well play a more extensive role.

HARDWARE MODIFICATIONS. Unlike the fuels examined so far, the question here is not so much modifying a gasoline engine as improving an electric one. Electric vehicles have failed so far in the marketplace because of their inferior performance, high cost, and short driving range. The most important technological breakthrough will be a battery that can provide increased energy density and power, along with reduced charging time. The goal is an operating range of at least 150 miles and acceleration comparable to conventional vehicles (DeLuchi et al. 1989b).

Until the battery breakthrough comes, there are several options. The Impact, a prototype EV made by General Motors, uses a commercially available, inexpensive lead/acid battery. Sodium-sulfur batteries are a better option; they can go twice as long between recharges as the lead-acid variety. Nickel-iron batteries, which have shown high durability after repeated recharging, should also be superior to lead/acid.[12]

The supply infrastructure for electricity is well in place and needs no modification, but additional generating capacity may be required if EVs become general-purpose vehicles. We can avoid having to expand peak capacity—the most expensive electricity—if pricing encourages recharging during off-peak hours.

At the individual level, a 50-amp, 240-volt outlet is sufficient for recharging in most cases. Most homes have adequate electrical service to recharge an EV in the garage as long as all major appliances are not operating simultaneously.

RESOURCE BASE AND SUPPLY. Electricity is not a fuel per se; it is a form of energy that can be used to power electric vehicles. Electricity in the US is currently generated, on average, from coal (55 percent), nuclear power (20 percent), natural gas (10 percent), hydropower (9 percent), oil (6 percent), and geothermal, wood, waste biomass, and wind (totaling less than 1 percent) (EIA 1989). However, different regions use different mixes of energy sources.

The Energy Information Administration (part of the US Department of Energy) projects substantial increases in natural-gas-generated electricity by the year 2000, with only a negligible change in oil-generated electricity (DeLuchi et al. 1989b). Beyond 2000, it is likely that a greater proportion of renewable sources will be used. One study suggests that by 2000 the share of the US energy supply provided by renewable energy sources could be 15 percent, double the present fraction. In the longer term—by the year 2020—renewable sources could be supplying as much as 50 percent of US energy if major changes in energy policy are implemented (Brower 1990).[13]

Today transportation uses less than 3 percent of US electricity. Given the extensive electric-power infrastructure in this country, increased usage by the transportation sector should be feasible. Electricity can also serve to wean the transportation sector from oil and diversify its supply base.

With current overall operating efficiencies and electrical-system losses, it would take approximately 1,460 billion kilowatt-hours (kWh) of electricity—about half of the annual output of US electrical generating plants—to "fuel" all US cars on the road (EIA 1990a).[14, 15]

FUEL PROPERTIES AND SAFETY CONCERNS. EV storage batteries (the "fuel cells" that power the vehicle) can deliver about 60 percent of the energy stored in them. Prototypes have efficiencies up to 97 percent. In terms of overall operating efficiencies, measured in miles per kilowatt-hour, standard passenger EVs are estimated at 2.4 to 3.4 miles per kWh—25 to 34 miles per gallon of gasoline-equivalent (DeLuchi et al. 1989b). Prototypes such as GM's Impact are projected to get 6.7 miles per kWh. EV vans are much less efficient, achieving only one to two miles per kWh (DeLuchi et al. 1989b, EPRI 1989). Isuzu has recently tested prototypes of an electric-power-storage system that has 40 percent greater starting power than conventional EV batteries, 20 times greater output energy, and the capacity to be recharged in under 30 seconds (Maskery 1990).

GREENHOUSE-GAS AND OTHER EMISSIONS. EVs shift emissions away from vehicles themselves to electrical-generating facilities. Thus their greenhouse-gas emissions depend on the type of fuel used to generate electricity. If new coal plants are used, the net result would be a 23-percent increase in CO_2-equivalent emissions (DeLuchi et al. 1989a). Additionally, using coal to produce electricity results in methane releases from coal mining and produces CO_2 and N_2O from coal combustion. If electricity is generated from new natural-gas plants, a 30-50 percent reduction in current net CO_2-equivalent emissions is estimated (Plotkin 1990). Renewable sources of electricity, including solar, wind, hydroelectric, geothermal, and biomass, would add nothing to current net CO_2-equivalent emissions.[16]

In addition, these renewable sources produce little or no emissions of hydrocarbons, carbon monoxide, and nitrogen oxides compared with conventional electricity sources. Both power-plant and independent power producers are regulated as to emission levels of CO, NO_x, hydrocarbons, particulates, and sulfur oxides (SO_x).

Today, most US electricity is generated from a primary energy input of coal, nuclear fuel, natural gas, and hydroelectric sources, which results in some form of air pollution. Typical emission controls remove up to 90 percent of NO_x emissions from natural-gas and coal-fired plants and about 95 percent of the SO_x emissions from coal-fired plants. Fueling EVs with oil-fired and natural-gas-fired electricity is projected to produce fewer emissions of hydrocarbons, CO, and NO_x than current gasoline vehicles (DOE 1988a).

Electric vehicles themselves are entirely emission-free—they have no tailpipe. All other fuels have some tailpipe emissions. This is an important air-quality distinction between EVs and the other alternative-fuel vehicles discussed previously. The many variables affecting other vehicles—emission-control systems, fuel volatility, vehicle maintenance schedules, operational elements—are irrelevant to EVs.

Depending on the chemicals used to charge the battery and the types of fuels used to generate electricity, water quality and solid-waste streams could be adversely affected. Two major studies have found that EVs could worsen water quality and solid-waste problems at the local level. The studies that cited the worst environmental impacts of EVs considered only the manufacturing and disposal of lead/acid, zinc/nickel, and nickel/iron batteries, and the production and use of nuclear and coal fuels to generate electricity (DeLuchi et al. 1989b). Neither study considered sodium/sulfur batteries and renewable energy sources to generate electricity, both of which would be much more environmentally benign.

EXISTING REGULATIONS. The goal of the Electric and Hybrid Vehicle Research, Development and Demonstration Act of 1976 was to further R&D efforts and eventually produce economically competitive, consumer-accepted EVs.[17] This program had a funding level of $15 million in 1988 (DOE 1989b). DOE considers the current legislation sufficient to stimulate EV technologies to a point where the private sector has the option to continue their development into marketable products.

Lately manufacturers have been encouraged by the serious consideration being given to laws that could make commercial production of EVs practical within a decade. For example, the Southern California Air Quality Management Plan sets out to eliminate all combustion-engine vehicles (passenger and freight) altogether and replace them with "extremely low-emitting vehicles" using electric batteries, fuel cells, and solar cells by 2007 (SCAQMD and SCAG 1989). In response to such regulations a market for EVs is emerging. To date, California has signed contracts for 10,000 EVs to be on the road by 1995 in an effort to reduce air pollution (Egan 1989). The state will offer subsidies of $1,000 to $10,000 for each electric vehicle (Callahan 1990).

Electric utilities themselves are the target of both federal and state regulation. Regulations range from conservation measures to the internalizing of social costs (which cut CO_2 emissions), to development of alternative technologies and adoption of financial incentives to decrease demand growth. All of these could improve the future prospects of EVs.

Although any number of energy sources can supply the electricity needed for expanded EV use, including fossil fuels and renewables, solar energy is one of the most promising options.

Solar Power

ADVANTAGES	DISADVANTAGES
+ Renewable resource	- Requires storage "cells"
+ Vehicle is emission-free	- Photovoltaic vehicles are currently
+ No greenhouse-gas emissions	limited by low-efficiency designs
+ Vehicle is noise-free	- Currently very expensive energy source
+ Vehicles can be 100-percent	- Full-cycle energy use may be very high
recyclable	

Solar Energy

COST AND AVAILABILITY. Solar technologies have become much more cost-effective in recent years. Solar-thermal electric systems can now generate power for as little as 8 cents per kWh, and photovoltaic (PV) cells generate power at about 25 cents per kWh—one-tenth of their cost in the early 1980s (Brower 1990). (By comparison, coal-generated electricity costs roughly 6 cents per kWh.)

Solar vehicles are not yet available to consumers. At least one company is ready to produce them, at an estimated capital start-up cost of $5 million (Egan 1989). Another company has plans to build a solar-car factory in Hawaii in the next two years (Lomont 1989). And there are other environmental entrepreneurs planning to build solar vehicles, as well as General Motors, whose prototype version costs a whopping $8 million.

The market niche sought for today's solar vehicle is the second household car used around town for errands and short daily work commutes. Solar vehicles are best in areas with the greatest incidence of sunlight. The first markets for these cars will likely be the sunny Southwest US and Hawaii. Such commuter models are expected to be available sometime in the 1990s and cost $10,000 to $12,000 (Egan 1989, Lomont 1989).

HARDWARE MODIFICATIONS. Because the power source of a solar vehicle is so unrelated to the gasoline-powered internal-combustion engine, modification is not an issue. Solar-powered vehicle engines will not resemble gasoline engines in any form.

RESOURCE BASE AND SUPPLY. There is more natural-resource potential available with solar energy than with any other energy resource. Some 44,000 quadrillion Btu, or quads, of sunlight shines on the United States each year—2,000 times the entire US transportation sector's current level of energy consumption (Brower 1990).

The amount of solar energy that could be collected and converted into available energy is limited by space and conversion efficiency. Nevertheless, enough solar energy could be generated to supply 100 percent of the nation's primary energy use. For example, if the same 1 percent of total US land area required to generate electricity from coal were used for solar collection, nearly 100 quads of energy would be available each year, more than the US uses in a year (Brower 1990).[18] However, current solar-energy supplies account for a scant 0.075 percent of US energy demand (Brower 1990).

Solar energy is a promising source of future transportation energy, especially for regional applications. It can be used to generate electricity for electric vehicles and hydrogen fuel as well as for vehicles fueled directly by solar energy.

FUEL PROPERTIES AND SAFETY CONCERNS. Solar-thermal collectors, which concentrate sunlight to temperatures of as high as 1500 degrees C, are one means of generating electricity. Another, photovoltaic systems, produces electricity directly by the interaction between a semiconductor and sunlight. Neither presents any safety problems.

Solar energy resources are unevenly distributed geographically. While these distributional differences are less important in terms of supply requirements, they can significantly affect the economic feasibility of solar energy. Northern latitudes have an average daily insolation of about 13,000 Btu per square meter, while southern latitudes can be twice that.

Since solar energy is unavailable at night, energy-storage systems are required. Pumped hydroelectric storage (the transfer of water between low and high reservoirs) is already in wide use, and advanced batteries and compressed air are promising options for vehicles themselves. Energy may also be stored in the form of hydrogen produced by the splitting of water molecules with electricity generated from renewable sources. There are several storage systems that can be used for direct transportation energy, including batteries, hydrogen, and possibly compressed air.

Current prototypes of photovoltaic vehicles are powered by single-crystal silicon panes with efficiencies of about 10 percent. These prototypes weigh only 600 pounds, seat two, and can travel 50 miles per day (Egan 1989). They incorporate aerodynamic form and their motors have very small state-of-the-art DC batteries with few moving parts.

There are several options for recharging the batteries of these vehicles. It can be done while the vehicle is sitting idle in a parking lot; backyard PV "tracking stations" can collect solar power and store it in the vehicle's batteries; or the batteries could be recharged from a standard household electrical outlet.

GREENHOUSE-GAS AND OTHER EMISSIONS. Generating solar energy in itself results in no greenhouse-gas emissions or other air pollutants whatsoever. And solar vehicles are completely nonpolluting and noise-free. They can also be designed so that they are 100 percent recyclable—from the body to the battery (Lomont 1989). Manufacturing solar collectors, however, will result in some emissions of greenhouse gases and other air pollutants.

EXISTING REGULATIONS. Several solar-energy policies were enacted in the 1970s, but many were rescinded by the Reagan administration. Despite progress with solar-energy supplies, elimination of federal renewable-energy tax credits and reduced R&D funding have caused this market to shrink. Additional market incentives and strong government leadership will be required if solar energy is to become a substantial US energy source in the near term.

One example of creative local policymaking to encourage solar energy can be found in Hawaii. The Energy Division of the Hawaii Department of Business and Economic Development has set up a program in regional high schools to design and build solar cars. Because these vehicles do not need Detroit's technological know-how, they can be built anywhere. This opens the door for innovative, decentralized manufacturing.

Fuel Cells

ADVANTAGES	DISADVANTAGES
+ Direct energy conversion means efficient generation (e.g., twice as efficient as a standard internal combustion engine)	- Nonrenewable resource when powered by fossil fuels
+ Lower NO_x, hydrocarbon, CO, and particulate emissions	- Current designs are heavy and voluminous
+ Lower greenhouse-gas emissions	- Current technologies are expensive
+ Well suited to large fleet vehicles (e.g., buses)	
+ Low maintenance costs	
+ Long vehicle life	
+ Future technology could reduce weight, size, and cost	

Fuel Cells

COST AND AVAILABILITY. Fuel cells are batterylike units that convert fuel directly to electricity. A fuel cell provides direct generation of electrical energy by electrochemically combining hydrogen and oxygen, which forms water and releases up to 90 percent of its chemical energy as electricity. Thus fuel is transformed directly (and more efficiently) to electricity without an intermediate conversion to heat. Although they are promising enough to have aroused the interest of several federal agencies, they are still too expensive and bulky for use in cars. They are, however, well suited for use in buses and other heavy-duty vehicles. Fuel cells should cost less to maintain than diesel engines because they have fewer moving parts. Buses running on fuel cells could last up to 20 years, nearly twice as long as the average diesel bus. Thus their higher up-front costs could be offset by lower maintenance costs and longer life.

Technological breakthroughs could make expanded fuel-cell applications even more attractive. A recent development, the proton exchange membrane (PEM), replaces the current phosphoric-acid electrolyte, and could reduce the fuel cell's weight by 25 percent, its volume by 40 percent, and cost by 25 percent.

Once fuel cells have been successfully demonstrated, wide-scale availability is the next hurdle. By the turn of the century, fuel-cell vans and cars could be in prototype (Saricks 1990). However, DOE estimates that the demand for fuel-cell vehicles must be at least 100,000 annually before a major automotive manufacturer will market these vehicles.

HARDWARE MODIFICATIONS. Current fuel cells are larger, heavier, and more expensive than conventional gasoline car engines. However, because size and weight are not a problem in buses and other heavy-duty vehicles, a prototype fuel-cell bus will probably be completed by 1992 with demonstration fleets to follow in 1996. Fuel-cell vehicles must be modified to include a fuel processor to combine air and fuel, a fuel cell to electrolytically combine air with hydrogen gas released from the fuel processor, and an electric motor to run the vehicle. Of these three modifications, the fuel cell itself requires the most development. Several fuel-cell technologies are being tested: alkaline, phosphoric acid, proton-exchange membranes (PEM), molten carbonate, and monolithic solid oxide. Phosphoric acid and PEM hold the most promise for near-term applications, the latter for passenger vehicles and the former for buses (Barber 1990).

RESOURCE BASE AND SUPPLY. A wide range of fuels such as hydrogen, natural gas, propane, methanol, ethanol, biomass, and water can be converted to electricity in a fuel cell. This is much more efficient than burning the fuels to generate electricity or using them directly in a standard combustion engine. Fuel cells are cited as 40-80 percent efficient, compared with power-plant efficiencies of 25-40 percent and state-of-the-art spark-ignition engine efficiencies of about 25-35 percent (Barber 1990, Shreve and Brink 1977). Thus fuel cells are twice as efficient as internal-combustion engines and power plants.

FUEL PROPERTIES AND SAFETY CONCERNS. Fuel cells are similar to common dry-cell batteries. Both convert the energy of a chemical reaction directly into electricity. Unlike a battery, however, a fuel cell does not undergo a material change. In fuel cells, the gaseous or liquid fuel and the oxidizer are introduced from the outside, whereas a battery stores its solid fuel and oxidizer on plates. In other words, fuel cells operate electrochemically, serving as reaction vessels in and of themselves. Thus they do not run down or require recharging; they operate as long as fuel and air are supplied.

Fuel cells produce direct current; a power inverter is required to convert this output to alternating current. A fuel-processing unit (or reformer) may be required to convert the input fuel to a hydrogen-rich gas.

Safety concerns about fuel cells are similar to those for electric vehicles (discussed above). Exposure to harsh chemicals and shock dangers from the electric motor are potential safety hazards for technicians repairing fuel-cell vehicles. The presence of hydrogen gas can be a safety hazard if not properly vented. High temperatures of certain fuel-cell configurations (molten carbonate at 1,200 degrees F [650 degrees C] and monolithic solid oxide at 1,800 degrees F [980 degrees C]) are another potential safety problem.

GREENHOUSE-GAS AND OTHER EMISSIONS. Fuel-cell vehicles are much cleaner than their conventionally fueled counterparts. Fuel cells emit extremely low levels of NO_x (0.001 grams/mile), hydrocarbons (0.002 grams/mile), carbon monoxide (less than 2 ppm), and a negligible amount of particulates (Barber 1990). In fact, 1,600 fuel-cell vehicles have the equivalent total air emissions of one of today's gasoline vehicles.

In terms of greenhouse-gas emissions, methanol fuel-cell vehicles are estimated to emit about one-half of the carbon dioxide of gasoline-fueled vehicles, while hydrogen fuel-cell vehicles emit no carbon dioxide at all (Barber 1990). In addition to air-quality benefits, fuel cells operate quietly, greatly reducing noise levels compared to today's vehicles.

EXISTING REGULATIONS. There are currently funds in the federal energy budget for an R&D program to develop hydrogen and hybrid vehicles. However, DOE depends on partnerships with other agencies and industries to promote fuel-cell R&D efforts. The PEM Fuel Cell R&D Program, a joint effort of DOE and the California South Coast Air Quality Management District (SCAQMD), with 20 percent industry cost sharing, is scheduled for test-vehicle demonstration by 1997. The Phosphoric Acid Fuel Cell/Battery Bus Program, cosponsored by DOE, DOT/UMTA, SCAQMD, with industry sharing 30 percent of the $15-million program cost, plans to have prototype methanol-fueled, fuel-cell/battery-powered bus fleets by 1995. The Monolithic Solid Oxide Fuel Cell (MSOFC) Program with eventual applications for cars, vans, trucks, buses, and trains is more formative in scope; a 60-kW power source is scheduled for development by 1997 (Barber 1990).

In addition to their potential for transportation, fuel cells have played a key part in NASA's research efforts. Recently, the space agency spent $20 million on fuel-cell research for Project Apollo alone. And the Department of Defense has shown interest in perfecting fuel cells for military operations.

Hydrogen

ADVANTAGES	DISADVANTAGES
+ Renewable resource when made from water	- Nonrenewable resource when made from fossil fuel
+ Innovative storage techniques (carbon granules) are less bulky, lightweight, and safe	- Full-cycle emissions are difficult to quantify
+ Lower flammability limit in air than gasoline	- Metal-hydride storage is very heavy and voluminous
+ Disperses quickly upon release	- In gaseous form, costly to refuel and explosive
+ No CO, hydrocarbon, or SO_x emissions from the vehicle	- Asphyxiant at high concentrations
+ Minimal NO_x emissions	- Hydrogen-distribution and fuel storage systems remain major barriers
+ Nontoxic	
+ Well suited to certain fleet vehicles (e.g., buses)	- Engine redesign needed to optimize combustion
	- Currently very expensive

Hydrogen Fuel

COST AND AVAILABILITY. Hydrogen is a clean-burning, high-energy fuel whose major by-product is water vapor. It can be produced from coal, natural gas, and oil, and by splitting water into hydrogen and oxygen (electrolysis).[19] Predictions of the future price of electrolytic hydrogen vary widely, depending on the assumptions made. One assumption is that photovoltaic electricity will be more economical than fossil-generated electricity for producing electrolytic hydrogen. By the year 2000 the cost of hydrogen produced from photovoltaic electricity could range from $1.68 to $2.35 per gallon of gasoline-equivalent (Ogden and Williams 1989). Other predictions for solar hydrogen for 2000 range from $3.10 to $11.75 per gallon of gasoline-equivalent (in 1988 dollars) (DeLuchi 1989). Today, hydrogen from coal costs about $0.85 to $1.50 per gallon of gasoline-equivalent.[20]

As PV technology comes of age, PV hydrogen systems will become more competitive and PV could augment the off-peak conventional power source of hydrogen production. PV hydrogen may be best suited to fleet vehicles in the near term. An estimated 7,000 MW of PV generating capacity, installed on about 22 square miles of land area (probably in the US Southwest), could fuel 10 percent of US fleet vehicles (such as buses, delivery trucks/vans, and other public and private fleet vehicles) with PV hydrogen (Ogden and Williams 1989).

It could take several decades to switch the US transportation sector over to hydrogen fuel, but the transition could begin in the 1990s. Commercial demonstrations of both the manufacture of hydrogen using photovoltaic electricity and hydrogen-powered transport systems themselves are the next step to making hydrogen fuel market-ready.

Fuel storage is another important cost issue. The three forms of hydrogen storage—as a liquid, as a compressed gas, and as part of a metal hydride (see Fuel Properties, below)—have varying costs. Metal hydrides may be the most appealing; their initial cost would be 30-50 percent of the cost of compressed-hydrogen storage (Ogden and Williams 1989). For liquid hydrogen, technological breakthroughs are needed to reduce storage costs.

HARDWARE MODIFICATIONS. Hydrogen vehicles look like gasoline vehicles, with a similar engine, but have a very different fuel-storage system. In theory, hydrogen vehicles can perform well enough for all highway applications. In practice, however, vehicle modifications, hydrogen distribution, and fuel storage remain as barriers that this fuel must overcome.

Hydrogen can be used in a conventional spark-ignition engine, but it is about 50 percent more efficient when burned in a stratified-charge engine (a spark-ignited, direct-injection system). Vehicles must be made much more fuel efficient in order to travel as far as gasoline vehicles. Efficient distribution of hydrogen will probably require upgrading of natural-gas pipelines. Pure hydrogen reacts at the surface of certain pipeline steels, embrittling them and causing fatigue cracks (Ogden and Williams 1989). Thus compounds that inhibit embrittlement must be developed before hydrogen can be shipped in natural-gas pipelines; otherwise dedicated-hydrogen pipelines would have to be constructed. Besides pipelines, hydrogen can be shipped in liquid form by rail car and tank truck, requiring no modification of existing systems, although this is prohibitively expensive on a large scale.

Research on fuel storage in metal hydrides is directed at finding hydrides that store a higher percentage of hydrogen by weight than is now possible. Research on storage as a liquid seeks to solve the problems of the bulkiness of the storage systems, the high cost of cryogenic technology, and evaporative fuel losses, which can range from 10-25 percent during refueling.

RESOURCE BASE AND SUPPLY. Hydrogen can be produced in several ways: by steam reforming natural gas (the most common method of large-scale hydrogen production), by steam gasifying coal, by partially oxidizing oil, or by electrolysis. Any number of energy sources can supply the electricity required to electrolyze water—fossil fuels and renewable energy sources are contenders.

Making hydrogen directly from fossil fuels is much cheaper and more efficient than using petroleum to make electrolytic hydrogen. Thus it is more likely that the electricity used to produce electrolytic hydrogen will come from a renewable source like solar energy. Furthermore, if and when fusion becomes feasible, electrolytic-hydrogen production could become cost-competitive.

Today, the hydrogen market is not large. In the US, only 0.6 quads of hydrogen—about 1 percent of total energy use—are consumed annually (Ogden and Williams 1989). And less than half of this is used as an energy source. Most is used in manufacturing glass, food, electronics, and steel, in producing chemicals such as ammonia and methanol, and in oil refining.

FUEL PROPERTIES AND SAFETY CONCERNS. Hydrogen can be used as a compressed gas stored in tanks at about 2400 psi, chemically bound in metal as a metal hydride (from which it is recaptured as needed), or in liquid form at extremely low temperatures. Other ways of storing hydrogen are also being developed.

Liquid hydrogen is appealing because it has more net energy content per unit volume than either compressed gaseous hydrogen or metal-hydride hydrogen—five times more than the former and twice as much as the latter. A 20-gallon liquid-hydrogen system weighs about 20 pounds (empty) and provides a 260-mile driving range (DeLuchi 1989). The Department of Energy estimates that a liquid-hydrogen system would require more than twice the volume of an equivalent amount of gasoline (DOE 1988a). Moreover, because hydrogen becomes a liquid at -423 degrees F (-253 degrees C), cryogenic containment is required, severely limiting distribution (liquid hydrogen cannot be piped more than one or two miles).

Compressed-hydrogen storage, on the other hand, is relatively simple. However, because of compressed hydrogen's low energy content per unit of volume, the vehicle's fuel economy must be increased drastically to store enough of the gas on board. Today's 35-mpg vehicle would require 60 to 100 gallons of storage space to provide a 200-mile driving range, thus sacrificing the vehicle's trunk space. Another major drawback of compressed hydrogen is its high refueling-station cost, estimated at 37 cents per gallon of gasoline-equivalent (Ogden and Williams 1989).[21]

The principle of the third storage method, metal hydrides, is simple: at low temperatures, hydrides store hydrogen in a metal; when the temperature is raised, the hydrogen is liberated. Unfortunately, an 80-gallon storage unit weighing up to 1,000 pounds contains only 0.5 to 2 percent hydrogen by weight. Hydride vehicles are limited by storage weight to a 90- to 180-mile driving range (DeLuchi 1989). Thus, like vehicles equipped with compressed hydrogen, hydride-equipped vehicles must be much more fuel-efficient to compensate for the low mass-energy density of the hydride fuel system.

Another means of storing hydrogen safely, now in development, is on highly porous carbon granules.[22] When these granules are chemically treated, they can expand their hydrogen-collecting abilities. The hydrogen fuel can be kept in a portable fuel tank, cooled to about -120 degrees F (-84 degrees C), at a pressure of about 700 psi. To retrieve the hydrogen, the fuel tank's temperature is raised and the pressure is lowered. Hydrogen granules have the advantage of being lighter than metal hydrides and closer to ambient temperature and pressure conditions than either liquid or compressed hydrogen. The total cost of carbon storage, including fuel-station cost and storage-vessel cost, would be less than for metal-hydride or liquid-hydrogen systems (DeLuchi 1989). This new storage method could be available in the 1990s and is most promising for heavy-duty applications such as buses.

Remember the *Hindenburg*? Its explosion is thought to be singlehandedly responsible for hydrogen's reputation as an unsafe fuel. Nevertheless, studies of the relative safety of hydrogen, methane (CNG), and gasoline have concluded that none of these fuels is *inherently* safer than the others (Ogden and Williams 1989).

Because hydrogen is lighter than air or any other fuel, it rises and disperses quickly upon release. Thus there are few problems with hydrogen leaks in free air from storage, pipelines, or the vehicle itself, since the fuel tends to disperse before it reaches flammable concentrations in air. From this perspective hydrogen is safer than gasoline, which is heavier than air and tends to linger near a leak, reaching hazardous concentrations more easily. Hydrogen releases do present a serious safety problem when leaked in enclosed areas with little dispersion. However, fires fueled by hydrogen burn rapidly and radiate little heat, making them short-lived.

Hydrogen itself is nontoxic, as are its by-products. Because hydrogen is odorless, colorless, and burns with an invisible flame, an odorant and flame colorant must be added to enable detection in the event of a mishap. Also, contact with liquid hydrogen destroys human tissue; gloves should be worn to reduce the risk of damage.

GREENHOUSE-GAS AND OTHER EMISSIONS. The composition and amount of these depend on how the fuel is produced. When hydrogen is generated from fossil-fuel electricity sources, CO_2-equivalent emissions will increase. If it is generated from nonfossil sources such as electrolysis powered by photovoltaic electricity, there are no additional greenhouse-gas emissions. But when hydrogen is made directly from coal, CO_2-equivalent emissions double for hydrides and increase by 140 percent for liquid hydrogen (DeLuchi 1989).

When hydrogen is burned in a vehicle's engine, only water and small amounts of nitrogen oxides are formed. Since hydrogen fuel is carbon-free, only trace amounts of CO and hydrocarbons are emitted from the lubricant coating in the vehicle's engine. Hydrogen vehicles do not produce particulates, sulfur oxides, benzene, or formaldehyde. The only pollutant of concern is NO_x, but these emissions from optimized hydrogen vehicles could be 10-50 percent less than those from gasoline-powered engines (Ogden and Williams 1989). Hydrogen fuel will not pollute water and land resources. Depending on how the hydrogen is produced, however, these other emissions (such as releases of toxins in coal-gasification plant wastewater streams) may increase.

EXISTING REGULATIONS. Of all the alternative fuels, hydrogen needs the most R&D to commercialize it for passenger vehicles. Yet in 1988, DOE's hydrogen R&D projects were phased out altogether (DOE 1989a). By comparison, countries like Japan and Germany provide significant government funding for hydrogen research efforts. Without government support, this promising fuel will remain only a very long-term option.

Conclusion

Which is the right alternative fuel? The answer depends on your objective. If the goal is to wean the US from imported oil, reformulated gasoline and oxygenated gasoline fuels are clearly not the answer. If the aim is to ensure sufficient long-term fuel supplies, the choice will not be ethanol from corn, methanol from fossil fuels, or LPG. If immediate availability is the object, then fuel cells, hydrogen, solar energy, and electricity will not fit the bill.

Moreover, there is no conclusive answer yet as to which fuel is the most environmentally benign and which may have harmful side effects that we are not yet aware of. Thus if the goal is to select an alternative to gasoline that will reduce pollution and greenhouse-gas emissions, more demonstration is needed.

Another complication in selecting alternatives is that certain fuels may be advantageous in certain regions but not nationwide. Determining the trade-offs that each alternative fuel offers is important before we give up our gasoline habit altogether and become dependent on another (potentially worse) fuel. We need a regional demonstration program to address the uncertainties that remain.

Nevertheless, based on what we know today, we can still make several assertions: Compressed natural gas is the most promising near-term alternative for the heavy-duty fleet, and fuel cells are the most promising long-term option sector wide (see box). Wherever clean fuels are indigenous to a particular region, it would be prudent to develop them and use them to further demonstrate the fuels' capabilities. For example, the Midwest could develop ethanol and other oxygenates; the South and Rocky Mountain states could test natural gas; the West could demonstrate electricity; Hawaii and the Southwest could test solar and hydrogen fuels; and the Northeast could use LPG. Such a scheme could reduce distribution costs in the near term, especially for fleet applications, and provide more data for long-term solutions.

Compressed natural gas (CNG) is available today for most motor-vehicle applications, and further advances could move this fuel into widespread use. CNG is attractive because of its competitive cost, low toxicity, low emissions, relative safety, and secure supply. However, it must compete with alcohol fuels, such as ethanol and methanol, which can be blended with gasoline in conventional engines and thus provide a convenient transition to alternative fuels. CNG cannot be blended with conventional fuels; CNG can be blended with hydrogen to make a fuel called hythane. Hythane holds promise as a clean-burning alternative fuel.

Given its limited resource base, LPG cannot contribute significant amounts of future transportation fuel. Moreover, it is not expected to reduce emissions to any appreciable extent.

Even though methanol and ethanol can be mixed with gasoline, easing the shift to these alternatives, dedicated use of these alcohol fuels will probably not become cost-competitive with gasoline, CNG, and LPG without government mandates or incentives. Alcohol fuels may

Comparing Alternative Transportation Fuels by Criteria

Criteria

Fuel	Adequate Resource Base	Manageable Fuel Properties	Greenhouse Gas & Other Emissions	Feasible Hardware Modifications	Cost Competitive (Currently)	Available (Market-Ready)	Effect of Existing Regulations
CNG	+	+	+	+	+	+/–	–
LPG	–	–	+/–	+	+	+	–
Methanol	–	–	+/–	+	–	–	+
Ethanol (corn)	–	+	+/–	+	–	–	+
Reformulated Gasoline	+/–	–	+/–	+	+	–	+
Oxygenates (MTBE/ETBE)	+	–	+/–	+	–	+	+
Electricity	+/–	+/–	+/–	–	–	+/–	+
Hydrogen	+	+/–	+/–	–	–	–	–
Solar Energy	+	+/–	+	–	–	–	+/–
Fuel Cells	+	+	+	–	–	–	+
Ethanol (woody biomass)	+	+	+/–	+	+/–	–	–

\+ Advantageous
– Disadvantageous
+/– Both advantages and disadvantages

have limited air-quality benefits in certain regions, although methanol will increase greenhouse-gas emissions if new coal sources are used as feedstocks. Ethanol can reduce greenhouse gases if woody biomass is used as feedstock instead of corn and other food crops.

Reformulated gasoline was designed as a first effort to address the air pollution in our dirtiest cities. In the near term, many of these cities would benefit from a switch to reformulated gasoline. In the long run, it has nearly all the problems of gasoline: resources are not adequate or secure, greenhouse-gas emissions will increase, and oil spills will continue.

Oxygenated additives such as MTBE and ETBE reduce only selected air emissions and are thus best used in regions where carbon monoxide standards have been exceeded. Again, these additives do not reduce greenhouse-gas emissions.

Electricity and hydrogen both hold promise for the future but only if they are made from nonfossil resources. If coal were to supply either of these resources, both greenhouse and other emissions would rise.

Solar energy, especially solar cars, could dramatically reduce the social and environmental costs of transportation. This alternative is longer-term and holds promise for those regions where sunlight is abundant.

Fuel cells are the best long-term transportation fuel source. They could promote a healthy diversity in the transportation sector because they can use a wide array of fuels, including hydrogen and biomass fuels. Since fuel cells generate electricity on board, the vehicles they power produce virtually no emissions. Further research is needed to reduce the technological and cost barriers of this alternative.

Before closing this chapter, the relationship between alternative fuels and vehicle fuel efficiency bears mentioning. Since most alternative fuels have relatively low energy contents compared with gasoline, increasing vehicle fuel efficiency is absolutely necessary for both practical and economic reasons. Enhanced fuel efficiency will thus promote the feasibility and marketability of alternative fuels.

Notes

1. Note that fuel cost may not be as important to the consumer as the total cost of driving a given distance. Thus if alternative-fueled vehicles can be designed to be very energy efficient, the cost may be acceptable even with low oil prices.

2. These prices do not include externalities that could both directly and indirectly increase fuel costs.

3. These hazards are measured in part by autoignition temperatures (the temperature above which a mixture will automatically ignite), flashpoints (the temperature above which combustible mixtures form just above the liquid

surfaces of a fuel), and flammability limits in air (the range of mixtures of fuel in air that will result in a fire or explosion).

4. Full-cycle costs include production, distribution, marketing, and vehicle hardware modifications.

5. In an optimized CNG engine, this fuel uses its available energy 5 to 10 percent more efficiently than gasoline. CNG is capable of supporting higher compression ratios than gasoline, given its 33 percent higher octane rating. In fact, CNG has a higher octane rating than both methanol and ethanol.

6. The actual level of CO depends on the air-fuel ratio in the vehicle's engine.

7. The California Energy Commission projects that in 1993 the wholesale price of methanol fuel alone (excluding distribution, marketing, and hardware-modification costs) will be $0.86 per gallon of gasoline-equivalent (in 1988 dollars).

8. Certain gasoline components can be added to eliminate the flammability problem.

9. The California Energy Commission projects that by 1993 pure wholesale ethanol fuel will cost $1.88 per gallon of gasoline-equivalent (1988 dollars).

10. This cost amounts to roughly $9.30 per megajoule of ethanol fuel ($0.75 per gallon). And although ethanol has a 53-percent lower net energy content than gasoline, it is 10 to 20 percent more thermally efficient.

11. Following intense battling between Congress and the Reagan administration, the excise-tax exemption was raised from four cents a gallon in 1978 to five cents in December 1982 and then to six cents in January 1985. It is scheduled to remain at six cents per gallon until September 1993.

12. See DeLuchi et al. 1989b for details on different battery configurations.

13. Such changes to federal energy policies include: 1) re-instituting renewable-energy tax credits; 2) taxing fossil fuel consumption, with part of the revenue used to fund R&D of renewable energy sources and to offset the costs of renewable energy tax credits; 3) modifying PURPA to require electric utilities to take into account the social and environmental costs of energy technologies when contracting for new capacity; 4) steadily increasing renewable energy R&D funding by 20 to 30 percent per year, approaching $1 billion by 2000; 5) purchasing renewable-energy technologies for government owned facilities; and 6) expanding government efforts to encourage exports of renewable-energy technologies.

14. Calculated by dividing 1,357 billion vehicle-miles for cars by an operating efficiency of 3 miles per kWh and multiplying by 3.25 to account for electrical-system losses. Similarly, total fleet-car-electricity requirements are estimated using 195 billion vehicle-miles. Calculations for vans assume 80 billion vehicle-miles of travel and an operating efficiency of 1 mile per kWh. For buses, 2 billion vehicle-miles and an estimated 1 mile per kWh were assumed. Figures are for 1987.

15. US net electricity generation was 2,780 billion kWh in 1989.

16. As long as biomass is not grown on existing forest land or generated from waste products that otherwise would not have oxidized, this energy source is carbon-free.

17. The three major domestic automobile manufacturers are involved in cost-sharing contracts with DOE and the Electric Power Research Institute (EPRI); other program participants include component and propulsion-system companies, battery companies, universities, and fleet-testing site operators such as GTE, Detroit Edison, and the US Navy.

18. This assumes a conversion efficiency of 25 percent. Note that regional differences in solar exposure change the economic viability of solar energy significantly.

19. The cost of producing hydrogen fuel from coal depends on the technology used, feedstock cost, and the size of the plant. Hydrogen produced from coal is estimated to cost from $6 to $20 per million Btu, whereas electrolytic hydrogen costs from $2 to $15 per million Btu, and solar hydrogen costs from $27 to $70 per million Btu (DeLuchi 1989).

20. This assumes $7 to $13 per million Btu hydrogen (DeLuchi 1989) and 116,000 Btu per gallon of gasoline.

21. This estimate considers the cost to compress low energy-density hydrogen from distribution pressures of 150 psi to storage pressures of up to 3600 psi.

22. Dr. J.A. Schwarz, professor of chemical engineering and materials science at Syracuse University, is the patent holder of this new technology.

6 Ultra-Fuel-Efficient Vehicles

In a recent poll, well over three-quarters of adult voters responding said they would be willing to pay for an increase in the average fuel economy of automobiles to 45 miles per gallon (RSM 1989).[1] Yet few new cars today achieve even 40 mpg; instead, they are fast and flashy. As *Fortune* magazine recently noted, "Consumers prefer steak, but Detroit continues to market sizzle" (Moore 1990). High fuel economy seems to be far from the top priority of car makers. Consumers have a right to ask why they are not being given a reasonable range of choices of truly high-mileage automobiles.

Only since the first oil crisis have relatively fuel-efficient vehicles been marketed. In 1975 cars still averaged only 14 miles per gallon. Concerned about the high level of oil imports devoted to motor vehicles, Congress enacted fuel-economy standards for new cars and light trucks. The CAFE (corporate average fuel economy) standards required manufacturers to sell increasingly more efficient vehicles starting in 1978. These standards prompted a doubling of new-vehicle fuel efficiency, to 27.5 mpg, in just 10 years (Figure 24). The legislation mandated no higher level than this (and actually allowed relaxation down to 26 mpg); thus fuel-economy gains first leveled out and then began to backslide. Because cars and light trucks still consume a disproportionate share of our oil imports (1990 CAFE levels are 27.5 mpg for cars and 20.2 mpg for light trucks), dramatic increases in fuel economy—which are technologically feasible—are advisable.

Cars

Available technologies could produce immediate gains in automotive energy efficiency. They include such innovations as four-valve-per-cylinder engines; intake valve control; continuously variable transmission (CVT); electronic transmission control; greatly reduced drag; improved tires, lubricants, and accessories; advanced weight reduction;

| Figure 24 | Recent Trends in New-Car and Light-Truck Economy |

Fleet-wide average fuel economy and corporate average fuel economy (CAFE) standard, from CAFE enactment (1978) to 1990.

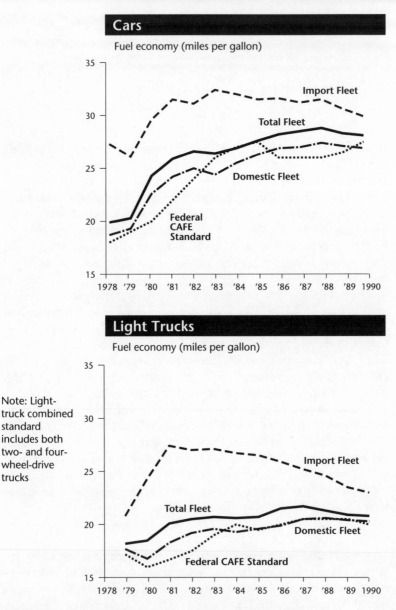

Cars

Fuel economy (miles per gallon)

Import Fleet

Total Fleet

Domestic Fleet

Federal CAFE Standard

1978 '79 '80 '81 '82 '83 '84 '85 '86 '87 '88 '89 1990

Light Trucks

Fuel economy (miles per gallon)

Note: Light-truck combined standard includes both two- and four-wheel-drive trucks

Import Fleet

Total Fleet

Domestic Fleet

Federal CAFE Standard

1978 '79 '80 '81 '82 '83 '84 '85 '86 '87 '88 '89 1990

Source: Langer, National Highway Traffic Safety Administration, 1990.

and various other engine improvements. The problem is that they are not yet being built into today's new cars. Once they are, fuel economy could increase from today's new-car average of about 28 mpg to 40 mpg (Ledbetter and Ross 1990) (Table 14).[2]

Unfortunately, current technological improvements are focused on making cars ever more powerful and faster. Since 1982, average horse-power has steadily increased and average acceleration time has dramatically decreased. The reduction in acceleration time alone may have caused at least a 6-percent decline in average fuel economy (Ledbetter 1989a). Fuel economy is marketed predominantly on stripped-down, low-cost models. Because of manufacturers' marketing tactics, fuel economy is linked to the cheapest models, but not to all models. In fact, all of the 1990 cars with a combined EPA fuel-economy rating of over 40 mpg are basic subcompacts (EPA and DOE 1989). A consumer who wants a fuel-efficient compact or mid-size car is simply out of luck.

A recent study calculated that if average automobile size and acceleration performance were held constant at their 1987 levels, new-car fuel economy could cost-effectively be improved to about 44 mpg by the year 2000, at an average cost of 53 cents per gallon of gasoline saved. (That is, this level of improvement would cost only 53 cents per gallon of gasoline even compared to an estimated 1990 price of $1.25 a gallon—a 70-cent-a-gallon difference.)

On a national scale, an increase in new-car fuel economy to 44 mpg by 2000 would reduce US highway-transportation fuel consumption by about one million barrels a day (nearly one-fifth of daily consumption) and 2.5 million barrels a day by 2005 (Ledbetter and Ross 1990, Ledbetter 1990). These future fuel savings represent nearly twice the amount of oil the United States was importing from Iraq and Kuwait prior to the Iraqi crisis of August 1990.

To achieve this level of fuel economy, and higher, numerous ultra-fuel-efficient cars, with mileage ratings of 52 to nearly 110 mpg, have been developed as prototypes (Bleviss 1988) (Table 15). These cars seat from two to five passengers and incorporate radical innovations such as the extensive use of plastics and light materials, flywheel improvements, and supercharged diesel injection engines. Experts say that these cars, equipped with good space and performance characteristics, can be built for no additional cost beyond the manufacturer's initial retooling (Ross 1989).

One of the most promising technologies is the two-stroke engine, which is lighter, smaller, and simpler than its four-stroke counterpart. These engines are common in motorcycles and lawnmowers, but not in passenger vehicles. Over 20 years ago, Sweden's Saab sold a small two-stroke-engine car in the US, but when emission controls went into effect in 1968, sale of these cars was discontinued. Two-stroke engines develop power once every two strokes of the piston—up and down—rather than requiring two complete turns of the crankshaft to develop power from

Table 14
Efficiency-Improving Technologies[a]

Technology	Percent Fuel Economy Gain	% Market Penetration (Over 1987 Levels)	Fleet % Fuel Economy Gain
Front wheel drive**	10	20	2.0
4 valve per cylinder (4 & 6 cylinder engines)**	6.8	80	5.4
Intake valve control**	6	40	2.4
4-speed automatic/ Continuous Variable Transmission (CVT)**	4.7	40	1.9
Electronic transmission control & torque converter lock-up**	3	85	2.6
Aerodynamic improvements**	4.6	100	4.6
Tires**	0.5	100	0.5
Lubricants**	0.5	100	0.5
Accessories**	1.7	100	1.7
Engine improvements			
-Roller cams**	1.5	80	1.2
-Low friction rings/pistons**	4	80	3.2
-Multipoint fuel injection**	3.5	10	0.4
-Overhead cam**	6	40	2.4
Weight reduction**	6.6	80	5.3
Advanced tires	0.5	100	0.5
Aggressive transmission management	8	100	8.0
Idle off	9	100	9.0

TOTAL RESULTING FUEL ECONOMY[b] = 43MPG

Notes:
**Technologies already in production.

a. This analysis is not meant to predict exactly how the industry will seek to comply with a standard that would establish a new automotive fleet fuel economy by 2000 of 40 mpg. Rather, this assessment is meant to show the feasibility of this target as well as to illustrate one way the industry could meet such a target.
b. 1987 base year with fuel economy of 28.3 mpg.

Source: Ledbetter and Ross, Supply Curves of Conserved Energy for Automobiles, *prepared for Lawrence Berkeley Laboratory, Applied Science Division, March 1990.*

Table 15
Ultra-Fuel-Efficient Prototype Vehicles

Manufacturer	Model Name (fuel)	Number of Passengers	Fuel Economy (mpg)	Innovative Features	Development Status
General Motors	TPC (gasoline)	2	61 city 74 hwy	Aluminum body & engine	Prototype complete, no production plans
British Leyland	ECV-3 (gasoline)	4-5	41 city 52 hwy	High use of aluminum & plastics	Prototype complete
Volkswagen	Auto 2000 (diesel)	4-5	63 city 71 hwy	Plastic & aluminum parts, fly-wheel, stop-start	Prototype complete
Volkswagen	VW-E80 (diesel)	4	74 city 99 hwy	Modified 3-cylinder, stop-start, supercharger	Ongoing research, possible production
Volvo	LCP 2000	2-4	63 city 81 hwy	Heat-insulated DI[a] engine, high mag-nesium use	Prototype complete
Renault	EVE+ (diesel)	4-5	63 city 81 hwy	Supercharged DI[a], with stop-start	Prototype complete
Renault	Vesta2 (gasoline)	2-4	78 city 107 hwy	High use of light material	Prototype complete
Peugeot	VERA+ (diesel)	4-5	55 city 87 hwy	DI[a] engine, high use of light material	Ongoing development
Peugeot	ECO2000 (gasoline)	4	70 city 77 hwy	2-cylinder engine, high use of light material	Ongoing development
Ford	un-named (diesel)	4-5	57 city 92 hwy	DI[a] engine	Research
Toyota	AXV (diesel)	4-5	89 city 110 hwy	High use of aluminum & plastic, CVT[b] & DI[a] engine	Ongoing development

See notes on following page

Notes:
a. DI = Diesel injection
b. CVT = Continuously variable transmission

Source: Bleviss, The New Oil Crisis and Fuel Economy Technologies, *1988.*

---

each cylinder, as a four-stroke engine does. Besides improving fuel economy by an estimated 20 percent, the two-stroke engine equipped with a fuel-injection system and advanced electronics can meet anticipated emission-control requirements (Fisher 1990). And because the two-stroke has about 200 fewer parts than a conventional engine, it costs manufacturers about $400 less to make and saves consumers in maintenance expenses. An Australian manufacturer, the Orbital Engine Company, is planning to make up to 250,000 of these engines in the US by 1993.

Given the many promising technologies, why the disinterest in meaningful improvements in fuel economy? A strong case can be made that, with the low gasoline prices of the 1980s, the dollar value of fuel-economy savings to consumers was relatively small compared to the overall cost of driving. In 1989, fuel costs represented only about 12 percent of the cost of operating a car (Ledbetter 1990). Even Iraq's invasion of Kuwait has not significantly changed the equation. As long as the total cost of driving varies only slightly with fuel economy, prospective buyers will continue to be indifferent to fuel economy (Ross 1989).[3]

Yet even if higher fuel prices and supply disruptions are brought on by events like the Iraqi oil crisis, market forces alone are unlikely to boost fuel economies into the 40-mpg range. In Western Europe and Japan, where gasoline prices are $2-$4 a gallon, new-car fuel economies are only 27-36 mpg. Thus ultra-fuel-efficient vehicles will not achieve a market niche without specific regulatory and economic signals such as increased corporate average fuel economy (CAFE) standards, higher gas-guzzler taxes and gas-sipper rebates, and consumer incentive programs like DRIVE+ (see Chapter 8). Other programs, such as outright purchase of old vehicles, can also help. And public policies that affect fuel economy indirectly, such as the Clean Air Act, could serve to promote ultra-fuel-efficient cars.

Light Trucks

Light-duty trucks can also be made much more fuel-efficient. Given their current low numbers (20 mpg on average for new trucks) and their increasing popularity (one-third of new light-duty vehicle sales), light trucks are a prime target for energy-efficiency improvements. Many of the same technologies that will improve cars will work with light trucks as well. Average efficiencies of 35 mpg are feasible for light trucks in the near term (Ledbetter 1990).

The large majority of light trucks are used as passenger cars; a 1982 Department of Commerce survey found that 73 percent of light trucks do not carry any freight (DOC 1982). Thus in the longer term, a new type of vehicle could be designed to replace light trucks for passenger transport. A radically redesigned two-seat, ultra-efficient utility vehicle may appeal to light-truck consumers if packaged with the right set of incentives (such as appearance and cost).

An increase to 35 mpg by the year 2000 in new light-truck fuel economy, coupled with new-car fuel economy improvements to 45 mpg, would reduce US oil consumption by 3.2 million barrels a day by 2005. These improvements will save consumers $38 billion annually and reduce carbon dioxide emissions by 650 million tons a year (Ledbetter 1990).

Heavy-Duty Trucks

Fuel economy is a fundamentally different question for heavy trucks than it is for light trucks because their freight load is such a large part of the vehicle's weight. Thus weight reduction and materials substitution in the truck itself are not promising strategies. But since energy use by heavy-duty trucks is projected to increase steadily through 2010, innovative economizing strategies are necessary (Carlsmith et al. 1990).

There are several options for both medium- and heavy-duty vehicles. Cab-mounted air deflectors; fairings to reduce the gap between tractor and trailer; radial tires; high-torque, low-rpm engines; variable-speed fans; improved lubricants; electronic transmission and engine controls; advanced methods for controlling aerodynamic drag; and better matching of truck specifications to missions can all improve fuel economy. With these technologies, heavy-duty trucks could make efficiency gains of 20 percent in the next 30 years (Carlsmith et al. 1990).[4]

Aircraft

Nonhighway vehicles, commercial aircraft in particular, could be more fuel-efficient as well. If 1990s-generation and post-2000 aircraft incorporate advances in engine, airframe, and control technology, significant efficiency improvements could be realized. These improvements are necessary if we are to keep pace with expected increases in air travel. Experts forecast US passenger air travel to increase at a rate of 6 percent annually for the next 15 years (Greene 1989). At this rate jet-fuel consumption would overtake automotive gasoline consumption in less than a decade.

The National Aeronautics and Space Administration has established the following near-term fuel-economy goals for commercial aircraft: reduce fuel consumption of jet engines by 20-30 percent, reduce aerodynamic drag by 15-20 percent, and reduce weight by 15-25 percent.[5] New ultra-high-bypass (UHB) engines will be up to 20 percent more energy efficient, and other engines using advanced propeller designs are expected to increase efficiency 20-50 percent.

Advanced ceramic and other high-temperature materials can further improve thermodynamic efficiency of the core turbine engines. Improved airframes can generate further efficiencies by reducing drag and weight. Lightweight composite materials can reduce fuel consumption by up to 15 percent. In addition, aerodynamics can contribute a potential energy-efficiency improvement of over 25 percent.

The trend toward larger aircraft, which are generally more efficient, will increase fuel economy. To combat increasing airport congestion, facilities are becoming more efficient, as automated tools for flight planning, airport operations planning, and air-traffic control all continue to improve. Overall, these efficiency improvements range from 46 to 104 percent (Table 16).

In the long term, supersonic and hypersonic aircraft could become important passenger carriers. By 2010, these aircraft could operate on engines 40 percent more efficient than current subsonic engines.

Trains

Railroads may not seem a likely candidate for a chapter on ultra-fuel-efficient vehicles. Overall railroad fuel efficiency is projected to improve at a rate of only 0.3 percent per year from 1990 to 2010 (Carlsmith et al. 1990). But railroads have a head start: they are already four times as efficient as trucks at moving freight.

On the passenger side, new, far more efficient trains are on the drawing board—and in some cases in prototype. Magnetically levitated (maglev) trains will run just inches above elevated guideways at speeds of up to 300 miles per hour. Maglev and steel-wheel high speed rail promise to be more energy efficient than the modes they would replace—the automobile and commercial aircraft. It could reduce regional auto congestion and air traffic on shorter, less-efficient routes. A system of maglev and steel-wheel high-speed trains operating in the most highly traveled corridors between cities 300-500 miles apart could save 280,000 barrels of oil a day if passengers were shifted away from automobiles and airplanes. (Carlsmith et al. 1990). And the development of high-temperature superconducting materials could increase maglev's energy efficiency even more. (See Chapter 7 for efficiency improvements in freight shipped by rail.)

Pipelines and Water Vessels

Unlike other transport modes, both pipelines and marine transport are expected to become less energy efficient over the next two decades. In 1985, pipelines transported freight at an efficiency of 1.16 TMT/kBtu (ton-mile-traveled per thousand Btu), but by 2010 efficiency is expected to drop to 0.97 TMT/kBtu—a 16-percent drop. Marine vessels are projected to become about 3 percent less efficient from a 1985 baseline of 2.72 TMT/kBtu (Carlsmith et al. 1990). The reasons for these pro-

Table 16
Efficiency-Improvement Potentials
for Advanced Airplane Technology
(Percent Improvement in Seat-Miles per Gallon)

Technology	Improvement Range		
	Maximum	Median	Minimum
ENGINES[a]			
Ultra-high Bypass	17%	10%	5%
Propfan	27%	23%	19%
Thermodynamics	27%	18%	15%
WEIGHT	18%	15%	9%
AERODYNAMICS[b]			
Hybrid Laminar Flow	18%	16%	15%
Advanced Aerodynamics	33%	26%	18%
TOTAL POTENTIAL SMPG GAIN[c]			
Ultra-high Bypass	94%	69%	46%
Propfan	104%	82%	60%

Notes:
a. Ultra-high bypass and turbofan engines are mutually exclusive.
b. The efficiency for hybrid laminar flow control is included in aerodynamics, and thus is left out of the total to avoid double counting.
c. Assume percent improvements in seat-miles per gallon are additive, which is a mathematically conservative approach.

Source: Greene, Energy Efficiency Improvement Potential of Commercial Aircraft to 2010, *1989.*

jected drops in efficiency are unclear, but it may have to do with the aging fleet of ships and pipeline systems.

Fuel Efficiency and Safety
Most of the fuel-efficiency gains realized from 1974-1989, which saved nearly 13 billion gallons of gasoline, were achieved by making vehicles smaller and lighter. During this period, while fuel economy doubled from 14 to 28 mpg, traffic fatalities dropped by 40 percent, to 2.2 deaths per 100 million vehicle miles traveled (Ditlow 1990b).

Higher fuel economy does not necessarily mean smaller—or less safe—cars. Improved engines, aerodynamic styles, and more advanced transmissions, tires, and other components can all increase fuel economy without sacrificing size or weight (Bleviss 1988, Ross 1989). Some experts argue that if manufacturers choose to further downsize vehicles rather than opt for other technological improvements (without enhancing safety equipment), safety will be compromised (Crandall and Graham 1989). Other experts claim that safety is a matter of vehicle design—that although downsizing has thus far been the primary means of increasing fuel economy, there is no reason why smaller cars cannot be designed to be safer. Occupant-restraint systems, air bags, and the ability

Volvo LCP 2000.

of a car to absorb energy can play a significant role in safety (Ledbetter 1989b). In fact, large differences have been found in the crashworthiness of automobiles, independent of their weight (OTA 1982, Ledbetter 1989b).

Data collected by the Insurance Institute for Highway Safety from 1986 to 1988 show little, if any, correlation between fuel economy and safety (vehicle death rate). In fact, one of the least efficient cars on the market, the GM Corvette, is less safe than several of the highly efficient models (Sprint, Civic, and Tercel). This underscores the fact that vehicle design and driver behavior have much more to do with safety than the fuel economy of the car itself.

The 1982-84 2,000-pound Volkswagen Rabbit with automatic seat belts had a lower rate of serious injury than the 3,700-pound Chevrolet Impala and 3,900-pound Ford Crown Victoria (Ditlow 1990b). Moreover, further research can improve both auto safety and fuel economy simultaneously. The Volvo LCP 2000, a prototype high-efficiency car, weighs less than half of today's average car, gets 81 mpg on the highway, and can withstand frontal and side impacts of 35 mph and a rear impact of 30 mph—more than current US regulations require (Ledbetter 1989b).

Ironically, many of the same technologies that could be used to improve fuel economy, without diminishing automobile safety, are instead being used to increase acceleration capability. And the faster a car accelerates, the less safe it is.

Fuel Efficiency and Vehicle Speed

At the height of the 1973 oil crisis, Congress imposed a national 55-mph speed limit to conserve energy. In 1985, the benefits of this speed limit were calculated at $3 billion a year in fuel savings and $195 million in the direct costs and $3.3 billion in the indirect costs of motor-vehicle accidents (Winston and Associates 1987). Despite this, enforcement of the law became increasingly lax in the 1980s, and although the Department of Transportation urged otherwise, many states raised the speed limit to 65 mph on certain roads or curtailed enforcement of the 55-mph limit.

The Iraqi oil crisis and the increase in prices it has brought highlight our continued dependence on oil imports. This is a good reason to reconsider the national 55-mph speed limit. Increasing passenger-vehicle speed from 50 to 60 mph wastes some 20 percent in average fuel use, and at 65 or 70 mph even more fuel is wasted. As much as 30 percent is sacrificed when speed is increased from 55 to 75 mph. Even the most fuel-efficient models may not save much fuel if the vehicle is driven over 55 mph (McGill 1985).

Conclusion

For each degree of improved energy efficiency, carbon dioxide emissions and energy consumption are reduced simultaneously—one for one. In other words, if the transportation sector could double its energy efficiency, CO_2 emissions from transportation would be cut in half, as would energy use.

Beyond technological fixes, the transportation sector's energy and environmental problems can and must be addressed by innovative strategies to reduce solo driving, overall vehicle miles traveled, and inefficient freight transportation. Such strategies can induce changes in both demand and supply of transportation services. Technology alone cannot solve our problems; innovative transportation strategies, examined in the next chapter, are an important element in reducing the overall social costs of transportation.

Notes

1. The poll was conducted by RSM, Inc., of Washington, DC, in November 1989 for the Union of Concerned Scientists and the Communications Consortium.

2. The Department of Energy estimates very conservatively that new-car fuel economy could be increased to 36 mpg by 2000 (Hirst 1989).

3. And, according to the "von Hippel-Levi effect," as fuel economies rise to the 30-40 mpg level, consumers will be even less inclined to make higher fuel economy their top priority.

4. Baseline efficiency in 1985 for heavy trucks was 0.37 ton-mile-traveled per thousand Btu (TMT/kBtu), whereas efficiency in 2010 is projected to be 0.45 TMT/kBtu.

5. All of the technological improvements to aircraft described in this section are from Greene 1989. This source should be referred to for technology specifications on aircraft improvements.

7 Innovative Transportation Strategies

■

There are several strategies that can help reduce transportation energy consumption, pollutant emissions, and traffic congestion. These range from alternative transportation services to innovative transportation-demand (and system) management strategies. Some of these strategies are best implemented at the federal level because they require comprehensive planning and coordination; others merit adoption at the state and regional level in response to specific needs.

In recent years transportation policies have increasingly had a regional focus, conforming to the "new federalism" policy introduced by the Reagan administration. Such a focus, which shifts the burden of support from federal to state and local governments, is expected to continue. The lack of federal leadership and financial support in addressing our transportation problems is clear in the Bush administration's draft "Statement of National Transportation Policy" of February 1990. Its message is plain: it is up to state and local governments to tackle on their own the US transportation system's problems.

A national transportation system is, of course, a federal responsibility. If the policy burden is passed to state and local governments, the federal government should accompany this shift with adequate resources. Without federal support for these improvements the public could be hesitant to fund new transportation projects and modernization of existing transit systems, which may take decades to prove their worth.

Several strategies—ridesharing, high-occupancy-vehicle lanes, better land-use planning, bicycling plans, improved freight transport, and many more—have the potential to ease transportation problems, but none can bring significant change by itself. Rather, a combination of innovative approaches, selected for each area, has the best chance of solving that area's transportation problems (in conjunction with the use of alternative fuels. As James Mills of San Diego's Metropolitan Transit Development Board noted, "The greatest [transportation] problems are solved if a lot of people do whatever is within their power to do" (TRB 1988a).

Building more highways cannot alleviate our transportation problems. Even if advanced technology like "smart" cars and highways is developed, technology alone cannot address the mounting congestion and pollution (OTA 1989b). Moreover, focusing on highways can mean ignoring or slighting alternatives to the automobile such as transit, bicycles, and pedestrian mobility.

Commuters need viable alternatives both to using their own cars and to the ways they use them. Intercity travelers must be able to choose between high-speed trains and airplanes, especially for shorter trips where delays and connections are most time consuming. And freight hauling must become more diversified, combining the services of trains, ships, pipelines, and trucks. This chapter discusses ways of encouraging these alternatives while reducing energy use, emissions, and congestion.

Mass Transit

The concept of mass transit—moving large numbers of people in a single vehicle—was born before the age of the single-passenger automobile (see Chapter 1). At the turn of the century, trolleys dominated urban transport. By the end of World War II, however, the changeover to buses was pretty much complete. In the 1960s the promise of high-tech rapid transit beckoned, but by the early 1970s the promised revolutionary changes had not materialized, and dependence on the automobile continued to rise.

Suburban sprawl encouraged the move away from public transit. As commuters spread out in all directions at ever greater distances from city centers, urban population densities fell. US population density in 1960 averaged 3,290 persons per square mile, but by 1980 this figure had fallen by 33 percent, to 2,177 persons per square mile (Lowry 1988). These development patterns hurt public transit, which is not as effective as the automobile at serving low-density, decentralized areas and the increasingly common suburb-to-suburb commutes. Nevertheless, better co-ordination between land-use development and transportation planning could encourage the use of mass transit and other alternatives to the car.

Mass transit includes buses, ferries, and railroads[1]—rapid rail (subways), light rail, trolleys, commuter rail, and intercity rail (Amtrak)—and runs underground, on surface streets, within freeway medians, overhead, and on abandoned railroad rights-of-way. The costs and attributes of the various mass-transit modes are summarized in Table 17.

Some 5,000 mass-transit agencies, authorities, and companies, operating more than 100,000 vehicles, provide nearly two and a half billion vehicle-miles of services each year (DOT 1988b). In 1985, urban-transit

Table 17
Key Characteristics of Different Mass-Transit Modes

Characteristic	Transit Mode						
	Light Rail	Bus	Commuter Rail	Rapid Rail	Personal Rapid Transit[c]	Automated Guideway	Maglev[c]
SYSTEM COSTS							
Initial Capital	$$	$[a]	$ to $$$	$$$$	$$	$$$	$$$$
Operating and Maintenance	$$	$$$	$$$	$	$	$	$$
ATTRIBUTES							
Schedule Reliability	***	*	**	***	****	****	***
Grade Separation	varies	varies	varies	yes	yes	yes	varies
Automated Operation	no[b]	no	no[b]	varies[b]	yes	yes	varies
Entrained Vehicles	yes	no	yes	yes	no	varies	no
PUBLIC PERCEPTION							
Comfort, Ride Quality	**	*	**	**	**	**	****
Route Comprehension	easy	hard	easy	varies	easy	easy	easy
Social Acceptability	***	*	***	**	***	***	***
RAILROAD INVOLVEMENT							
Operating Labor	no	no	yes	no	no	no	varies
Freight Coordination	varies	no	varies	no	yes	no	varies

Key

$ = Low	* = Fair
$$ = Moderate	** = Good
$$$ = High	*** = Excellent
$$$$ = Very High	**** = Superior

Notes:
a. Bus/HOV lane cost per mile can be higher.
b. May have automated train stop without full automation.
c . Characteristics are projected since not yet in full-scale operation.
Source: Adapted from Schumann, "What's New in North American Light Rail Transit Projects?" *1989.*

Double-stack commuter rail, subway, trolley, and light rail.

ridership amounted to over eight billion individual one-way rides, and rural service accounted for another 300 million (DOT 1988b).[2] Twelve million people rode mass transit each day—about half for work-related commutes (DOT 1988b). Of the nearly 42 billion passenger-miles traveled on mass transit in 1989, half were on buses, 29 percent on heavy rail, 17 percent on commuter rail, and the remaining 4 percent was split between light rail, trolley bus, ferryboats, and other transit services (Neff 1990).

Although the numbers sound large, they are actually small in terms of national averages; public transit accounts for only 3 percent of all trips nationwide and 6 percent of all work-related trips. However, when the largest metropolitan areas in the US are considered, transit accounts for 19 percent of the work trips (AASHTO 1988). Since major metropolitan areas have the greatest share of public-transportation ridership, ranging from Denver at 25 percent to New York City at 88 percent of all central-business-district work trips, it is in these areas where increasing ridership can make the biggest difference (AASHTO 1988).[3]

Today in a typical metropolitan area, suburb-to-suburb commuters outnumber suburb-to-central-city commuters six to one (Orski 1987). And the proportion of commuters who live and work in the suburbs is growing. Such arrangements make it difficult to design effective mass transit that will persuade drivers to abandon their cars.

Yet only when ridership is high can public transit both cover its direct costs and reduce the social costs of transportation—pollution, excessive energy use, and congestion. Not only must mass transit increase the sheer number of riders, it must also, in order to reduce these social costs, lure them away from personal passenger vehicles and not from other forms of transit or ridesharing.

Well-planned mass transit can reduce congestion, benefit the environment, aid in sound development, and be cost-effective as well. It can also help channel future development to prearranged layouts, better integrating transportation and land-use planning. New mass-transit systems can help revitalize older cities and can spark new business activity in others. But mass transit is not a panacea for all of our transportation problems. Rather, it is one of the various options available to centralized metropolitan areas. Weighing the benefits and costs of each alternative is the only way to arrive at the best transportation solution for a particular area.

Generally, small cities rely on private transportation (the automobile); medium-size cities should have a balance of private and public transportation; and large metropolitan areas must be served by extensive high-performance transit systems. Automobiles should be discouraged wherever public transit can be provided (Vuchic 1990).

SOCIAL BENEFITS OF MASS TRANSIT. Mass transit has two principal advantages over single-passenger cars: less pollution and greenhouse-gas emissions, and less energy use. Although some transit options pollute less than others, all result in fewer emissions than driving solo. According to EPA data, electric rail, followed by vanpools and buses, emits the least reactive hydrocarbon (HC) and carbon monoxide of any transportation mode. Vanpools and carpools emit the least nitrogen oxides, sulfur oxides, and particulates (Platte 1990, Pane 1990, Stevenson 1990, EPA 1989).[4] Regional emission reductions from mass-transit expansions and improvements can range up to 20 percent (AOR 1989).

Moreover, using alternative fuels some mass transit could be even cleaner without becoming significantly more expensive. Buses can be designed to run (and some are already running) on CNG, hydrogen, methanol, and fuel cells. Tests on CNG buses (the most popular near-term alternative) indicate that CO and NO_x emissions can be reduced up to 70 percent over 1991 emission standards; HC emissions can meet the 1991 standard without extra tailpipe controls; and particulates can be reduced by a factor of five.[5] Early versions of the CNG bus have sold for about $200,000—about 20 percent more than a conventional diesel bus.

Not only do mass-transit vehicles emit less pollutants than single-passenger cars, they also emit less carbon dioxide as well as use significantly less energy per passenger-mile: 40-60 percent less during the work commute. Although increasing mass-transit ridership may not result in large reductions in national energy use, state energy use and local congestion and emission levels can be greatly reduced.[6] Table 18 details

Table 18
Percentage of Energy Saved (or Wasted) by Switching Commute Vehicle

Passenger Switches to:

Original Mode	Car	Truck	Carpool	Vanpool	Transit Rail	Commuter Rail	Transit Bus	Amtrak	Airplane	Bike	Walk
Car	—	(15)	48	88	75	73	71	84	35	97	96
Truck	13	—	55	89	79	77	75	86	43	98	96
Carpool	(91)	(121)	—	77	(53)	49	(44)	70	n/a	95	92
Vanpool	(722)	(848)	(329)	—	(103)	(119)	(140)	30	n/a	77	66
Transit Rail	(305)	(367)	(112)	51	—	n/a	(18)	n/a	n/a	89	83
Commuter Rail	(274)	(332)	(96)	54	n/a	—	(10)	n/a	n/a	n/a	n/a
Transit Bus	(242)	(294)	(79)	58	16	9	—	n/a	n/a	91	86
Amtrak	(532)	(630)	(231)	23	n/a	n/a	n/a	—	(313)	n/a	n/a
Airplane	(53)	(77)	n/a	n/a	n/a	n/a	n/a	76	—	n/a	n/a
Bike	(3,523)	(4,081)	(1,794)	(341)	(795)	n/a	(961)	n/a	n/a	—	(50)
Walk	(2,315)	(2,687)	(1,163)	(194)	(497)	n/a	(607)	n/a	n/a	33	—

Notes:
Refer to Table 4 for original data used in this table.
n/a means that these modes are not typically substituted for one another.

Sources: Davis (ORNL) 1989; UCS calculations.

the energy savings associated with switching to more efficient transportation modes during the work commute. For commute travel, transit rail is 16 percent more efficient than transit bus, and vanpools are 77 percent more efficient than carpools. Mass transit is nearly four times as energy efficient as cars and trucks at moving passengers during rush-hour commutes.

The potential of mass transit to ease traffic congestion is impressive: one fully occupied train can remove as many as 100 cars from the road during rush hour, a bus can eliminate 40 cars, a vanpool subtracts up to 13 cars, and each carpool removes two to three cars. Moreover, the fewer cars and trucks on the road during commuting hours, the more efficient other vehicles (such as transit and bicycling) become because they can operate more effectively.

How a person gets to mass transit—by driving to a Park&Ride, biking, or walking—also affects overall energy use and has a significant effect on pollution. The first few miles traveled in today's cars produce high emissions due to a condition known as cold start, when the emission-control system is not yet heated up. Because of cold start, about 90 percent of total trip emissions (not including carbon dioxide) occur during the first mile of an average seven-mile car trip (AOR 1989).

Thus for each Park&Ride commuter diverted to Bike&Ride, roughly 150 gallons of gasoline are saved annually.[7] The savings are even greater, of course, for each auto commuter diverted to Bike&Ride—over 400 gallons of gasoline each year (Totten 1989). Not only do commuters who bike or walk to transit instead of driving there cut their average annual fuel use by one-third, but they also cut emissions of carbon dioxide by one and a half tons and air pollutants by 160 pounds annually.[8] In addition, walking or biking to transit instead of driving saves parking fees.

PUBLIC COSTS OF CURRENT MASS TRANSIT. Transit systems have public costs as well that are often measured in terms of safety, comfort, and convenience—or, more accurately, the lack of these. Such costs are important because they may explain why certain forms of public transit have lower ridership than others. Some transit systems, for example, are plagued by risks to riders' safety (mugging, rape, and other crime), certainly a substantial deterrent to transit use. Crowding, discomfort, excessive noise, and general unpleasantness are also costly in terms of lost ridership. Additional riders that might otherwise ride transit are lost because the system cannot provide them with adequate flexibility in their daily routines.

Another social problem—homelessness—is also affecting transit ridership. The rising number of homeless people who have taken up residence along rail lines, in terminals, and on transit vehicles themselves are forcing systems to struggle with service disruptions, complaints, lawsuits, injuries, and even death. The situation is driving riders away from transit. Lost ridership, along with additional operating and maintenance costs for dealing with the homeless, is expensive. In New York

City, for example, the Metropolitan Transit Authority spent $20 million in 1989 in extra expenses and lost fares as a result of the homeless problem.

Crime on mass transit is also costly. The new Los Angeles rail system, which recently opened the first leg of its multibillion-dollar commuter transit network, is spending one-third of its $12-million annual operating budget on security measures. Because trains pass through the heart of Los Angeles' gang territory, the transit system will have to combat problems ranging from vandalism to theft to drug possession. Ridership may well suffer because people will be deterred by these risks.

Nevertheless, mass-transit systems can be designed with security in mind. The new rail systems in Washington, Atlanta, and Baltimore, for example, are among the safest places in those metropolitan areas (Wachs 1989). Far less attention, however, is given to bus stops, which are usually poorly lit and vulnerable to crime. By comparison, however, public safety is much more at issue with automobiles than transit. For example, the death rate per passenger-mile-traveled in autos is seven times that for passenger trains and over 90 times the rate for transit buses. In terms of crime, the risk at transit stops is probably comparable to that of walking alone some distance to a parked car.

PRIVATE COSTS OF MASS TRANSIT. Building even the most basic mass-transit system can be a huge financial undertaking—commonly provided for by government subsidies and direct public funding. In 1985, about $2 billion was spent on local transit nationwide—compared to $32 billion for roads (Casler and Hannon 1989). Studies have found that it costs $5-$19 million per mile to build a busway system; $5-$83 million per mile to build a light-rail network; and $25-$100 million per mile for a subway (DOT 1988b, Parody et al. 1990). Recently, several light-rail systems have been built at the lower end of the range, for under $20 million per mile (NARP 1989). The rule of thumb for new transit construction is that whatever it costs to build the system at grade level, it will cost double to elevate the system and quadruple to build it underground (Lemov 1989). By comparison, highways cost from $10 million to $100 million per mile to construct.

Federal funds devoted to transit construction are raised by the gasoline tax; one cent of the 9-cent federal gasoline tax is used to fund urban mass transit-related projects. State and local funds are usually raised through bond measures that must be approved by a popular vote.

In terms of capital costs of vehicles, buses are generally cheaper than all kinds of trains. A bus costs about $170,000 and has about a 15-year life. Both light- and heavy-rail trains last at least three times as long but cost almost 10 times as much (Lemov 1989).

Historically, capital expenditures on mass-transit systems have been about 35 percent of transit operating costs (DOT 1988b). Typically, revenue from fares covers 30-45 percent of total system operating costs for buses and 65-90 percent for light and heavy rail (subways)—although the lower ends of these ranges are probably more common for older systems (NARP 1989). In 1985, US mass-transit operating costs were over $11 billion, of which fares made up about 44 percent, state and local subsidies covered 48 percent, and federal subsidies made up only 8 percent (DOT 1988b).

Comparing various mass-transit modes, the Transportation Research Board found that in 1983 buses had the greatest net cost per passenger-mile, $0.24, while trains cost $0.17 per passenger-mile (Parody et al. 1990).[9] By comparison, cars cost $0.15 per passenger-mile to operate (Davis et al. 1989).[10]

PRIVATE BENEFITS OF MASS TRANSIT. Innovations can simultaneously help promote the attractiveness of mass transit and the economic vitality of the community it serves. One idea entails creating a commercial center around transit activity. For example, Union Station in Washington, DC, which serves Amtrak and local public transit, was renovated and is now a thriving hub of shops and restaurants. Likewise, the bus terminal in Roanoke, Virginia, covers all of its $2 million in annual operating costs through commercial rents and parking fees. This popular bus station/ shopping facility has played an important part in the 12-percent increase in area bus ridership since its opening in 1987 (Lemov 1989).

In Dallas, the regional transportation district (DART) offers a demand-responsive van system. Operator-dispatched vans that can travel within suburban zones and to main-line bus routes serve people living in areas that do not have the ridership to support regularly scheduled bus routes. DART's van program carries about 800 passengers a week and is increasing ridership at a rate of 5-10 percent each month.

Communities can also enjoy economic benefits that are spillovers from transit projects. For example, the new light-rail system in Portland, Oregon, was followed by over $500 million worth of development along its route, and San Diego and Buffalo have experienced similar benefits. Likewise, the subway systems built in Washington, DC, and Atlanta have spurred successful commercial

DartAbout van-bus transit in Dallas, Texas.

developments in those cities (Parcells 1990).

INTERCITY BUS TRANSIT. Intercity bus services have historically linked urban and rural America. Since partial deregulation of intercity buses in 1982, established carriers (such as Trailways) have gone bankrupt and other carriers (such as Greyhound) have dropped many routes that they considered unprofitable.[11] While all carriers are undertaking cost-cutting measures to improve their competitive positions, these actions have not been enough to reverse the trend of decreasing profits. As a result, much of rural America, already without train service, is being cut off as it loses bus service. From 1983 to 1985, rural communities lost intercity bus service at unprecedented rates. Today one-third of the rural communities that Greyhound serves may lose their intercity bus service, a void that regional bus carriers may or may not be able to fill.

Bus ridership has dropped since deregulation because of increased auto travel and greater competition from small air carriers that started service following airline deregulation in 1978 (Thompson and Sek 1989). And after eight years of bus deregulation, the economic situation for carriers is so dire that the country's only remaining major intercity bus service is threatened with bankruptcy.

AMTRAK. The National Railroad Passenger Corporation—better known as Amtrak—was established by Congress in 1970 in response to the sharp decline in passenger-train travel following World War II.[12] Amtrak provides intercity rail passenger service mostly along the Northeast corridor plus a few other north-south and east-west transcontinental routes.

Amtrak has received nearly $11 billion in federal grants in its 20 years. Even though it is now covering an increasing portion of its operating costs, continued federal support is needed to sustain passenger-train operations for the foreseeable future. Amtrak covers 72 percent of its $2.2 billion operating cost with system revenues, requiring only a 28-percent federal subsidy; just eight years ago, Amtrak made up only 48 percent of its cost in system revenues (GAO 1990c). Today it may well have the highest revenue-to-cost ratio of any passenger rail system in the world (Parcells 1990). But Amtrak is in desperate need of about $1.2 billion over the next five years, in addition to normal federal subsidies, to replace aging equipment and make infrastructure improvements.

The trains of Amtrak carried 21.4 million passengers in 1989, half of them along the Northeast corridor (Parcells 1990). This rail service plays a valuable role in relieving traffic on highways and in airports. Amtrak commands over one-third of the New York-to-Washington, DC, air/rail transportation market (NARP 1990). And nationwide, Amtrak passenger-miles rose in 1989 for the eighth consecutive year, to nearly six million passenger-miles (Parcells 1990).

Because Amtrak links passengers between downtown areas rather than the outlying areas where airports are usually located, and because riders don't have to deal with traffic congestion, train travel can be more attractive than either flying or driving. To make it attractive enough to ensure Amtrak's future success, however, continued government funding will be necessary, including money for system improvements such as upgrading certain routes to high-speed service.

HIGH-SPEED RAIL. High-speed rail (HSR) can operate at speeds of over 200 mph, although recent trials of France's TGV (Très Grande Vitesse) reached record speeds of 320 mph (Walker 1990, HSRA 1990). Amtrak's Metroliner between Washington, DC, and New York City reaches 125 mph. HSR trains use standard steel wheels, operate on traditional train tracks, and are powered by electricity. HSR is envisioned as an intercity passenger mode in the US, much like Amtrak. Although it has not yet been built in this country, the technology is proven; for over a decade, HSR systems have routinely operated in France, Japan, and western Germany.

Many consider HSR service to be complementary to air and automobile *France's TGV Atlantique is a high-speed train that runs on steel-wheel tracks.* travel, rather than a replacement. Indeed, HSR can best serve trips of intermediate length, between 150 miles—where cars leave off—and 300 miles—where airplanes pick up (Walker 1990).

Perhaps the greatest benefit of HSR is that it builds on and improves what we already have in place. For this reason (and given the similarity between HSR and Amtrak's intercity service), Amtrak has offered states its assistance in developing and operating HSR systems. However, Amtrak does not have the fiscal resources to upgrade to HSR itself.

Even though federal funds are committed at fairly low levels, several states are moving ahead with privately constructed and operated HSR projects. Texas, for example, has requested proposals to serve the Dallas-Houston-San Antonio triangle; one 300-mile leg is expected to be operating by 1998. Capital and construction costs for the Texas Triangle HSR are forecast at $4.4 billion—approximately $6 million per mile (Walker 1990). Ohio is planning a $2.5-billion HSR project to connect Cleveland, Columbus, and Cincinnati. And a bistate HSR project running from Las Vegas to Los Angeles has estimated costs of $3.5-$4 million per mile. Because HSR is so affordable and it takes advantage of current infrastructure, it is considered the most attractive option for expanding the US rail network in the near term.

MAGNETIC-LEVITATION TRAINS. The magnetic-levitation, or maglev, train employs powerful electromagnets to raise rail cars about six inches above a guideway and propel them at speeds of up to 300 mph (Johnson 1990). Because of its high speed, maglev is well suited to replace airplanes traveling shorter distances (300-500 miles). Although the US explored maglev technology two decades ago, it remains in the study phase today. While we have studied it, Germany and Japan have built and run full-scale, passenger-carrying maglev prototypes.

Maglev has several advantages over conventional transit vehicles and airplanes. First, maglev trains are not affected by adverse weather conditions, the single largest cause of airline delays. This is so because they don't touch the track, because snow does not accumulate on the track to impair mobility, and because poor visibility is not as much

Transrapid maglev in Germany.

of a deterrent with a fixed-guideway system as with the takeoff and landing of an airplane. Because maglev never touches the track, there is little noise—and also little maintenance. A two-way maglev system requires only 50 feet of land and can be elevated over existing rights-of-way along highways, avoiding costly and disruptive land acquisitions. A single maglev line has a capacity equal to six lanes of interstate highway, and an intercity maglev network has the capacity of a major airport.

The use of maglev (as well as steel-wheel high-speed rail) would reduce greenhouse and other air emissions as well as energy consumption. Maglev emits one-fourth the carbon dioxide of airplanes and reduces hydrocarbon, carbon monoxide, nitrogen oxide, and particulate emissions. And maglev uses only a quarter as much energy per passenger-mile as airplanes (Johnson 1990). According to the Department of Energy, by 2020 a transportation mix that included maglev and high-speed rail could result in a drop in energy consumption of 14 percent, CO_2 emissions of 20 percent, and CO and NO_x emissions of nearly 30 percent, compared with an airline-only scenario (Rote 1990).

Today, half of all airline flights are less than 500 miles; these shorter trips are expensive and inefficient, both in terms of fuel and operations, tying up takeoff and landing slots for long-distance flights (Johnson 1990). To relieve airport congestion due to short-distance travel, individual maglev trains (each with the capacity of a medium airplane) could carry passengers to major "hub-and-spoke" airports for connections to long-distance air travel.

Germany has such an integrated air-train system. Lufthansa passengers can fly into Frankfurt and continue to their final destinations either by air or by Lufthansa's Airport Express. About half of the passengers choose the Airport Express (currently a conventional train) because there are fewer delays and it takes travelers closer to their end destinations. Lufthansa has recently received government approval to connect two medium-size German airports with a maglev train, thus creating one super-airport for longer-distance, more profitable air travel (Johnson 1990).

In the United States maglev and high-speed rail could serve as a regional carrier where distances between cities are relatively short and conventional tracks have not been laid—in the Northeast, the Midwest, the Southwest, California, Florida, and Texas. Several states are already pursuing this state-of-the-art transit as a way to modernize rail lines to compete with regional air and highway travel. Plans include routes from Boston to Washington, Philadelphia to Harrisburg, Pittsburgh to Cleveland, Miami to Jacksonville, Tampa to Orlando, and San Francisco to San Diego (Rote 1990).

Florida has passed a Magnetic Levitation Demonstration Act to help create a 15-mile maglev link between the Orlando airport and major tourist attractions, which could be built as early as 1994. Las Vegas put out a request for proposals for a 230-mile maglev system that would link this city with southern California, possibly by 1998 (Johnson 1990). These projects could be the first to introduce millions of Americans to maglev.

Ultimately, the Department of Energy envisions a 2,000-mile intercity maglev network at a cost of $15 million per mile for tracks and vehicles (Katauskas 1989). Individual systems, however, could cost as little as $10 million a mile or as much as $50 million a mile to build. It is important to note that maglev is two to 10 times more expensive to build than high-speed rail. Thus HSR may present serious competition to maglev. In fact, for the high cost of even a limited maglev network, a much more comprehensive "backbone" intercity rail network could be created or revived, serving even more cities nationwide.

In order for a maglev network to become reality, the federal government would have to formulate a clear plan for integrating maglev into our current transportation system. The commitment would require several steps. The first step is funding. The president's proposed 1991 budget slated $10 million to explore the potential of maglev (Johnson 1990). Clearly this funding level is much too low to accomplish anything other than a preliminary study of the technology. Significantly more federal money will have to be devoted to maglev if the US ever hopes to build an expanded system.

The second step is congressional hearings to examine the benefits to US manufacturers, other businesses, and state and local governments. A maglev program office that cuts across the many agency jurisdictions over this technology should be headed by a lead agency to accelerate progress. Industry must be involved in the development of the technology. The national laboratories and universities can further research efforts, given clear direction from the government. Finally, continued funding must be committed to maglev development, on the order of $500 million to $1 billion over the next seven years (Johnson 1990).

GUIDEWAY TRANSIT. Guideway transit (or automated guideway transit,

AGT) uses a rail or channel to maneuver either buses or trains along an exclusive path. Guideways are usually fully automated and have no crew on the vehicle itself. These systems usually have small and medium-size vehicles that operate on guideways with exclusive right-of-ways. Guideways are rare in North America, although guided buses are popular in other developed countries.

Miami's People Mover.

One example of a US automated guideway transit system is Miami's People Mover, which operates along a downtown guideway loop (Zimmerman 1990). The guided bus has shown itself to be a cost-effective intermediate between busways (a special roadway designed for exclusive use by buses) and light-rail lines in Japan, Germany, England, Belgium, and Australia (Nakadegawa 1990). Buses require only minor adaptations to use guideways, which require less space than busways.

Guideway rail transit has been studied in the US over the past several decades and has not been found cost-effective. When elevated guideways are designed to carry multicar trains, massive structures are required; these systems are typically costly, unsightly, and problematic in terms of snow removal. Smaller guideway systems such as personal rapid transit are more cost-effective than previously proposed guideway systems.

PERSONAL RAPID TRANSIT (PRT). These are small, lightweight, computerized personal vehicles that run on elevated guideways and can be summoned electronically within 30 seconds from a station. They can take up to three passengers to a destination preprogrammed by the passenger before entering the vehicle. One example of a prototype PRT system is TAXI 2000, which features nonstop,

TAXI 2000 personal rapid transit.

on-demand, automated service. Each of TAXI 2000's essential elements has been demonstrated.

Designers of PRTs like TAXI 2000 claim they combine high operating efficiency and low cost. Since vehicles are in use only when a passenger is present, inefficient operations during off-peak hours are eliminated. Once capital costs are met, the argument goes, the system can operate more economically than bus and rail because of its small guideway and fully automated, non-labor-intensive operation. Also, freight can be transported during off-peak hours to further reduce operating costs. Operating and maintenance costs can range from $0.20 to $0.90 per passenger-mile (compared to the $0.36 per passenger-mile for today's average transit system). Capital costs are estimated at $5-$10 million per mile (ATA 1988).[13]

CONCLUSION. Mass transit can be cleaner, more fuel-efficient, and more cost-effective than alternatives such as driving solo and flying. The key is high ridership. Therefore mass transit is a solution to urban pollution and mobility problems only to the extent that there is a sufficient ridership base.

In most metropolitan areas around the US, public transit plays a vital role in reducing the social costs of transportation. Large numbers of people moving along common routes from suburb to city center are most effectively shuttled by transit. For suburb-to-suburb travel, however, transit may not be capable of attracting enough ridership to be effective. In some cases, mass-transit incentives and auto disincentives can play a role in luring travelers out of their single-passenger automobiles and onto transit. But depending on personal preferences and lifestyle, incentives may not always work.

In order to compete with other modes, transit will require continued technological improvements. High-speed rail and new light-rail systems are prime candidates to ensure the future success of mass transit. The ultimate technology chosen should be fully integrated into the existing transit system. Clean alternative fuels should also play a role in mass-transit systems, especially buses fueled by compressed natural gas and fuel cells. And, of course, transit should provide bicycle and pedestrian access for the greatest energy and environmental benefits.

Strategies for Commercial Freight Movement

Today freight is transported by a number of modes—truck, train, ship, aircraft, and pipeline. Each carries a nearly equal share of US freight. But this was not always the case. Early in the 20th century, railroads had a near monopoly on hauling commercial freight. Because of rail's dominance and the barriers to entry facing other modes, the Interstate Commerce Commission (ICC) subjected the rail industry to heavy regulation. When trucks were brought under ICC regulation, in 1935, the regulations were as much to protect the burgeoning trucking industry from railroads as to regulate it. In fact, ICC regulation of the trucking industry at first generated a high volume of new service in that industry, then protected it when it became established, thus forming undesirable oligopolies (DeJarnette 1989). Indeed, throughout much of this century, ICC regulations have led to the poor physical and financial health of the railroad industry (DeJarnette 1989).

By the mid-1970s, the move to deregulate all of transportation had gained considerable momentum. In 1978 the airlines were deregulated, and in 1980 both trucks and railroads followed suit.[14] Deregulation has led to distinct changes in freight movement in both the trucking and rail industries. There are many new trucking firms, and service in general has greatly expanded since 1980 (Thompson and Sek 1989). The rail industry has seen the opposite development: fewer routes are now available to shippers, and rail investments have steadily declined as investors pursued more attractive opportunities elsewhere.

Both regulation, in the early 1900s, and deregulation, in the 1980s, were advanced to promote economic competitiveness in the freight industry. But competitiveness is not the only issue; the growing social costs of freight transportation, such as excessive energy use and pollution, have now assumed substantial if not equal importance.

TRUCKING. Trucks are an attractive target for energy conservation and emission reductions. They consume 59 percent of all energy used to haul freight, yet they haul only 21 percent of the total (Davis et al. 1989). Advanced truck technologies (see below) and an increased shift to intermodal transport (combining trucking with ship, rail, and other modes) would reduce energy consumption and pollutant emissions.

Truck technologies that reduce energy consumption and carbon dioxide emissions include radial tires, drag-reduction devices, more-efficient diesel engines, and alternative engine technologies (see discussion of fuel-efficient heavy-duty trucks in Chapter 5). These improvements are most effective for high-speed, long-haul travel. Other measures to reduce energy consumption, emissions, and traffic congestion in urban areas include off-street truck-loading zones, improved terminal design and location, and computerized delivery routing and scheduling (Stowers and Boyar 1985).

For example, rescheduling and rerouting of truck deliveries away from congested areas during peak-commute hours alone could result in up to a 3-percent reduction in highway emissions, according to the South Coast Air Quality Management District in Southern California (OTA 1989a). Despite these improvements, on-road fuel efficiency is dependent on the driver and driving conditions; both idling and speeding waste energy.

Federal standards allow trucks of up to 80,000 pounds and 53 feet in length. The trucking industry is pressuring regulators to increase these limits by allowing triple trailers and longer twin trailers. But although multiple-trailer trucks may be more energy efficient than single trailers, they are much less efficient than intermodal carriers (see below). Furthermore, multiple trailers can cause more accidents and worsen traffic congestion. Another major concern is that the infrastructure is often not designed to handle their excessive weight and size. Add to this the facts

Triple-trailer trucks, legal in some states, are less efficient and less safe than intermodal transport (single or twin-trailer truck plus rail).

that pollution is aggravated as freight is shifted away from rail to these larger trucks, and that energy use rises dramatically (Lafen 1990).

Intermodal transport—combining trucks, rail, and ships—holds the most promise for moving freight with the least social cost. It can provide more-efficient transport with fewer emissions, using less energy, at lower costs, and delivering faster service than trucking alone.

RAILROADS. Although railroads move a full 30 percent of all intercity freight, they consume only 5 percent of the energy used to transport freight (Stowers and Boyar 1985, Davis et al. 1989). And because trains can use cleaner and more diversified fuel sources than trucks, such as electricity, shifting freight from trucks to trains would reduce both emissions and US demand for imported oil. Moreover, greater use of trains would reduce highway congestion and traffic accidents. As intermodal transport increases, such a switch to railroads is likely to occur.

Double-stack containers for intermodal freight.

A recent intermodal technology known as double-stacking containers has helped integrate train, truck, and ship hauling. In 1988, there were 105 double-stack trains in operation, twice as many as in 1987 (Nicholas 1989). Since tunnels and bridges can present a problem for double-stack containers, drop-frame or deep-well flatcars (similar to those used by trucks hauling heavy equipment) are employed.

Even though rail is relatively energy efficient, it can be even further improved. In the near term, operation and maintenance—train handling and dispatching—offer the largest energy-saving potential. Additionally, older diesel locomotives can be retrofitted to reduce fuel consumption by an estimated 2 percent (Stowers and Boyar 1985).

INTERMODAL FREIGHT TRANSPORT. Because shippers find that pickup and delivery by truck is the most convenient, a scheme that combines the energy-saving and pollution-cutting attributes of rail and ships with the convenience of trucks should win widespread use. Such a scheme is intermodal (or "piggyback") freight movement. Intermodal systems are well suited to handle the continued growth in import and export traffic, especially with the advent of double-stack trains and railmaster technologies (see below).

Over the past two decades, intermodal systems have handled an increasing volume of freight, growing at an annual rate of 4 percent. A system developed in 1983 called Railmaster, in which trucks are fitted with two sets of wheels, one for the road and one for the rails, eliminates the need for separate flatcars and complex loading systems. This enables freight-carrying truck trailers to be shipped by rail less expensively, with much greater (70 percent) operating efficiency and substantially greater (about 25 percent) energy efficiency than previous systems. Railmaster transports its backhauls with nearly a full load, and its delivery times are close to those of average truck deliveries (Mintz and Zerega 1989).

"RoadRailer," an intermodal freight technology.

Double-stack containers also promote intermodal freight transportation. Used on trains and trucks, they can cut fuel use by 35 percent and operating costs by 40 percent, and offer faster transit times than previous systems (Nicholas 1989).

With a promising future, intermodal freight transport should expand further, provided that larger trucks are not allowed on highways, more rail flatcars are made available, and the hub system for rail freight is optimized to reduce fuel- and time-wasting empty backhauls.

PIPELINES. Pipelines transport water and a variety of petroleum products, including crude oil, natural gas, and coal slurry. They handle roughly 20 percent of all freight and use 10 percent of the energy consumed for hauling freight in the US. Oil and gas pipelines are very energy efficient, coal-slurry pipelines less so. Pipelines are one of the cleanest means of transportation; thus wherever possible, shifts to this mode should be considered.

SHIPS. Water vessels are an important component in intermodal transport, especially for international freight. Ships and trains can be combined with the inland movement of marine containers by train. Water vessels hauled 30 percent of US freight while using only 17 percent of the energy (Davis et al. 1989). Domestic ship traffic alone accounted for 55 percent of the total tons shipped in waterborne commerce in 1986 (Davis et al. 1989). Internal and local traffic accounted for 62 percent of domestic marine cargo transportation, most of which was barges. In terms of energy efficiency, ships are second only to oil pipelines, about equal with trains, and almost five times more efficient than trucks.

CONCLUSION. A combination of strategies will ensure the most efficient movement of freight and reduce the social costs of commercial shipping in the future. The strategies: first, freight should be shifted to the most energy-efficient, lowest-polluting, and most operationally efficient mode; second, intermodal handling should be used wherever possible; and third, advanced truck technologies should be developed and put in place as soon as possible.

The freight industry is still in a state of flux following deregulation in the 1980s. Since all efforts focus on maximizing profits, externalities such as pollution, congestion, and accidents should be reflected in the private costs of hauling freight. Only then will shippers bear the proper responsibility for moving goods.

Fleet Vehicles

Fleets constitute a broad category of public and private vehicles that are typically dispatched in large numbers for varied tasks. On average, fleet vehicles are driven more than twice as many miles a year as vehicles in general use. In 1987, nearly 10 million vehicles belonged to fleets of four or more, and eight million belonged to fleets of 10 or more (Davis et al. 1989). Business fleets made up the bulk—44 percent of all fleet vehicles—while those leased by individuals accounted for 26 percent, daily rental agencies held 10 percent, government vehicles represented 8 percent, utility fleets had 7 percent, police fleets made up 3 percent, and the remaining 2 percent was accounted for by taxis (Davis et al. 1989).

Each year, 1.7 million new fleet cars and trucks are purchased and regularly refueled at central locations (Tilley 1990). Thus fleet vehicles, especially government fleet vehicles, utility-company fleets, and certain business fleets, are prime candidates for operating on cleaner alternative fuels. Taxis could operate more cleanly and fuel efficiently by rerouting and routine maintenance service.

GOVERNMENT FLEETS. These centrally fueled, maintained, and dispatched fleets offer an excellent opportunity for improvements in fuel economy and emission reductions. Fleet-management programs can reduce fuel consumption and tailpipe emissions through training and technical assistance on driving techniques, preventive vehicle maintenance, optimized routing, and better record keeping. In addition, alternative-fueled government fleets are being used as a trial ground for alternative fuels such as natural gas, electricity, methanol, fuel cells, and hydrogen.

In Colorado, for example, 10 percent of all new vehicles bought or leased by the state are required to run on alternative fuels by 1991. In Pennsylvania the state energy office committed $5 million to local governments and private companies to convert nearly 200 fleet vehicles to natural gas (Tilley 1990). Other states have enacted requirements that government fleet vehicles run on cleaner fuels, and state-regulated utility companies continue to work with fleet operators on fleet conversion to natural gas.

TAXIS. Although they account for only 2 percent of vehicle fleets, taxis play a key role in urban mobility and traffic congestion. If the 125,000 taxis in the US were well maintained and efficiently operated, they would be a relatively efficient way to travel. For example, shared-ride taxis, because they are more efficient than traditional exclusive taxi rides, can be considered a form of ridesharing. All too often, however, taxis carry a single passenger in an older vehicle that may not be especially well maintained. Such a vehicle may use up to 20 percent more fuel than necessary (Mintz and Zerega 1989).

Other problems with taxis have more to do with their routing than with the vehicles themselves. Some taxi regulations do not permit return fares, which cuts efficiency in half and doubles the pollution of taxis that are free to pick up passengers on both the outbound and return trip.[15] The political and economic reasons for such regulations merit further analysis, although the energy and environmental benefits of amending them are clear.

MINIVAN FLEETS. Private and public minivans, holding up to 16 passengers, link airports with city centers, provide connections to mass transit, and serve other commuting purposes. Minivans can be especially effective in rural areas where commuting distances are long, residents' vehicles may be unreliable, and public transit is not widely available. These fleets can provide greater flexibility, convenience, and cost-effectiveness than buses (because they offer door-to-door service) and taxis (because they are more economical).

From an energy and emission-reduction perspective, minivans are the best choice to achieve the above purposes. Commuters using minivans (often called vanpools) consume 88 percent less energy than if they use their personal autos and over 70 percent less energy than if they take mass transit (see Table 18). The same savings are realized for greenhouse-gas emission reductions.

ALTERNATIVE FUELS. Centrally fueled fleets will probably be switched to alternative fuels before vehicles in general use (OTA 1989a). Natural gas, for example, can be used by heavy-duty fleet vehicles like street sweepers, garbage trucks, mail and other delivery trucks, some municipal construction equipment, and buses. The Office of Technology Assessment estimates that dedicated CNG-fueled fleets can reduce hydrocarbon emissions (which form smog) by at least 56 percent and possibly up to 90 percent at a cost of $0-$7,400 per ton of hydrocarbon reduced.[16] OTA also estimates that methanol fleets have a cost-effectiveness of $3,200-$51,000 per ton of hydrocarbon reduced. Thus dedicated-CNG fleets are estimated to be three times more cost-effective than methanol fleets (OTA 1989a).

FLEET-VEHICLE MAINTENANCE. Vehicle-maintenance programs can drastically reduce both the energy

A natural-gas-fueled transit bus.

consumption and the emissions of fleet vehicles, especially when they are maintained on a periodic schedule at a central facility. Such measures produce the following estimated fuel and carbon dioxide savings (Mintz and Zerega 1989):

- proper air/fuel mixture: 5-20 percent
- tuned engine: 3-7 percent
- correct wheel alignment: 2 percent
- regularly changed motor oil: 5 percent
- correct tire pressure: 3 percent

Together these measures can yield substantial savings in both fuel and carbon dioxide emissions.

CONCLUSION. Fleet vehicles may be the first beachhead in the battle for widespread gains in energy efficiency and emission reductions. The central operation and maintenance of fleets makes switching to alternative fuels and improving vehicle maintenance feasible. In addition, fleet vehicles are ideal candidates for alternative fuels because they are often heavy-duty and can accommodate the extra weight of these new fuel systems. A regional alternative-fuel demonstration program with government fleet vehicles could provide more information about different transportation fuels and their social benefits. Finally, there is room to improve taxis by keeping these vehicles maintained and operating efficiently.

Air Quality and Congestion Relief: Transportation Demand Management and Transportation System Management

Transportation demand management (TDM) and transportation system management (TSM) consist of a wide range of measures aimed primarily at improving air quality and relieving traffic congestion. In the process, these strategies can result in energy savings as well.

All too often, transportation planning takes projected demand as a given and attempts to satisfy it rather than trying to reduce it. The goal of TDM strategies is to influence people to shift to more-efficient modes of transportation and to travel during off-peak hours. Some strategies attempt to manage transportation demand with regulations and pricing schemes, such as parking management and time-of-day charges for roads; others manage demand by promoting alternative-mode choices, such as ridesharing and telecommuting. In complementary fashion, TSM strategies aim to affect the supply of transportation services. The most successful policies integrate supply and demand strategies to create a transportation network that promotes efficient, low-polluting choices.

Specific TDM/TSM strategies include:

- alternatives to parking
- ridesharing
- high-occupancy-vehicle (HOV) facilities

- variable-pricing schemes
- telecommuting
- alternative work schedules
- bicycle and pedestrian use
- innovative land-use planning
- retimed traffic signals and "intelligent" highway/vehicle systems

As a cautionary note, many of these strategies take at least two years to develop fully. In addition, the desired outcome does not always materialize; furthermore, immediate results do not ensure long-term benefits—initial successes can turn to failure if left unattended. Thus localities must be prepared to monitor these strategies carefully over the long term to ensure continuing success.

PARKING STRATEGIES. Abundant, low-cost parking further enhances the attraction that Americans feel for their personal autos. Indeed, current parking policies strongly encourage the use of personal autos. Recent studies have found that 75 percent of all commuters park in free, employer-provided, off-street spaces; an additional 18 percent park for free in on-street spaces. Even those who must pay for parking often do so at prices well below market levels. Studies conclude that "free" parking costs employers $166-$1,657 per space per year (in 1985 dollars) (Pucher 1988).

Parking is expensive: an above-grade space can cost up to $18,000 to build, and underground parking is at least twice that much (DOT 1987b).[17] Moreover, a 500-car parking lot requires an estimated 170,000 gallons of gasoline to construct and 1,200 gallons of gasoline for annual maintenance (Replogle 1984).

Parking has hidden costs as well. Land devoted to parking means lost revenues from the tax-generating activities it precludes—residential, commercial, and industrial. In the case of transit Park&Ride facilities, parking can reduce the ability to capture revenue from foregone commercial development that would otherwise have located next to transit as real-estate values appreciate. In addition, more parking can generate more traffic, which can significantly increase road-maintenance costs.

On another level, the hidden costs of parking can be seen as a consequence of societal expectations. Many employers and employees see free parking as part of an overall benefits package. Retailers consider parking availability a vital part of doing business and remaining competitive. As a result, parking benefits often become hidden costs, embedded in lease terms or absorbed as a tax-deductible operating expense.

Despite these expectations, the private sector can benefit from reducing parking supply in exchange for providing alternative transportation. Cost savings per parking space eliminated can range from $1,000-$15,000 depending on land cost and type of parking facility (DOT 1987b).

Parking management plays an important role in developing successful TDM programs (DOT 1989). Studies have found that either introducing paid parking where it was previously free or removing parking subsidies can reduce single-passenger driving by as much as 30 percent

(Higgins 1990a). And others studies have found that doubling the cost of driving by increasing parking fees alone could reduce traffic by 10-30 percent (AOR 1989).

A study of parking-management strategies for several communities was conducted in 1980 by the Department of Transportation (DOT 1987b). It examined residential parking-permit programs, preferential parking for HOVs, restrictive parking caps, flexible off-street parking requirements, parking pricing mechanisms, parking fringe benefits, and parking-violation enforcement (see below), all of which were in effect in one or more cities in the US. A decade later, most of these programs continue to yield reductions in traffic congestion and long-term parking volume.

Preferential HOV parking—assigning favorable parking locations and subsidized rates to HOVs—can pay off when HOVs operate at high occupancy rates. High enforcement costs are required, however, to ensure that HOVs receiving benefits are fully occupied.

Local parking caps (where a community limits the total number of available parking spaces) can backfire. Research conducted on the parking policy of Montgomery County, Maryland, warns that too restrictive a cap may divert development to other, less desirable locations unless affordable alternative transit is readily available (DOT 1987b).

Residential parking permits (a variation of local parking caps) are a common method of regulating on-street parking supply. However, the various restrictions on nonresident parking can cause outlying areas to be burdened with a high concentration of parked vehicles. Also, parking restrictions require high levels of enforcement, which can be very expensive.

The minimum amount of parking required by local zoning codes can be relaxed in return for support by developers and employers for alternative transportation strategies. Such strategies are often cheaper than supplying parking. For example, Sacramento, California, has revised its zoning laws to reduce parking requirements by 5 percent when bicycle facilities are provided, by 15 percent for marked rideshare spaces, and by 60 percent for transit-pass subsidization (DOT 1987b).

Another strategy is simply raising the price of parking. However, the relationship between parking demand and parking price is thought to be very inelastic—it takes a large price change to reduce parking demand appreciably. Moreover, reduced parking demand depends to a large extent on what alternatives are available. For example, Montgomery County employees have indicated a willingness to take mass transit (and walk longer distances to their destinations) to avoid increased parking charges (DOT 1987b).

A different strategy is to stop subsidizing parking at a higher level than transit. A 1985 federal law allows employers to subsidize mass transit at the rate of $15 per month; anything over this amount must be added to employees' reported earning for tax purposes. Parking benefits provided to employees, on the other hand, are not taxed at all. Furthermore, employers can deduct their parking maintenance and operating costs for tax purposes. This kind of inequality must be removed if we are to discourage personal-auto commuting.

Although enforcement costs are high, aggressive parking enforcement and adjudication can be another effective way to reduce traffic volume. Care must be taken, however, to balance this strategy against the anger it can arouse among voting motorists.

Taken together, parking pricing and other parking regulations are potent demand-management tools. But these policies depend for their effectiveness on the availability of inexpensive, safe alternative transportation. Policymakers thus should emphasize parking strategies where they bolster other options such as ridesharing, mass transit, and nonmotorized transport.

RIDESHARING. Ridesharing became popular during the Arab oil crisis, and it has maintained a steady level nearly two decades later. During the 1980s, however, the motivations for ridesharing changed. Conserving energy was no longer the major reason people carpooled; avoiding traffic congestion and saving time were the more likely incentives. But the Iraqi crisis and the subsequent rise in gasoline prices have reminded commuters why ridesharing became popular in the first place.

Rideshare programs are the most energy-efficient form of passenger transport after walking and bicycling, more so even than mass transit. A van carrying nine passengers can reduce energy consumption by almost 88 percent if each rider gives up his or her single-passenger auto, while a three-person carpool reduces energy use by 48 percent (see Table 18). (Carpools are slightly less efficient than vanpools because energy savings depend on the number of passengers occupying the vehicle.)

In 1983, 15 percent of all commuters carpooled or vanpooled, reducing US transportation energy consumption by 4 percent, or nearly 400,000 barrels of oil a day (Hillsman and Southworth 1990). These energy savings resulted in a 1-2 percent reduction in CO_2 emissions.[18]

Ridesharing reduces energy consumption, greenhouse-gas emissions, vehicle miles traveled, and pollution. Studies have found that metropolitan ridesharing programs reduce work-related VMT by almost 5 percent and carbon dioxide emissions by 4 percent. Moreover, rideshare programs can reduce employee parking demand by over 20 percent (DOT 1987b).

Carpools and vanpools can offer substantial savings over personal vehicles, and are often less expensive to ride than mass transit. Moreover, ridesharing has the greatest benefits for long-distance commutes originating in low-density areas that encounter congestion en route and terminate where parking supply is limited or expensive. Under these conditions, ridesharing is more attractive because transit is not as efficient in less densely populated areas, and high-cost parking makes the use of personal cars expensive.

Carpools work best for those who live 15 miles or more from work, and vanpools are cost effective for those living more than 25 miles from work (AOR 1989). Unfortunately, ridesharing can encourage greater trip lengths and "sprawl" development. Despite this, ridesharing can be an effective means of serving low-density development not well suited to transit, while mass transit can be used to encourage more clustered land-use patterns and shorter traveling distances.

Ridesharing mechanisms vary, from employer-based vanpool programs to casual carpools that accept different passengers daily at central locations. The number of employer-based vanpools more than doubled between 1980 and 1985, and some 3,000 to 5,000 individually owned and operated vanpools operated in 1985 (Stowers and Boyar 1985). Employer rideshare promotions as well as guaranteed-ride-home services and emergency taxi services can boost rideshare participation rates.

HIGH-OCCUPANCY-VEHICLE (HOV) FACILITIES. One of the benefits of ridesharing in many metropolitan areas today is access to high-occupancy-vehicle facilities. These are designed to manage urban peak-period travel demand, and can reduce work-related VMT by 5-15 percent (Burke 1989). They are usually multidirectional highway lanes separated from the flow of traffic by concrete median barriers. HOV systems are designed to reduce highway congestion and travel time for buses, carpools, and vanpools. A well-designed HOV lane with adequate support services, including active ridesharing programs, can carry as many people as four general-purpose highway lanes (Burke 1989,

High-occupancy-vehicle facility.

Christiansen 1990). Today, about 1 percent of major US freeways have HOV lanes (Burke 1989).

In 1985, experience with HOV facilities showed that during the peak commuting period each HOV lane handled at least 30 percent of the total passenger volume on the highway and 40 percent during the peak hour (Lancaster and Lomax 1987). And preferential treatment can help boost these numbers. In Los Angeles, for example, HOVs are allowed to bypass the stoplights on freeway ramps, which has helped to more than double use of HOVs in that city (Higgins 1990a). But even if HOV use does not double, if it can increase the average volume a highway can carry by 10-15 percent, an HOV project is considered successful (Christiansen 1990).

Perhaps the greatest benefit to HOV users is time savings. Based on Houston's experience, the estimated time saved is 20-30 minutes for its 10-mile HOV facilities (Lancaster and Lomax 1987). A "spillover" benefit is the reduced loads on main highway portions, leaving more space for all users. User operating costs are also reduced, as are energy consumption and air pollution. Specific savings depend on the class of HOV used—bus, carpool, or vanpool.

When adequate support services exist, HOV facilities can deliver significant benefits: vehicle occupancy increases, fuel is saved, and travel times are reduced. But successful HOV facilities require a steady level of high occupancy—at least four passengers. Thus, passenger requirements should not be relaxed in an effort to increase utilization of HOVs.

Busways, another type of HOV facility, typically permit entry to only the highest-occupancy vehicles—buses. Exclusive bus lanes are usually designed with a physical barrier separating them from traffic, or as so-called contraflow lanes to avoid enforcement problems. Busways are not as popular in the US as they are in Canada and Brazil. In Ottawa, for example, buses have achieved a high level of performance in serving low-density areas (Replogle 1990).

The primary drawback of busways (as well as most HOV facilities) is that they are not as pedestrian-friendly as light-rail transit. An HOV lane or busway running down the middle of a busy road can be impossible to cross. On the other hand, it is relatively easy to cross a light-rail track because these vehicles move at slower speeds, and the track can provide a temporary median to protect the pedestrian while crossing a busy street.

A significant advantage of HOV facilities from a policy point of view is that they are relatively inexpensive and take little time to construct. HOV facilities cost $4-$12 million per mile to build, significantly cheaper than most other mass-transit infrastructures (Lancaster and Lomax 1987). Other incidental HOV costs include facility maintenance and enforcement. Maintenance costs $1,000-$10,000 per lane-mile, and enforcement costs are estimated at $100,000 per year per facility (Colberg and Jacobson 1988).

Care should be taken in designing HOV facilities because they can negatively affect land-use patterns. They can encourage dispersed, sprawled development patterns, as well as the location of transit where it is not accessible to pedestrians. And, as noted, they can make it difficult for pedestrians to cross the street. Therefore, HOVs should be seen as a transitional strategy to induce riders to get out of their single-occupant-vehicles, rather than a long-range policy goal.

VARIABLE-PRICING STRATEGIES. Variable distance and congestion (time-of-day) pricing can be an effective means of reducing VMT, energy use, and emissions. Variable road pricing assesses drivers for using roads during peak periods and over long distances. The same principle holds for mass transit: riders pay more for traveling during peak periods in the peak direction of travel and over longer distances. For air travel, variable pricing could be easily implemented by replacing current takeoff fees based on aircraft weight with fees based on time-of-day usage.

In economic terms, variable pricing is a highly efficient means of matching transportation supply with demand. In practice, however, pricing strategies can be a regressive form of taxation by disproportionately burdening those with lower incomes (Willis 1990). This can be corrected with income-tax credits and other public policies that provide economic compensation to those with low incomes.

The inherent efficiency of variable pricing has led several jurisdictions worldwide to consider it. Hong Kong tested electronic road pricing in the mid-1980s, and in 1989 the Dutch transport minister came out in support of road pricing. In the US, the North Dallas Tollway in Texas has installed a new system that automatically bills drivers a higher amount for traveling during peak hours (Winston 1990). The US Office of Technology Assessment recommends that congestion pricing be aggressively pursued nationwide (Willis 1990).

Variable road pricing can also be used for heavy-duty trucks in order to allocate the cost of road damage caused by excessive weight. A pavement-damage charge can be assessed based on the truck's weight per axle (the best measure of road damage) (Winston 1990).

Time-of-day pricing could address some of transit's financial problems. Each transit service should price its fares higher during rush hours because significantly more of its capital and operating budget is spent meeting peak-hour demand (Wachs 1989). Since the bulk of transit passengers journey to and from work or school during rush hours, transit revenues would increase. Moreover, lower fares during off-peak hours would ease the burden on the transit-dependent, who are often poor or too young or old to drive. A difference of 50 percent between on- and off-peak fares was found to cause about 4 percent of transit riders to shift to off-peak times and was thought to increase overall ridership slightly (Andrle et al. 1990).

Distance-based pricing is another promising variable scheme for both roads and transit. Most toll roads, and a few mass-transit systems, charge vehicles more the farther they travel. A recent distance-based-fare demonstration project for mass transit found that it is possible to implement a zone-fare system without disrupting riders, drivers, or system revenues (Andrle et al. 1990). Most European transit systems employ variable prices ("stage" or "zone" fares) in which payment varies with the length of trip. Since the cost of providing a longer trip is more than that of a shorter trip, such pricing is much more efficient. Monthly transit passes exacerbate the problem; since long-distance peak-hour travelers are more likely to purchase these passes, they obtain higher subsidies than many other riders.

Another European innovation that incorporates elements of variable pricing is the integrated transit fare system used by the Netherlands for nearly a decade (Replogle 1990). This system allows passengers to buy a single ticket that is valid for any transit system in the country—bus or rail. Because the system is both flexible and fully integrated, anyone can ride transit anywhere and at any time.

Automated toll-collection systems are one way to administer variable pricing along highways. These high-tech systems are currently being installed on many roads, bridges, and tunnels across the country (see below).

Variable congestion pricing could save the US $22 billion annually in lower maintenance costs and fewer system delays (Winston 1990).[19] The exact figures may vary, but clearly if travelers, commuters, and freight haulers pay the full cost (including social costs) of using the transportation system, the system will be less congested and in better repair.

TELECOMMUTING. Telecommuting entails transmitting information without transporting people. It means working at home instead of in the office, teaching by TV instead of in the classroom, and otherwise using electronic communications for transactions formerly done face to face. According to some experts, telecommuting can be a powerful weapon in the battle to ease congestion, reduce energy use, and improve air quality (Owen 1985).

In 1980, about 3 percent of US citizens worked at home—some seven million telecommuters (Black 1990). With advances in computer technology, telecommuting could be much higher by the year 2000, significantly reducing travel demand and fuel consumption. For the state of California alone, forecasts call for reductions of up to 30 billion passenger-miles of travel, 700 million gallons of fuel, and seven million tons of CO_2 in the year 2000 (Kitamura et al. 1990b). The Southern California Association of Governments estimates that by 2000 a 12-percent reduction in work-related travel through telecommuting could reduce area-wide air emissions by 2 percent (AOR 1989). Furthermore, the California South Coast Air Quality Management District estimates that telecommuting, along with alternative work schedules, could reduce highway vehicle emissions up to 7 percent (OTA 1989a).

Telecommuting has some potential problems that must be ironed out. It may violate zoning ordinances that do not allow residential and business uses in the same building. In a recent pilot program in Los Angeles in which 500 city workers telecommuted, the program was successful in reducing emissions, but there were threats to block the program because of violations of zoning ordinances (Bicker 1990).

Nevertheless, the future for telecommuting is promising. As the cost is reduced through the widespread use of communication satellites, fiber optics, and computerized information systems, telecommuting could become cheaper than motorized commuting, with no loss of worker efficiency.

ALTERNATIVE WORK SCHEDULES. Alternative work schedules are already widely implemented. There are three basic forms: staggered work hours, flexible work hours, and compressed workweeks. Staggered work hours allow groups of employees to work on fixed schedules with sequential or staggered starting and ending times. Flexible work hours ("flex-time") give employees some choice in organizing their own schedules. Employees on compressed workweeks put in a full week in less than five days.

One goal of these alternatives is to control travel demand by shifting it to less congested, off-peak periods. Research suggests that alternative work schedules may not be complementary with other TDM/TSM strategies and may, in fact, hurt ridesharing and transit programs (Higgins 1990a, Giuliano and Golob 1990). Nevertheless, modifying work schedules may be a way for a region to buy time while developing and implementing a comprehensive congestion-management program.

As expected, staggered work hours and flex-time have been shown to reduce on-peak travel volumes and travel time. Staggered work hours have yielded up to a 9-percent reduction in average estimated travel time. However, those employees who do not change their work hours can benefit even more than participants because they will save time without the inconvenience of having modified work schedules. In other words, there can be disincentives to participate.

Compressed workweeks may not reduce overall travel volumes whatsoever. In fact, because of added nonwork travel on extra days off, total travel volumes could even grow.

Voluntary alternative work-schedule programs are problematic in that they can have the effect of simply shifting the peak-hour commute rather than spreading out the peak (Giuliano and Golob 1990). Mandatory alternative work schedules require systematic enforcement and can create difficulties for employees who need to have control over their schedules. Costs like these, in added inconvenience and difficulty of enforcement, mean that policymakers should thoroughly evaluate alternative work scheduling in light of their primary objectives.

CONCLUSION. Parking pricing and other parking regulations can be powerful transportation-demand management strategies that should be considered especially where they support other strategies such as ridesharing, mass transit, and bicycle and pedestrian travel. Ridesharing is an effective demand-management tool especially in low-density areas over long commutes where parking is in limited supply. Thus ridesharing should be viewed as a way to best serve low-density development not well suited to transit, while mass transit can be used to encourage more clustered land-use patterns and shorter traveling distances.

High-occupancy-vehicle facilities have provided modest but measurable environmental benefits to date, and are a proven way to reduce vehicle-miles traveled and travel times. Moreover, the increased carrying capacity of vehicles means reduced fuel consumption as well.

Variable pricing schemes for roads, transit, and airports are merited because they are highly efficient means of matching transportation supply with demand. In fact, if such pricing is not instituted, it will be difficult if not impossible to reduce congestion throughout the US transportation system. Variable pricing can be especially effective if revenues are used to improve transportation alternatives and make system-wide improvements rather than going to general revenues.

As telecommunications technology advances, telecommuting will become an increasingly viable work strategy for reducing emissions and congestion during peak periods of travel. Telecommuting can reduce not only automobile travel but airplane travel as well.

Although perhaps not the best long-term policy, alternative work scheduling can serve as a way to buy time to manage congestion. Of the various alternative work schedule programs, staggered work hours and flex-time are the most promising possibilities for reducing on-peak travel volumes and travel time.

Since the work commute tends to stress the transportation system to the greatest degree, individuals can make a difference based on their decisions. Reducing single-passenger-auto commuting can offer energy savings, congestion relief, less pollution, and greater system-wide efficiency. The current commuting situation can be vastly improved by changing worker habits (see box).

Bicycling and Pedestrian Strategies

One end of the transportation spectrum—human-powered transport—has received little attention compared with the fanfare given to automobiles and mass transit. Yet bicycling and walking are important both as primary means of mobility and as links to mass transit.

In US cities, fewer than 10 percent of commuter trips are by walking or bike, compared with 40 percent in typical European cities. This is one reason we use four and a half times as much gasoline per capita as Europeans (Replogle 1990). To the extent that policymakers can promote these energy-efficient, pollution-free, cost-effective alternatives, all can benefit.

BICYCLING STRATEGIES. In 1978 Congress expressly endorsed the role of bicycles in our transport system. In the National Energy Conservation Policy Act, Congress asserted that

... bicycles are the most efficient means of transportation ... represent a viable commuting alternative to many people,

Bike-on-transit program, San Diego, California.

Individual Commuters Can Make a Difference:
How to Reduce Emissions, Congestion, and Energy Use

1. Avoid peak-period hours of travel. If possible, commute at off-peak hours. Idling and stop-and-go driving consume substantially more fuel and result in more air emissions than driving at a steady speed of 45 to 55 mph. Fuel consumption doubles when average speed drops from 30 to 10 mph, and emissions are triple what they would have been at a constant 55 mph.

2. When purchasing a new vehicle, buy a car instead of a van or light truck. Cars emit far less pollution—70 percent less carbon monoxide, 50 percent less hydrocarbons, and 20 percent less nitrogen oxides—and use 30 percent less gasoline over the same number of miles.

3. Walk, bike, or carpool to public transit instead of driving solo. These alternative connections to public transit can save up to 150 gallons of gasoline per person annually and cut air emissions by at least 50 percent.

4. Rideshare whenever possible. A two-person carpool reduces gasoline consumption and air emissions by 50 percent over driving alone; a three-person carpool cuts gasoline consumption and air emissions by 66 percent; and a 10-person vanpool cuts fuel usage and emissions by 83 percent.

5. Telecommute whenever possible. Work at home or at a teleconference center, if one is available to you. Also, take advantage of alternative work schedules to avoid peak periods of travel.

Source: California Energy Commission, *1990 Conservation Report.*

---

offer mobility at speeds as fast as that of cars in urban areas, provide health benefits through daily exercise, reduce noise and air pollution, are relatively inexpensive, and deserve consideration in a comprehensive national energy plan.[20]

In 1980 the US Department of Transportation estimated that bicycle use could be increased by 200-400 percent for work trips and 50-100 percent for other transportation purposes by 1985, with resultant fuel savings of up to 23.5 million barrels of oil per year (about 5 percent of all fuel required for auto commuting in 1985) (DOT 1980). Other experts estimate that bicycling currently displaces some 14 billion automobile-miles per year, or 1 percent of total auto miles per year (Komanoff 1990).

Of the 90 million US bicyclists in 1989, 23 million were "regular riders" and 3.2 million were "bicycle commuters" (BIA 1990). In that year, bicycling was the second most popular form of recreation in America; over half of all adults rode a bicycle. By 2010, bicyclists are expected to increase to nearly 120 million (LAW 1989).

Bicycles are the least energy-intensive form of transport. A 10-mile commute by bicycle requires only 350 calories of renewable energy. The same trip in an average car requires 18,600 calories of nonrenewable energy (about half a gallon of gasoline); a bus trip uses 9,200 calories, and a train trip 8,850. Even walking is more energy intensive than biking: a 10-mile walk requires 1,000 calories of renewable energy.

Bicycling has a low social cost. It saves energy, reduces pollution, and alleviates traffic congestion. Today's 3.2 million bicycle commuters save an estimated 550 million gallons of gasoline and six million tons of CO_2 annually by not using cars.[21]

Each person who cycles instead of driving alone saves *per mile* at least 2.6 grams of HC, 20 grams of CO, and 1.6 grams of NO_x (Table 10). In aggregate terms, if the current 0.5 percent of all trips now made by bicycles rose to 2.4 percent, CO and other emissions would decrease by 5 percent (EPA 1979).

For those who cannot bicycle all the way to their offices, cycling to mass-transit stations can also reduce energy use, pollution, and congestion. The average motorist driving to a Park&Ride facility could, by switching to a bike, save 150 gallons of gasoline annually, reduce CO_2 emissions by 3,000 pounds, and reduce emissions of CO, HC, and NO_x by two to five times (due to "cold-start" conditions) (Replogle 1988).[22] Bicycles also do not add to traffic and parking congestion; 12 bicycles can be parked in the space required for a single car (LAW 1989).

If only 2 percent of the US work force now living less than two miles from a transit route and currently commuting by auto were to bike to transit, 120 million gallons of gasoline would be saved each year—1 percent of total US fuel use for auto commutes (Replogle 1988).[23] Such a switch may be likely: in a recent survey of Washington, DC, Metro riders using Park&Ride facilities in Fairfax County, Virginia, 25 percent of those surveyed indicated that they would consider Bike&Ride transportation if access and parking were improved (Clarke 1990).

Moreover, the bicycle-transit link is extremely cost-effective. In an effort to serve the suburbs, transit agencies have historically relied on Park&Ride access to attract those living beyond normal walking distance to ride transit. This solution has been costly in terms of land, capital, and facility maintenance. Each parking space requires over 300 square feet of land and costs from $4,000 to as much as $20,000 to construct, including an additional $175 each year to maintain (DOT 1987a, Replogle 1984). Each bicycle parking space, on the other hand, uses less than 12 square feet of land at a cost of $50-$150 to build and costs just a few dollars to maintain (Replogle 1988).

Undoubtedly, the growth of bicycle use in the US has been hampered by the high theft rates. The Department of Transportation has recognized that "fear of theft is a significant disincentive to bicycle transportation." Bicycle thefts are at least three times more common than automobile thefts in the US, and less than 20 percent of stolen bikes are recovered (Replogle 1984). Secure bicycle parking facilities and bike-on-transit programs can alleviate this problem. Parking should be located close to station entrances, and high-security or guarded facilities are best. These are common in Europe and Japan but do not yet exist in the United States.

Safety (or the feeling of being safe) is one of the most important issues for bicyclists and pedestrians alike. Safety increases when bicyclists are given ample space for sharing the road. Recent studies have shown that widening the outside or curb lane to at least 14 feet can benefit *both* cyclists and motorists (TRB 1988b). Other factors affecting safety include the number of lanes, posted speed, traffic volume, traffic mix, pavement conditions, parking frequency, type of intersections, shoulder condition, and degree of enforcement protecting cyclists' rights-of-way. In addition to protection from automobiles, bicyclists should be separated from pedestrians; if this is not possible, wide lanes shared between pedestrians and cyclists should be clearly marked to divide traffic.

Bicycles are underrepresented in the US transportation system more for political than technical reasons. With no technological barriers to overcome, the only restraint on bicycles is the willingness of policymakers to give them the attention they deserve. According to the Department of Transportation:

> Many of the disincentives to increased bicycling are the result of the low level of integration of bicycling into our transportation system. Three root causes account for this situation: (1) lack of awareness and understanding of bicycling concerns among transportation professionals; (2) fragmentation of transportation planning and management; and (3) low level of policy and funding commitment to support bicycling. When combined these causes produce a situation common in federal, state, and local transportation agencies: bicycling is simply overlooked (DOT 1980, Replogle 1984).

In fact, until recently the Department of Transportation had no full-time staff person dealing with bicycle transportation. A recent congressional report on DOT appropriations directed the agency to appoint a bicycle program manager to develop a national plan for the promotion of bicycle ridership and safety (House 1990).

In the past decade bicycles have gained limited recognition as a viable, cost-effective form of transportation. A few cities and states have adopted successful bicycle programs, among them Seattle, Eugene (Oregon), and the states of Oregon and Florida. Thirty-three states have included bicycle promotion in their "State Implementation Plans" (SIPs) required by federal clean-air regulations. For example, Madison, Wisconsin, predicts that a 50-percent increase in bicycling commuting would lead to a 7-percent reduction in HC and CO emissions, and a 15-percent reduction in NO_x (LAW 1989). And Chicago has found that providing secure bicycle parking at mass transit is 13 and 310 times more cost-effective at reducing hydrocarbon emissions than either carpooling or Park&Ride service, respectively (LAW 1989).

PEDESTRIAN STRATEGIES. Enhanced pedestrian access to transit is another vital transportation need. Although census data show that almost 6 percent of US workers walked to work in 1980 (and this is probably an underestimate), many more walk to mass transit (Black 1990). The exact number is difficult to quantify because these pedestrians are not considered in ordinary origin-destination surveys.

Like bicycling facilities, pedestrian facilities should be planned in conjunction with mass-transit. When commuters Walk&Ride, along with the energy and environmental benefits, parking is also not required. This makes Walk&Ride much more cost-effective than Park&Ride. Moreover, walking and bicycling (in and of themselves or in conjunction with transit) can save commuters from buying a second car—a tremendously cost-effective decision.

Even land-use planners agree that it is desirable to encourage more people to walk. Integrating land-use and transportation planning is the key to providing maximum safe, efficient pedestrian movement. Studies support the planner's conventional wisdom that higher density and mixed-use development promote more walking (Black 1990). Furthermore, designing with the pedestrian in mind, so that those on foot are not inhibited by the auto, benefits the community at large.

CONCLUSION. Bicycling and walking are the cleanest and most energy-efficient forms of transportation, with virtually none of the social costs of other forms of travel. Planning and building more extensive facilities for both is also extremely cost-effective. Policies at all levels of government should be adopted to promote these transport modes to the fullest extent possible. This includes requiring those responsible for land-use planning and road building to integrate walking and bicycling into future plans.

Regional Development Strategies

Today's typical commute is not, as it once was, from suburb to central city; it is from suburb to suburb. Two-thirds of all new jobs are located in the suburbs, and suburb-to-suburb movement is now twice that of suburb-to-central city (Nakadegawa 1990). To handle the growing regional congestion this is creating, agencies and officials, notably land-use and transportation planners, have numerous tools at their disposal. Growth-management measures, including land-use strategies, job/housing balances, and zoning ordinances, will all be required to solve regional transportation problems.

LAND-USE PLANNING. Land-use and development policies, although they only indirectly affect transportation demand, are as important as transportation measures themselves in determining the evolution of regional networks and local travel behavior. Only by integrating regional land-use planning and long-range transportation planning can we hope to create livable suburban development.

In the past, regional land-use and transportation planning often took place only after congestion and pollution problems threatened to reach crisis proportions. One example of an exception to this, where an excellent vision of comprehensive growth policy is outlined, is in Montgomery County, Maryland (MCPD 1989). Although its reputation may be otherwise, southern California provides another example of comprehensive growth management of present and future transportation problems (SCAG 1989b). And three cities, San Jose, San Francisco, and Portland, Oregon, are partners in a sustainable-city program that sets out goals for comprehensive economic, housing, transportation, energy, and environmental planning (Deakin et al. 1989, Yesney 1989).

The following land-use planning tools can greatly assist transportation planning (DOT 1987b):

■ *Residential Density*

The higher the residential density, the higher the transit ridership and the shorter the trip length. Result: improved cost recovery and better level of transit service. Two rules of thumb for residential density that promote transit ridership are: 1) density should exceed 2,400 persons per square mile and 2) a minimum of seven dwelling units per fully developed acre should be built.

■ *Employment Density*

For significant transit use, there should be at least 50 employees per acre of business development (in areas with over 10,000 jobs). Densities of only 25 employees per acre result in ridership levels of only 1 percent of all employees, not enough to sustain transit services. At densities of 50-60 employees per acre, an estimated 6-11 percent of employees will ride transit.

■ *Development Location and Proximity to Existing Transit*

All too often, access to mass transit and other alternative transport is a low priority in deciding where to locate development. Clustering new and existing development creates a concentration of trip destinations. Ideally, activity centers (areas of significant development—business parks, for example) in urban areas should be planned at distances of three to six miles from one another, allowing for shorter work and shopping trips.

The rules of thumb for proximity to transit are as follows: People can be expected to walk up to 1,000 feet to a bus stop. Those over 45 years of age will not walk as far; senior citizens will not walk more than 750 feet to a transit stop (steep grades reduce these distances). Those with higher incomes are less inclined to walk any distance to mass transit. Bike&Rides attract cyclists from one-half to three miles away, while Park&Rides draw people from 1-10 miles away.

■ *Mixed-Use Development*

Balanced residential and commercial/industrial development in reasonably close proximity can lead to a reduction in transportation demand. Mixed-use development offers several benefits: reduced parking requirements, more open space, enhanced retail activity, reduced auto traffic, and increased safety during evening hours. For greatest benefits, the mix of housing should match the income structure of area employment in terms of affordability.

■ *Land-Use Design Considerations*
Pedestrians are more likely to Walk&Ride if transit delivers them to their front door rather than to a parking lot they must walk through. Accordingly, new developments should be designed with parking in the rear. Provisions for on-site bus turnouts and passenger shelters also encourage transit use. Foot travel is enhanced when connecting complexes provide pedestrian arcades. And, of course, for safety reasons adequate lighting is critical.

■ *Street Layout*
Designing transit routes early in the development process can minimize distances to stations and ensure that roads will support heavy buses, reducing maintenance costs. Improved road design can cut costs by reducing street size. Gridded systems provide the easiest pedestrian access, while cul-de-sacs, popular in suburban developments, restrict transit and pedestrian passage. Sidewalks, the need for which is often ignored, must be provided. They attract pedestrians and provide safety. For bicycles, wide curb lanes (14 feet minimum), striped bike lanes, or separate bike paths provide easier and safer access to transit centers, Bike&Ride lots, freeway-flyer stops, and major bus stops.

TRANSPORTATION CONTROL MEASURES (TCMs). TCMs are defined as "a set of interrelated measures that have the general objective of reducing emissions by reducing driving or improving traffic flow" (OTA 1989a). These measures were introduced in the 1977 amendments to the Clean Air Act for areas that could not attain ozone or carbon monoxide standards (Gushee and Sieg-Ross 1988). Their aim is to change public behavior through information, mandates, and other economic means. TCMs can include modified work schedules, telecommuting, high-occupancy-vehicle lanes, bicycle programs, parking management, road fees, and land-use controls.

The Office of Technology Assessment (OTA) came to the following conclusions about TCMs (OTA 1989a):

■ TCM programs must be tailored to each area.

■ The success of many TCMs depends largely on public acceptance and participation.

■ Long lead times and sustained efforts are required to implement TCMs.

■ The effectiveness of one TCM may depend substantially on concurrent implementation of another.

■ TCMs must integrate planning at all levels—for transportation, land use, air quality, and resources—in order to be most effective.

Studies show highly variable results from TCMs ranging from no effect at all to a 30-percent reduction in single-occupant driving (Higgins 1990b). Using only a few TCMs, hydrocarbon and NO_x emissions have been reduced by 1-7 percent (Gushee and Sieg-Ross 1988). Implementing the full range of TCMs should lead to even further reductions.

ZONING ORDINANCES. Zoning can encourage development that supports alternative transportation. A few of the many zoning tools available to land-use and transportation planners include:

■ planned-unit development—gives developers incentives to meet pre-determined land-use goals

■ floating zoning—permits special uses within a jurisdiction in accordance with development criteria

■ bonus or incentive zoning—provides developers with bonuses and incentives to achieve increased development density

■ mixed-use zoning—requires a wide array of types of development aimed at reducing distances between houses and jobs

■ land banking—outright purchase of land by the public sector well in advance of any development to ensure appropriate land use

■ transit zoning districts—targeted development in areas with transit systems already in place (DOT 1987a, Replogle 1990)

Zoning codes all too often require that parking be provided as part of any urban development. The federal Urban Mass Transportation Administration reports that three to four parking spaces are required for every 1,000 square feet of office space (DOT 1989). Such zoning regulations encourage automobile use. Zoning can be better used by land-use and transportation officials to provide incentives for developers to provide access to alternative transportation.

Moreover, local governments tend to allow overdevelopment of commercially zoned areas. When commercial land is developed more than the infrastructure can handle, there is no room for residential development. Thus low-density urban sprawl—usually residential—rings these areas, and traffic congestion follows. Tightening control of commercial zones is an important step in influencing the pattern of regional development (Replogle 1990).

There are seemingly limitless schemes for integrating land-use planning and transportation-control measures. The Southern California Association of Governments (SCAG) has identified four main strategies focusing on planning, investment, financial, and regulatory mechanisms (see below) (SCAG 1989a).[24] A comprehensive growth-management policy geared to reducing the social costs of transportation would probably integrate elements from several of these strategies:

Planning strategies

■ Maximum limits on development area to encourage clustered growth with appropriate jobs/housing balance

■ Regional growth-management plans

Investment strategies
■ Land-acquisition programs to foster targeted development or preserve open space
■ Housing subsidies and investment programs to encourage affordable housing in key areas
■ Downtown-regentrification programs to promote mixed, high-density development
■ Employment programs to develop skills for job flexibility
■ Special transportation-service programs to facilitate access to jobs in nonresidential areas

Financial strategies
■ Fair-share bonuses and fee schedules to reward or penalize developers for meeting housing and nonresidential targets
■ Preferential and deferred taxation of undeveloped land to preclude nonclustered urban development
■ Tax deferral of selected developed property to reduce property-tax burdens on targeted development in certain areas
■ Interjurisdictional tax-sharing schemes to remove property- and sales-tax incentives that encourage local governments to approve unsound projects in order to raise tax revenues
■ Revenue financing plans that upgrade an area for targeted development and use increased property-tax revenues to cover the cost
■ Government funding and tax-exempt-bond financing programs to encourage desired development
■ Development fees to build facilities or provide necessary services
■ Agreements to share financial burdens of development between developer and community

Regulatory strategies
■ Mixed-use zones to reduce distances between houses and jobs
■ Small zoning districts to shrink zone sizes for greater land-use mix in each activity center
■ "Growth-sequence zoning" to control the timing and location of growth in order to divert residential growth from job-poor areas
■ Conservation zoning to limit development in environmentally sensitive areas
■ Conditional-use permits to allow uses different from those specified in ordinances
■ Development-timing permits to oversee the timing and location of urban development
■ Growth-management quota system to restrict growth to conform with regional growth policies
■ Impact zoning to evaluate proposals against specified criteria

■ Density regulations (cluster zoning, transferable development credits, and incentive zoning) to achieve increased development density
■ Intensity regulations to control the ratio between open space and development
■ Off-street parking and loading regulations to discourage vehicle trips
■ Temporary moratoriums on development to stunt growth during comprehensive planning
■ Contract zoning and development agreements to enable agencies to restrict development
■ Floating zoning to selectively permit special uses within a jurisdiction in accordance with development criteria
■ Planned-unit development procedures to improve site design by giving developers incentives to meet land-use planning goals

SCAG has assessed the ease of implementing these strategies and found that the easiest to implement are plan-intensity schemes, downtown-regentrification programs, tax-allocation financing plans, industrial-development financing plans, parking regulations, and planned-unit development procedures. Other studies estimate that, if effectively implemented, these strategies can result in a 10-percent reduction in air emissions (AOR 1989).

Since few regions have tried these ideas, the costs and benefits are not well documented. The costs of many of these policies are expected to be very high both to developers and the public. But it is fair to say that in areas with drastic problems, such as the Los Angeles region, these strategies may be cost-effective.

JOBS/HOUSING BALANCE. The job/housing (J/H) balance is a useful developer's tool, although no rule of thumb or actual values are available. Basically, when jobs and housing are not in balance, transportation problems are the likely result. Land-use planners can look at the range of incomes and housing costs to determine how far people have to move away from their jobs to find housing they can afford. The farther they must move, the more congestion, energy use, and air-quality problems an area will have. The regional-development strategies discussed above can bring jobs and housing into balance.

Innovative Transportation Technologies

To a limited extent, technological improvements can make the transportation system more efficient. These improvements include infrastructure changes and innovations in vehicle technology. It is important to note that these improvements offer only a partial solution to our transportation problems, and that although a technology may be state of the art, its energy and environmental impacts may not necessarily be reduced.

TRAFFIC-SIGNAL SYNCHRONIZATION. Overall energy efficiency can be increased by using centralized computers to optimize signal timing and coordinate groups of signals. Signal synchronization is not a new idea. Traffic engineers have timed traffic signals to improve traffic flow since the 1920s. Today, older fixed-timing systems are being replaced by computerized systems; one in five signalized intersections is now computer controlled.

Of all the easily implemented strategies, signal improvements can provide the greatest near-term energy and CO_2 emission savings. Depending on the system, reductions of 25 percent in travel time, 15 percent in delays, 13 percent in fuel use, and 10 percent in air emissions can be realized by computerized resignalizing (Willis 1990, AOR 1989).

These measures are very cost-effective. About 25 gallons of fuel are saved for every project dollar expended (Stowers and Boyar 1985). And signal-system improvements mean operating savings for all highway vehicles—cars, trucks, and buses.

Signal improvements need to account not only for motor vehicles but also for cyclists and pedestrians. Special signals can be installed for cyclists, allowing them a 10-second lead on the green signal to cross the intersection before cars. This can also reduce conflicts with right-hand turns at intersections. Many US cities and counties, such as Boston, Baltimore, and Montgomery County, Maryland, have an all-direction, pedestrian-only crossing signal in advance of the green signal for cars.

These improvements are relatively easy to make. North Carolina has retimed 980 intersections and gained an estimated annual savings of 12.2 million gallons of fuel, with an operating cost of $45.1 million—a ratio of cost savings to direct program costs of 98 to 1 (ITRE 1989).[25] In California, the retiming of 4,000 urban traffic signals reduced delays 15 percent, cut fuel use 9 percent and hydrocarbon and CO emissions 8 percent (AOR 1989).

ADVANCED VEHICLE/HIGHWAY SYSTEMS. Several interdependent vehicle and road technologies may offer reductions in traffic congestion, air pollution, and energy consumption. Known as advanced (or intelligent) vehicle/highway systems (AVHS or IVHS), they fall into four categories: advanced driver-information systems, advanced traffic-management systems, automated vehicle-control systems, and commercial and fleet operation technologies (OTA 1989b).[26]

According to the US Office of Technology Assessment, AVHS could help highways handle a greater volume of traffic, promote highway safety, and enhance the productivity of commercial and fleet operations. Estimated increases in throughput (volume) of 10-20 percent are anticipated from information-based AVHS technologies (discussed below).

AVHS technologies include advanced driver information systems (ADIS, sometimes called motorist information systems), which warn motorists of traffic congestion by providing timely information on road conditions so that motorists can plan their routes accordingly. These systems have many forms—standard radio traffic reports, interactive video displays, and vehicle-based navigation systems, which automatically optimize a driver's course.

Advanced traffic-management systems (ATMS, sometimes called "smart streets") are infrastructure-based monitoring systems that allow for on-road surveillance and control of traffic. These can include signal synchronization (discussed above), accident-detection systems, highway- and corridor-control systems, which can be used to signal rush-hour lane changes to motorists; and ramp metering systems, which stagger vehicle entry onto highways. Sophisticated ATMS can reduce travel time by 13 percent, number of stops (i.e., for signals) 35 percent, fuel consumption 12 percent, vehicle emissions 10 percent, as well as increase average speeds 15 percent (OTA 1989b). Moreover, studies indicate that ATMS have a benefit-cost ratio of over 10 to 1 (Ewell 1989).

Automated vehicle-control systems (AVCS, or "smart cars") attempt to automate all or part of a trip, requiring less driver interaction with the vehicle. These systems include collision-warning and -avoidance devices; automatic headway controls, which establish following distances between vehicles; and automatic steering controls. A car with a fully automated vehicle-control system has not yet been developed, but individual components exist in prototype. Many AVCS allow for faster travel speeds, closer following distances, and narrower lane widths than present automobiles. Given these reduced operating margins, safety must be proven before these systems are used.

The fourth group of advanced vehicle/highway systems is automated technologies for commercial and fleet operations, including automatic vehicle identification (AVI), weight in motion (WIM), automatic vehicle classification, and automatic vehicle location (AVL). AVI-equipped vehicles can maintain cruising speeds during information and financial transactions such as highway and bridge tolls and at state boundaries. Weight-in-motion technologies weigh heavy trucks in motion for compliance with weight regulations and for information purposes; and AVL systems can identify vehicle location and transmit the information to a central location.

Advanced technologies run the risk of making driving solo seem even more desirable, thus threatening to aggravate the problem they set out to solve. According to the OTA, automated systems alone cannot provide even a near-term solution to traffic congestion and vehicular air pollution; other transportation strategies are required as well (OTA 1989b). In any event, automated systems have many hurdles to clear before they become feasible. Given the high level of resources they require, other innovative transportation strategies should be adopted before AVHS.

ADVANCED TRAVELER INFORMATION AND SERVICES (ATIS). These technologies (sometimes termed "smart transit") can be used by transit and rideshare vehicles to provide information to the traveler that will make it easier to determine which HOV alternative to use. Accurate and up-to-date information is provided at both work and residence locations as well as en route, and in the vehicle itself through touch-tone telephones, cable television, videotex terminals, and computers. ATIS technologies include: (1) on-board replication of maps and signs, (2) pretrip electronic route planning, (3) traffic information broadcasting systems, (4) safety warning systems, (5) on-board navigation systems, (6) electronic route-guidance systems, (7) electronic signs showing transit routes and schedules, (8) audiotex/videotex (remote computer systems that permit residential and business users to interact over telephone lines to obtain timely transportation information), and (9) automated carpool-matching capabilities.

European countries and Canada are well ahead of the US in applying ATIS technologies to public transportation. For example, Germany currently operates an automated command-and-control system that integrates fixed-route transit buses, dial-a-ride minibuses, and contract taxi services. These services provide operators and passengers with arrival and destination data which greatly facilitates transit operation and use. In France, the public is using personal computers and microcomputer terminals to purchase up-to-the-minute information on bus and train fares and schedules. Over five million French currently subscribe to these videotex systems. "Smart-cards" fare-collection devices are also installed in many French and German buses. Smart-cards are plastic credit cards with microcomputer chips which permit more convenient fare payment, thus increasing ridership and raising employee productivity while electronically reporting ridership levels (Behnke 1991).

The Urban Mass Transit Association (UMTA) has developed an Advanced Public Transportation Systems Program to undertake research and development of innovative applications of advanced navigation, information, and communication technologies that most benefit public transportation. The program elements include market development, customer interface, vehicle operations, and HOV preference and verification.

The objectives of UMTA's program are to make travel on public transportation easier and more convenient by providing audio and visual information on service schedules and routes, and expanding the options for those who have selected a public-transportation mode. One feature of UMTA's "smart transit" development program is simplified fare payment by electronic media. A second objective is to present potential users, especially commuters who normally drive alone, with audio and visual information on the range of transit and ridesharing options available. A third objective of the program is to encourage travelers to shift to HOVs by providing faster and more relaxed trips by granting preferential treatment or access to facilities reserved for vehicles carrying a set minimum number of passengers. The final objective is to use vehicle-location and communications technologies to monitor, control, and manage public-transportation services in order to provide the most efficient public transportation systems.

Resources spent on making transit and ridesharing more user-friendly through smart-transit technologies are very promising. To the extent that they can attract travelers to transit and ridesharing, traffic congestion, air pollution, and energy consumption will be reduced.

AUTOMATED TOLL-COLLECTION SYSTEMS. These automated systems (a subset of AVHS technology) have already been put to use on several roads and bridges across the nation. They allow tolls to be charged automatically from cash accounts previously established by commuters; thus motorists do not have to stop and pay. Such systems can reduce congestion, pollution, and energy use. They also make variable road-pricing schemes (congestion pricing charges, discussed earlier in this chapter) technically feasible.

While tolls are efficient user fees for roads, they add to the problem of congestion. It takes about 12 seconds to stop and pay a toll to a human collector, five seconds to throw exact change into a toll-collection machine, and less than one second to pass a vehicle through an automated toll-collection device. Automated tolls also reduce air pollution because vehicles are not idling, and accidents because drivers do not have to stop.

Several bridges already use automatic tolling. The Crescent City Bridge in New Orleans, Michigan's Grosse Ile Bridge, and Philadelphia's Benjamin Franklin Bridge use bar-code labels (like those used in grocery stores) placed on cars' side windows for scanning by lasers. As soon as electronic tolls are tested on the San Diego-Coronado Bridge, nine other California toll bridges are slated for retrofit with these automated systems.

Roads are also scanned electronically. On the Dallas tollway, electronic tags (about the size of a credit card) are carried on vehicle windshields for automated toll collection. Ten Oklahoma turnpikes (six existing and four planned) are also scheduled to get automatic toll systems. Other toll roads under construction, like those in Orange County, California, are being equipped with automatic toll-collection systems, and tests are planned in Orlando and Denver for future use of these systems.

So far, use of these systems is optional. In Dallas and New Orleans, about 25 percent of all commuters have chosen to participate, and the numbers are growing. Cameras that can take pictures of license plates are used to deter cheating. Culprits are fined and denied the right to reregister their cars until the fines are paid.

AUTOMATED POLLUTION DETECTION. Yet another type of AVHS that has received attention, especially in highly polluted areas, is a highway radar trap that measures carbon monoxide emissions from passing cars in a fraction of a second. These systems could be used as an alternative to annual inspection-and-maintenance tests if similar systems were developed to measure hydrocarbon and NO_x. In the meantime, an automated pollution-detection system linked to a video camera that records a vehicle's license plate could generate a letter to a car's owner requiring that the vehicle be brought in for an inspection.

An estimated 10-30 percent of all cars on the road produce half of the pollution. Tests performed in Illinois with this device established average failure rates of 25 percent for pre-1974 cars. Some experts think this device could prove useful in reducing air pollution because it provides actual emission data on high-emitting vehicles as they operate. But other experts are concerned that such measuring devices are unsuitable for general screening because they cannot factor in the condition of the car and whether it is accelerating.

Conclusion

As this chapter has shown, there is no shortage of innovative ideas for improving our transportation system and reducing its social costs. The key question is which options to choose to bring these changes about. For most problems, a regional focus is best, although it may make more sense to implement some strategies at the federal level, such as funding for mass transit, and some at the local level, such as bicycling and pedestrian schemes.

The way to put innovative ideas into practice is to foster a policymaking environment that encourages them. Chapter 8 discusses specific policies—regulations, economic incentives, information, quasi-governmental measures, and comprehensive plans—that can help create such an environment.

Notes

1. Rapid (or heavy) rail is better known as subway, Metro, or rapid transit. Light-rail systems are sometimes referred to as trolleys or streetcars. Intercity rail is best known as Amtrak and other commuter rails. Light and heavy rail are generally electrified. Commuter rails vary among cities: they can run on either diesel or electricity, and travel at speeds comparable to rapid rail (about 70 mph). See Glossary for definitions.

2. In 1985, the nation's mass-transit fleet was comprised of about 60,000 buses, 10,000 subway cars, 1,000 streetcars, 4,000 commuter-rail cars, 400 commuter-rail locomotives, 30,000 vans, and 125,000 taxis. The transit infrastructure included 1,600 miles of rapid-rail track, 860 rapid-rail stations, 430 miles of light-rail track, 4,300 miles of commuter-rail track, 890 commuter-rail stations, and hundreds of mass-transit maintenance facilities.

3. Public-transit ridership figures for central-business-district work trips in other cities are: Atlanta—38 percent, Boston—59 percent, Chicago—77 percent, Dallas—35 percent, Los Angeles—36 percent, Philadelphia—62 percent, San Francisco—52 percent, and Seattle—45 percent.

4. Data are based on these sources and author's calculations.

5. The emission tests were done by Cummins Engine Company and Brooklyn Natural Gas Company.

6. Even if mass transit carried 30 percent of all commuters to work nationwide (rather than the current 5 percent), there would only be a 4 percent reduction in total energy use for all US work-related travel.

7. This assumes an auto-commute distance of six miles one-way, a 20-mpg auto, and 250 work days per year.

8. This assumes an auto-commute distance of six miles one-way, 250 days per year, auto averaging 20 miles per gallon, annual fuel use of 500 gallons, 25 grams per mile of total hydrocarbon, carbon monoxide, nitrogen oxides, sulfur oxides, and particulate emissions.

9. 1983 costs are reported in 1987 dollars using a CPI factor of 1.141. (The CPI is the consumer price index, used for inflating 1983 dollars to 1987 values.)

10. Cost per mile is divided by an average passenger occupancy of 1.7 to arrive at cost per passenger-mile (1988 cost reported in 1987 dollars for comparison).

11. The Bus Regulatory Reform Act of 1982 (P.L. 97-261) was enacted on September 20, 1982. This law gave greater freedom to carriers to set rates and reschedule services.

12. The enacting legislation was the Rail Passenger Service Act of 1970 (P.L. 91-518).

13. Contact the TAXI 2000 Corporation, Revere, Massachusetts, for more information about this system (TAXI 2000 Capital and O&M Cost Fact Sheet).

14. The Airline Deregulation Act of 1978 (P.L. 95-504) phased out federal control over airline fares and routes, thus allowing new airlines to form and existing airlines to expand into new markets and abandon old ones. The Motor Carrier Act of 1980 (P.L. 96-296), deregulating trucking, was enacted July 1, 1980. The Staggers Rail Act of 1980 (P.L. 96-448) was enacted October 14, 1980, to deregulate railroads.

15. The situation at Washington's Dulles International Airport is a good example of this inefficiency. Dulles taxis have exclusive rights to pick up passengers at the airport, but they can also pick up passengers downtown on the return trip to the airport (although they often return without a passenger). However, non-Dulles taxis bringing passengers to the airport cannot solicit fares for the return trip to the city. Thus taxis serving Dulles average only one-half a passenger per round trip—highly energy inefficient, highly polluting, and not cost-effective.

16. The price tag on dual-fueled CNG fleets is a little higher—$400 to $12,000 per ton of hydrocarbon reduced.

17. This assumes that industrial land costs $7-$10 per square foot and construction costs add $4-$6 per square foot (in 1985 dollars).

18. This assumes 4 percent overall transportation energy savings and that the transportation sector is responsible for one-third of US carbon dioxide emissions.

19. This figure represents estimated net savings; the cost of providing this service

system-wide is estimated at $3 billion annually. Moreover, when congestion pricing (for highways and airports) is coupled with a sound infrastructure investment policy, this is even more efficient.

20. The Energy Policy Conservation Policy Act of 1978 (P.L. 95-619) also required the Department of Transportation to develop a Comprehensive Bicycle Transportation Program to increase bicycle use for energy conservation. While DOT did establish a bicycle program, funding has remained very low over the years.

21. This assumes an average commute of 7.5 miles one way, average vehicle occupancy of 1.15 passengers, average car mileage of 19.2 miles per gallon, 250 work days per year, and 20 pounds CO_2 per gallon of gasoline.

22. Cold-start engine conditions usually occur during the first mile of travel. Because the car's engine is not warmed up, it is operating inefficiently, using two to five times more fuel and releasing two to five times more emissions than a fully warmed-up engine.

23. This assumes one-third of the 4.18 million barrels of oil per day for all automobile transportation is used for work-related commutes.

24. This study provides only an overview of SCAG's strategies. For details on each strategy, refer to the Regional Growth Management Plan (SCAG 1989a).

25. Annual fuel savings per signalized intersection average 12,410 gallons, and operating costs include fuel, delays, and stops.

26. This OTA report (Advanced Vehicle/Highway Systems; see bibliography) provides detailed documentation on AVHS and should be referred to for questions on the subject. This section is adapted from this report unless otherwise noted.

8 Public-Policy Options and Recommendations

The public sector—federal, state, and local government—has traditionally assumed the lead role of transportation policymaker. Perhaps this is because transportation services are considered by many to be "public goods," meaning goods that are consumed by everyone. The goal historically has been to establish an optimal allocation of resources that provides a high degree of mobility to all Americans. The mobility has been achieved for a substantial portion of American society, but at the cost of a less than optimal allocation of resources. Moreover, for too long the negative side effects of our transportation system—pollution, excessive oil use, and congestion—have been overlooked. In light of continuing conflict in the Middle East and constantly fluctuating crude-oil prices, the increasingly dirty air in American cities, and the mounting traffic on our nation's roads, it is urgent that these problems be addressed by fresh transportation policymaking.

But setting transportation policy is not, nor should it be, the responsibility of government alone. More than most issues, transportation policy directly affects, often on a daily basis, the welfare of individuals and institutions throughout society, from consumers to corporations. As a result, transportation policy, to be effective, must take into account the range of interests at stake and encourage wide public participation.

Several strategies aimed at reducing the transportation sector's social costs have been discussed previously. Three major questions emerged: Which strategies hold the most promise? What policy instruments should be used to induce these changes? Who is best suited to formulate and implement these policies?

As for the first question, the most promising strategies include:

- increasing the fuel efficiency of the US transportation sector
- commercializing clean-burning alternative fuels
- increasing vehicle occupancy

- stabilizing vehicle miles of travel on US roads
- improving intercity rail
- increasing mass-transit ridership
- promoting the use of intermodal freight transport

These seven strategies are the most important energy and environmental components of a sound transportation policy.

Policymakers have several options in the types of policy instruments they use. Generally speaking, these instruments fall into four broad categories:

- regulations
- economic incentives
- information
- quasi-governmental measures

Within each of these categories, specific policy options and recommendations are discussed below.

Regulatory Policies

Regulatory policies are mechanisms that can "push" the market by "command and control" to a desired goal. An example is automobile fuel-economy standards (see below). Regulatory policies entail setting standards, establishing procedures for permits and licenses, and enforcing regulations.

The government uses regulations to coerce, rather than induce, certain behavior. Many experts agree that the current regulatory system whereby government sets limits on the private sector can be administratively burdensome, resulting in an inefficient distribution of resources (Dower and Repetto 1990). Nevertheless, there are several regulatory policies that are both practical and desirable for the transportation sector.

STANDARDS. Standards provide a generic way to internalize the social costs of transportation by setting limits on producers. Such command tactics are one certain way to control pollution, excessive oil use, and other negative side effects of transportation.

The trade-off for certainty is that standards raise producer costs and market prices and also affect trade patterns, sometimes with unforeseeable results. Standards also have important limitations: implementing them requires technical expertise, and enforcing them requires authority to be effective. Moreover, because standards provide a ceiling for compliance, manufacturers may have a disincentive to go beyond what the standards require for fear that further regulation will follow. This leads to inefficiency in the marketplace and can discourage innovations.

Two examples of successful federal transportation standards are the vehicle emission-control standards and the CAFE (corporate average fuel economy) standards. Both have proved effective since their enactment in the early 1970s. But raising these standards takes enormous political effort; neither regulation was amended throughout the 1980s even though air quality worsened and autos consumed the lion's share of oil in the US. In 1990, the Senate narrowly defeated a bill that would have increased CAFE standards 40 percent by 2000.[1]

The 101st Congress finally undertook the challenge of tightening the Clean Air Act, enacting the first amendments since 1977. The new act includes provisions on vehicle tailpipe emissions, alternative transportation fuels, toxic emissions, acid rain, and ozone-layer depletion.

Following are details on three standards that should be revised or adopted:

Increase the federal CAFE standards for cars, vans, and light trucks. The federal CAFE legislation was enacted in 1975 in response to the Arab oil embargo of 1973. CAFE applies to each manufacturer's fleet of new cars and light trucks in a given model year. Manufacturers must meet the CAFE standard each year based on a sales-weighted average. Compliance with the standard is calculated for each manufacturer as follows:

$$\text{CAFE} = \sum M_i / \sum (M_i/E_i)$$

where: M_i = volume of sales of model i, and

E_i = fuel efficiency of model i, based on 55% city and 45% highway driving

Failure to meet the standard in any given model year subjects a manufacturer to a civil penalty of five dollars for each one-tenth of a mile per gallon the manufacturer's fleetwide average fuel economy falls short of meeting the standard, multiplied by the number of vehicles in that fleet. In order to avoid these fines, a three-year carry-forward and carry-back provision was added in 1980 to allow an internal credit system for calculating an individual manufacturer's compliance with the standard.

However, the federal standard has been stagnant for the past five years. After reaching its ceiling of 27.5 mpg in 1985, it was repeatedly relaxed from 1986 to 1989, and the average fuel economy of all American cars on the road has been stuck at about 19 mpg. The only way to guarantee increases is to raise the CAFE standard for new cars. Congress must require manufacturers to sell cars that average more than the current CAFE standard of 27.5 mpg. The same is true for light trucks, which today average only 13.5 mpg, 20.2 mpg for new models.

A revamped CAFE level of at least 40 mpg for new cars and 30 mpg for new light trucks by the year 2001 is feasible with available technologies. The improvements could save nearly three million barrels of oil a day by the year 2005 (nearly half of current passenger transportation use), and if vehicle miles of travel are stabilized, even more fuel will be saved (Ledbetter 1990). Carbon dioxide reductions would be in the range of 460 million tons annually.

Allow states to establish individual fuel-economy standards. If Congress fails to enact significantly higher CAFE standards, several states are eager to do the job. New York, Vermont, and Iowa have each considered legislation to increase the fuel economy of state-owned vehicles and may tackle all vehicles if allowed by the federal government. (States are currently preempted under the 1975 CAFE legislation from setting their own fuel-economy standards.)

One option might be to maintain the federal CAFE level (either current or future) as the floor while allowing individual states to adopt higher standards. This would give state and local governments the ability to increase the fuel efficiency of the vehicles registered in their own jurisdictions. Several states may already have higher fleetwide fuel economy averages based on their current statewide sales weighted mix. For example, California currently attains about 30 mpg even though the federal CAFE standard is set at only 27.5 mpg.

Encourage states to adopt California's stricter emissions standards for motor vehicles, and tighten transportation control measures. The 1990 amendments to the Clean Air Act include several transportation-related provisions. These include requirements to:

■ sell reformulated gasoline in the nine smoggiest cities by 1995

■ sell oxygenated fuels in carbon monoxide "non-attainment" areas in 1992

■ reduce emissions from cars and trucks in fleets of 10 or more in polluted cities by 80 and 50 percent, respectively, starting in 1998

■ install hose-and-nozzle controls at gas-station pumps to capture vapors during refueling and install fume-catching canisters on new cars, starting in the mid-1990s

■ adopt transportation control measures such as carpooling programs, driving restrictions, and HOV lanes to counteract VMT growth

■ produce 150,000 cleaner nongasoline alternative-fuel vehicles by 1996 under a California pilot program

■ phase in tighter tailpipe standards (30 percent HC reduction and 60 percent NO_x reduction) starting in 1994 and require manufacturers to certify these higher levels for 10 years or 100,000 miles

Many of these requirements focus on tailpipe emissions because these emissions are responsible for about half of urban air pollution. If fully implemented, the amendments will generally result in substantial improvement in air quality. Unfortunately, the new tailpipe standards are less stringent than California's (see below). Even more troubling, however, are provisions requiring the sale of reformulated gasoline in the nation's dirtiest cities. Several alternative-fuel options (CNG, biomass ethanol, hydrogen, electric vehicles, and fuel cells), either alone or in combination, would have been a better choice in reducing smog-forming emissions, greenhouse gases, toxic by-products, and oil-import levels.

Under the Clean Air Act, only California has the right to set different (i.e., higher) emission-control standards than the federal government. Any state can then follow suit by adopting these stricter standards. In September 1990, before the Clean Air Act was amended, California adopted the most stringent emission standards on cars and light trucks in the nation, and New York followed suit. (Together California and New York represent 20 percent of all new-car sales.) These standards will phase in progressively cleaner vehicles as follows:

■ Between 1994 and 1996: at least 10 percent of new vehicles sold in these states would have to meet a standard of 0.125 grams per mile (gpm) of HC—40 percent less than today's cars. These vehicles would probably run on natural gas, methanol, ethanol, propane, or reformulated ultra-clean gasoline (with enhanced emission-control systems).

■ In 1997: 25 percent of all new cars sold in these states will have to be "low-emission vehicles" (LEVs), emitting only 0.075 gpm of HC and 0.2 gpm of NO_x. LEV sales will increase by 25 percent annually.

■ In 2000: 96 percent of all new cars sold would be LEVs, with the remaining 4 percent made up of even cleaner, ultra-low-emission vehicles (ULEVs). Ultimately, by 2003, 10 percent of all new sales must be ULEVs, probably running on fuel cells, electricity, or hydrogen.

We believe other states should be encouraged to follow the lead of California and New York. This would substantially improve the likelihood that the nation's clean-air objectives will be met in the years ahead.

PERMITTING AND LICENSING. Permits and licenses are used to ensure compliance with existing regulations before a project can get under way. Failure to obtain the necessary permits usually delays a project, which can be costly and can stop the project altogether. In some cases, compliance with permitting regulations can be a precondition for obtaining funds (such as federal highway funds). The benefit of permits is that they can provide comprehensive review capability to both regulators and the public at the outset of a proposed development. In practice, permits and licenses can serve to create new markets and establish prices for remedial technologies.

An appropriate arena for permits is land-use-development projects. Each one affects the transportation system and the environment. A new office park or shopping center can increase traffic levels, resulting in increased emissions and energy use. Accordingly, land-use, transportation, energy, and environmental planning should be linked more directly through permitting requirements.

The National Environmental Policy Act (NEPA), the principal federal environmental permitting regulation, requires government agencies to prepare environmental impact statements (EIS) on actions affecting the quality of the environment prior to a project's construction. The EIS serves as an environmental disclosure law, providing information to the public about the particular environmental costs involved in a project. Several states have adopted permitting regulations similar to NEPA, including California, Minnesota, New York, and Texas (GAO 1990d). Assessing the impacts of transportation on energy consumption and the regional environment should be a central element in these environmental permitting documents. Thus permits should reflect goals established by a region's comprehensive growth-management and regional transportation plans. Permitting can be improved in the following ways:

Close the loopholes and correct inadequacies in environmental permitting requirements. Through regulatory reform, loopholes can be closed and regulations modified to include critical energy- and environment-related transportation priorities. Ideally, the permitting process should:

■ address energy-related transportation issues, such as energy efficiency, in project construction and operation

■ identify and preserve major transportation corridors, such as railroad rights-of-way, as long-term resources for future trains and other uses such as bike paths ("rails-to-trails" programs)

■ avoid the use of averages and aggregates in transportation planning because these figures do not account for hours of highest use, which are the most environmentally costly (Deakin 1988)

Require coordination of land-use plans with environmental and energy goals. Transportation and land use are intimately related activities. They are usually regulated by very different authorities, however. Land-use planning is traditionally done by local governments, while transportation planning is more likely to be a state or regional function. Interaction between the two can often be cursory. Usually the only regulatory requirement consists of weighing the proposed development against the capacity of nearby roads and intersections to decide if the development burdens existing infrastructure. Impacts on energy consumption and overall environmental effects are rarely a concern.

Better coordination would result if a few guiding principles were followed in assessing land-use impacts. These include:

■ promoting development in areas with existing mass-transit services

■ encouraging increased population density of new developments in order to make transit services easier to provide

■ promoting housing construction in job-rich areas and employment opportunities in residential areas (OTA 1989a)

Currently, regional transportation plans are required under the Surface Transportation Assistance Act and the Urban Mass Transportation Act. These plans are prepared by metropolitan planning organizations and must be approved by the Federal Highway Administration. Once approved, they serve as the master plans for federal transportation funding.

These regulations should be reformed to incorporate specific language that promotes the attainment of air-quality and fuel-use standards as well as land-use planning goals. Developments could be required to account for pollution and increases in energy use attributable to traffic growth. As another example, developers could be required to provide alternative transportation strategies that lower emissions and vehicle miles traveled as a condition of both highway and UMTA funding.

State implementation plans for air-quality attainment and regional transportation plans also need to be better coordinated to reflect the importance of the air-pollution and energy impacts caused by transportation. The results of such coordination would set goals for states and localities to reduce congestion, energy consumption, and environmental degradation associated with the transportation sector.

REGULATORY REFORM. Regulations are often relaxed in response to political pressure. The national 55-mph speed limit is an example. Compliance with the 1973 federal law became lax in the 1980s, and Congress, responding to pressure, allowed states to raise the limit to 65 mph on rural interstates. The negative side effects of this relaxation include increased energy use, increased pollution, and increased traffic fatalities. To rectify this situation, policymakers should take the following actions:

Enforce federally mandated speed limits. To minimize fuel economies lost at higher speeds, the states should enforce current speed limits. Doing so will both increase highway safety and reduce fuel use. This policy can be made even more effective by initiating a public-information campaign so that individuals realize the benefits of fuel conservation for national security and improved highway safety.

Allow federal funds to be transferred from highway projects to alternative-transportation projects in areas with poor air quality. Most federal funds are dedicated to highway projects regardless of the environmental consequences of new roads. Governors and/or legislators in areas with air-quality and congestion problems should be permitted to transfer available federal funds to alternative transportation projects designed to reduce vehicle pollution and congestion. This would give states the flexibility to shift federal resources to meet local priorities. Permissible alternatives could include mass-transit projects, HOV facilities, fleet-vehicle conversion programs to alternative fuels, and bicycle and pedestrian projects.

DEREGULATION. During the late 1970s, deregulation reduced the federal government's control over private enterprise, and transportation was a prime target. The result was widespread deregulation of the US transportation network—airlines, railroads, trucking, and buses. In terms of economic efficiency, advocates of deregulation claim that it has been successful, at least in the short term, because it has increased both profits and ridership (Buchholz 1982).

However, long-term social objectives must be kept in mind if policymakers deregulate further. The private sector best serves itself by maintaining high profits, and is not equipped to maximize social benefits. Thus when transportation services that show little or no profit but serve a legitimate public purpose are in the hands of unregulated private interests, they run the risk of being prematurely abandoned or poorly maintained. In physical terms, deregulation has already devastated parts of the nation's railroad lines and intercity bus network, and aggravated airport congestion. Following railroad deregulation in 1980, 30,000 miles of track were abandoned, threatening rural farming communities with economic ruin because they could not move their goods to market. Before the tracks are all abandoned, the federal government should tighten the requirements under which railroad companies can abandon, sell, or lease track. At the least, the government should assess substantial fines on companies that shut down lines without abiding by what remains of federal regulations.

Economic Incentives

Economic incentives, in contrast to regulation, tend to "pull" the market by changing price signals, thereby inducing behavior rather than commanding it. Taxation, subsidization, user fees, and other pricing schemes are typical economic incentives. One advantage of these policies is that they can enhance economic efficiency by internalizing social costs (such as pollution and congestion) that are not reflected by current market prices. Historically, roads and highway vehicles (autos and trucks) have been subsidized at a much higher level than alternatives such as railroads, bicycles, and walking. Future economic incentives must correct this to properly reflect the social costs of highway vehicles.

TAXATION. Taxation can improve our transportation system and ameliorate some of the environmental problems caused by it. To the extent that taxes are used to internalize social costs such as vehicle pollution and excessive energy use, their economic burden is reduced insofar as they correct existing market failures. Such taxes usually can provide better long-run solutions than regulatory approaches because taxation costs less than regulation, encourages innovation, gives clear price signals to consumers, and minimizes government intrusion. Nevertheless, many solutions draw on both regulation and taxation. Taxes, especially on gasoline, lack popularity with most voters today and are therefore politically risky. But there is mounting evidence that voters will support higher gas taxes if revenues are targeted for specific transportation improvements rather than for general deficit reduction (National Journal 1990).[2]

Depending on how a tax is structured, it can encourage either substitution of goods or reductions in consumption. Taxes can stimulate changes in consumer behavior, product development, industrial processes, investment decisions, and provide necessary revenues for alternative transportation services. The level of the tax determines the effect: small taxes serve only to raise revenue, while high taxes shift demand. The major limitation of taxation is the political resistance to setting high enough taxes to change demand and promote innovation.

Another pitfall of taxes is that they may be regressive and regionally discriminatory, disproportionately burdening low-income individuals or those living in certain areas of the country. However, most gasoline and other fuel taxes can be made more socially equitable through income-neutral "tax shifts," whereby rebates or targeted social benefits flow to those with low incomes and in certain regions.

Taxation of transportation goods and services can take several different forms: commodity taxes, output taxes, and tax incentives, to name a few.

Commodity Taxes. Commodity taxes (also termed excise taxes) are taxes on goods that serve both to raise revenue and dampen demand. Gasoline, diesel, and jet-fuel taxes are the most familiar commodity taxes in the transportation sector. The primary purpose of these taxes to date has been more to raise revenues for deposit into the Highway and Airport Trust Funds than to reduce demand for these fuels. But because the social costs of high fuel consumption are mounting, gasoline and other transportation-fuel taxes should be increased as follows:

Increase federal and state gasoline taxes and other transportation-fuel taxes by a combined total of $0.50 to $0.75 per gallon over the next five to 10 years. Increasing the current $0.09-per-gallon federal gasoline tax (and the $0.15-per-gallon diesel tax) could reduce both energy consumption and emissions by stimulating energy-efficiency gains and reducing driving. Moreover, fuel taxes could enhance national security and reduce the trade deficit by cutting oil imports. However, unless increases are substantial—$0.50 a gallon or greater—energy use will continue to increase and only revenue will be generated (about $1 billion for every one-cent-per-gallon increase).

The relationship between the price of gasoline and the demand for automobile travel is estimated in terms of the short-term "elasticity" of miles traveled to changes in the price of gasoline. The ratio of the change in miles traveled to the change in the price of gasoline ranges from -0.1 to -0.5 (OTA 1989a). Thus for every 100-percent increase in gasoline price, there is a 10-50 percent decrease in VMT. Likewise, the short-term price elasticity of the demand for gasoline itself is on the order of -0.2 in the short-term and -0.7 over the long term (Chandler and Nicholls 1990). In the short term, a combined federal and state gas-tax increase of $0.50 per gallon would lead to an estimated 20-percent reduction in automobile travel and 40-percent reduction in gasoline use.

Congress increased gasoline and diesel fuel taxes by a mere $0.05 per-gallon in its 1990 budget legislation. Revenue from this increase is estimated at $5 billion annually and is planned for budget-reduction purposes, with at most half of the funds transferred to transportation-related spending. Clearly, this increase is not an effort to change consumption patterns, promote efficiency gains, or further alternative-transportation options. A better solution would be a $0.25-per-gallon tax increase phased in over the next five years, at least half of which would be devoted to transit and other alternatives to the automobile and the remainder used to repair and maintain transportation infrastructure.

This would have to be combined with state taxes to reach the $0.50- to $0.75-per-gallon level that would be necessary to reduce fuel consumption and VMT.

States also levy both excise and sales taxes on gasoline. As of January 1990, gasoline excise-tax rates ranged from $0.04 per gallon (Florida) to $0.22 per gallon (Nebraska), and averaged $0.163 per gallon (TFI 1989). In recent years these levels have been increasing; 23 states raised their gasoline taxes in 1989 alone. California, the state that led the tax revolt in the 1970s, doubled its $0.09-per-gallon gas tax in June 1990 (by popular vote), earmarking the revenues for transportation-system improvements.

At least eight states currently impose a sales tax on gasoline: Illinois, West Virginia, Indiana, Michigan, New York, California, Georgia, and Florida. These sales taxes are on the order of $0.04 to $0.06 per gallon above the state gasoline excise tax.

The bulk of a gas-tax increase should occur at the state level because states can earmark revenues for specific alternative-transportation services more easily than federal policymakers, who are inclined to use the money for general revenue. Thus states should increase their gasoline taxes by $0.25 to $0.50 per gallon, phased in over five to 10 years.

Experts conclude that a combined federal and state gas-tax increase on the order of $1 per gallon would reduce the negative side effects of our fossil-fuel habit. Based on current projections, a $1-per-gallon gasoline tax phased in over three to five years could reduce US energy consumption by about 4.2 quads, cut crude-oil imports by about two million barrels a day, reduce carbon emissions by about 90 million tons annually, and raise net tax revenues of about $80 billion (Chandler and Nicholls 1990).[3] This represents roughly a 28-percent reduction in gasoline use based on current consumption levels.

The important issue remaining is how best to spend gas-tax revenues. The majority of these receipts should be spent on the transportation sector: for infrastructure repair, intra- and intercity rail enhancements, programs that promote use of the most socially beneficial forms of transportation (mass transit, intermodal freight, ridesharing, bicycling, and walking), and for compensation to those low-income individuals least able to afford tax increases.

Finally, a consumption tax on transportation fuels should be imposed when oil prices drop below a predetermined level in order to keep the price at the pump relatively constant. Increasing the tax when the price falls below a floor would discourage overconsumption of cheap petroleum. This will help consumers and businesses make sound long-term decisions regarding the purchase and ultimate use of efficient vehicles, alternative fuels, and auto options.

Increase the current gas-guzzler tax and extend it to light trucks. Currently a gas-guzzler excise tax is levied on vehicle manufacturers based on their new products' fuel-efficiency ratings. The federal gas-guzzler tax levies a tax on manufacturers for each vehicle sold that gets less than 22.5 miles per gallon. This level should be raised in line with proposed fuel-economy standards and applied to light trucks, vans, and utility vehicles as well. Specifically, guzzler taxes should be extended from the current 22.5 mpg to at least 27 mpg as the CAFE standard is increased to 40 mpg. And new light trucks and vans should be assessed similar taxes starting at 20 mpg as the CAFE standard is increased to 30 mpg. This excise tax would encourage the manufacturing of more fuel-efficient vehicles as well as discouraging the production of highly inefficient vehicles.

Such a tax is effective; there is evidence that the gas-guzzler tax played a major role in post-1983 fuel-economy improvements to lowest-mileage cars (Rothschild 1990). Moreover, based on historical experience with the gas-guzzler program, the tax has proved to be feasible in political, legal, administrative, and social terms.

Output Taxes. Output taxes are applied to goods and services on the basis of each unit of damage they cause society. Pollution taxes on motor vehicles and weight-distance taxes on heavy-duty vehicles are examples of output taxes. Policymakers should consider taking the following actions with regard to this kind of tax:

Levy vehicle pollutant taxes. A one-time tax assessed on new vehicles based on estimated pollution-emission rates could foster the transition to cleaner alternative fuels. Raising the price of gasoline vehicles would make cleaner-fuel vehicles more competitive. This tax would also raise revenue that could be used to fund a regional alternative-fuel demonstration program. According to the Congressional Budget Office, an average tax of $250 on new vehicles could provide nearly $13 billion in revenues from 1991 to 1995 (Montgomery and Marcuss 1990). This tax could be extended to all motor vehicles based on annual emission-inspection results.

Establish weight-distance taxes for trucks. Based on payload weight and hauling distance, these taxes would be assessed on the heavy-duty vehicles that cause the most road damage and are significant air and noise polluters as well. As trucks continue to get heavier and larger, social costs will grow, as will negative effects on all other vehicles and on infrastructure. One drawback of such taxes is that they are difficult to allocate fairly across different types of heavy-duty vehicles. Nevertheless, without weight-distance taxes, cars and light trucks will in effect subsidize heavy trucks, enhancing their competitiveness at the expense of more environmentally benign rail and intermodal means of hauling freight.

Tax Incentives. Tax incentives are another means of providing inducements to both consumers and producers of more socially acceptable transportation goods and services. Under one scheme, consumers would be given incentives to purchase new low-emitting, fuel-efficient motor vehicles rather than dirty, inefficient vehicles. Another example of a tax incentive is the tax-free monthly commuting allowance given to employees who ride mass transit. Policymakers should consider establishing the following incentive programs:

Offer consumers tax incentives for purchasing clean, fuel-efficient new motor vehicles. Incentive programs can be established to motivate consumers to buy superior vehicles and induce manufacturers to produce better vehicles. The tax incentive can be designed as a revenue-neutral program whereby rebates would be paid for by tax surcharges.

At the federal level, such fees and rebates could be provided through income-tax adjustments or a separate transaction through the dealer with the US Treasury. States, however, can assess variable sales taxes on new motor vehicles themselves.

Several states are considering such policies. The DRIVE+ Program (developed at the Lawrence Berkeley Laboratory) passed the California legislature overwhelmingly but was vetoed by the governor in 1990. DRIVE+ offered sales-tax rebates to purchasers of cleaner, more fuel-efficient new cars and light trucks; the rebates were to be paid for by buyers of dirtier, less efficient new vehicles (Levenson and Gordon 1990). Fees and rebates would have been offered based on a predetermined target, set higher than the current standards. Massachusetts has also formulated a variable sales tax on fuel efficiency (which has not yet been enacted in 1990), and Iowa, New York, and Oregon are considering similar tax schemes.

States would offer consumers who buy cleaner and/or more fuel-efficient vehicles a rebate on their new vehicles' sales tax. The program would be paid for by fees levied (higher sales taxes) on purchasers of vehicles that fail to meet targeted fuel-economy levels and stricter emissions standards. A safety component could also be added, thus creating incentives for manufacturers to employ only those technologies which simultaneously reduce emissions while increasing efficiency and safety.

If properly designed, these programs can be self-contained and self-financing, avoiding any overall impact on state budgets. Slight adjustments to the fee and rebate schedule could result in additional revenue.

Offer greater tax relief to both employers and employees for employee travel allowances. Providing more equitable tax treatment for employer-sponsored travel-allowance programs would give commuters incentives to use alternatives to private automobiles. The current federal tax law allows employers to provide only $15 per month tax-free to employees who commute via public transportation. Transit benefits that exceed this level are fully taxable, while parking is not. Waiving taxes on these commuting allowances given to employees for mass transit and ridesharing, and increasing the credit to at least $50 per month, could provide a needed incentive to rideshare and use public transportation. This tax policy benefits lower-income commuters, who rely heavily on public transit, and would partially compensate for any regressive effects of higher gasoline taxes.[4] Moreover, travel allowances should be offered to employees who bicycle and walk to work as well as those who rideshare and ride mass transit.

In addition to incentives given to employees, employers could be allowed tax credits (dollar-for-dollar) for providing rideshare and transit-incentive programs to their employees. This policy would make programs such as shuttle connections to mass transit and employer-owned vanpools in employers' financial interest to undertake.

SUBSIDIZATION. A subsidy is a direct or indirect payment for a good or service that provides financial incentives to producers and/or consumers to change their behavior. Subsidies can be directed to either private firms or other levels of government (better known as grants). Subsidization is used to correct an undersupply of goods; without subsidies, public goods such as transit and road maintenance would not be provided in adequate amounts.

One limitation of subsidies is that they are often subject to annual revision and thus lack an ongoing commitment to achieve long-term policymaking goals. Given the current federal budget deficit there is a general move away from subsidies as a means of financing transportation services. New taxes and user fees will be required as a monetary source for new subsidies.

All forms of transit have historically required subsidization, but highways and air travel have been the principal recipients. While intercity rail and public transit have received subsidies, the levels are much lower. Since urban public transit and intercity rail can provide clean, efficient alternatives to single passenger motor-vehicle travel and highly inefficient short-distance air travel, they should receive increased subsidization.

Continue subsidizing intercity rail transit. The National Railroad Passenger Corporation, better known as Amtrak, was created by Congress two decades ago to take over the nation's failing passenger railroad lines. Federal subsidies to cover operating costs have varied substantially over the years, from 60 percent in 1980 down to only 28 percent ($584 million) in 1989 (Nice 1989). In light of the expensive lessons we are learning today about the costs of rebuilding railways in US cities, as exemplified by the estimated $5 billion Los Angeles will spend to rebuild its rail system, it is economically prudent to keep Amtrak up and operating. This means a long-term commitment to subsidize operating costs, as well as either granting or loaning Amtrak the estimated $250 million a year it badly needs for capital improvements. Federal policymakers should work with Amtrak to meet its goal of covering all its operating costs by 2000. The railroad must be assured that subsidies are forthcoming when they are needed. Given reliable long-term funding to ensure efficient operation, Amtrak is more likely to receive additional funding from the private sector and state governments as new high-speed rail systems are integrated into the existing rail network.

Incorporating high-speed rail service into the Amtrak system will enhance the competition between Amtrak and air travel. This will reduce the social costs of shorter-distance air travel—airport congestion, fuel use, emissions, and noise. High-speed rail costs about $6 million per mile; thus upgrading Amtrak along the Northeast Corridor would cost some $2.5 billion, while five extensive routes in major US corridors would cost an estimated $20 billion.

Continue providing operating subsidies to urban and rural public transit. Historically, public transit has not covered its annual operating costs from farebox receipts alone. Commuters pay an average 35 percent of the actual cost of running a bus or train. However, new rail-transit systems have succeeded at covering more of their costs through fares, from 65 to 92 percent (Parcells 1990). Still, many older transit systems across the nation rely heavily on subsidies to maintain their operations.

Subsidizing transit helps shift commuters out of less efficient transport modes onto buses and trains, and in turn reduces rush-hour congestion, cuts pollution, and serves the poor and elderly. Studies show that ridership would increase with greater subsidies; as many as 25 percent of the respondents surveyed said they would consider riding public transit if their passes were subsidized (DOT 1988c). Studies put needed subsidies at $11 billion a year for urban transit and $160 million a year for rural transit (APTA 1989).

There are several sources of subsidies: local governments can require businesses to subsidize employees; state and federal governments can allocate a portion of gas-tax revenues toward greater subsidies; and creative techniques can also be used. New York City, for example, tacks a quarter of a percent onto its sales tax, while the state places a surtax on telephone bills, and certain regions of New York use a realty transfer fee to generate subsidies for mass transit.

Institute employee travel-allowance programs. Employers should be encouraged to give employees a commuting allowance, to be spent as the employee chooses. This gives employees maximum choice and clear economic incentives to choose less energy-intensive and more environmentally sound commuting options. Under one such policy employers would give employees monthly travel allowances equal to the cost the employer incurs to provide parking benefits. The employer can then charge an equivalent amount for parking, which was formerly free. Employees who choose to drive alone will not be affected because their subsidy will cover the new parking fee. However, an employee who chooses to rideshare, use mass transit, bicycle, or walk will be better off financially.

The City of West Hollywood, California, recently instituted a travel-allowance plan, providing $45 monthly, and an additional 15 percent of its employees stopped driving alone.

To the degree that worker parking demands are reduced, applicable state and local taxes can pay for providing parking spaces. The program would operate best if all subsidies are tax-free.

USER FEES. In their simplest form, user fees are economic instruments that are assessed for the use of goods or services (transit fares, airport-departure fees, and highway tolls, for example). User fees must be imposed on public goods or services in order to allocate resources efficiently. Thus user fees are one way to finance publicly provided infrastructures such as highways and airports. In fact, the secretary of transportation has repeatedly targeted user fees to help pay for overhauling the US transportation system. In addition to airport-departure fees, there are landing fees for airlines and various types of road pricing.

User fees are often considered more favorably than taxes because charges can be refined to target those consumers who use publicly provided services, rather than using general revenues, which charge everyone. Beyond highway tolls, drivers should be charged each time they get on a heavily traveled road and pay for these services based on the time and distance traveled. Such a scheme might work as follows:

Institute a mechanism for variable travel charges. Fees can be set to vary over time and distance so that higher charges at peak periods and over longer distances can compensate for the higher social costs of those travel patterns. Examples of such charges include differential road pricing at toll and bridge crossings and on automated roadways based on time and distance traveled. A new system in use on the North Dallas Tollway in Texas automatically bills drivers a higher variable rate for driving during rush hours (Winston 1990). Such charges are especially efficient if the revenues are used to provide alternatives for commuters who do not use the roads at peak periods. Zone-oriented, peak-period fares could be used for public transit as well, and peak-hour pricing could be used for air travel.

At the very least, peak-hour costs for road, airport, and transit in congested areas should be implemented wherever feasible. Differential pricing for on-peak versus off-peak trips, on the order of 50 percent, could help pay higher system costs during times of high use; it could also shift those passengers on the margin to off-peak travel, and could make alternative modes look more attractive. This would reduce the cost of off-peak travel, making transit more affordable for the poor and elderly, who often travel during noncommuting hours.

Another way to place user charges on those who drive in congested urban areas is to require commuters to purchase "environmental passes" for display on the vehicle's dashboard. Passes might cost $1 per day and could also be used for a single trip on mass transit.

Distance-based charges can also be assigned to roads, airports, and transit. Toll roads and public transit can institute such charges in order to pay the higher marginal costs of moving people and freight over longer distances. Airports can assess distance-based charges on shorter flights where the social costs attributed to more frequent takeoff, taxi, and landing are higher on a per-mile basis than for long-distance travel.

Admittedly, it is easier to design variable charges into a new system than it is to retrofit an existing network. Although this type of charge policy may be difficult to administer on all roads, it may work for certain toll and other heavily traveled roads, as well as bus and rail systems that use automated-toll and -fare techniques. Airport charges could be assessed based on the time of departure and distance traveled.

Establish a High-Speed Rail Trust Fund. A 10-percent tax is currently assessed on airline tickets, and the revenues are deposited in the Aviation Trust Fund. In 1990 the trust fund had collected $8 billion in tax receipts, which are dedicated to new and expanded airports and other aviation expenditures. New high-speed-rail (HSR) systems cannot compete with air travel given the large tax subsidy the latter enjoys. However, many airports are congested, and there is widespread public opposition to building new facilities or expanding existing ones. The last airport to be built was in Dallas-Ft. Worth in 1974, and the proposed Denver airport has taken a decade to get its permits.

HSR would operate from existing hub airports, with trips that would substitute for 100- to 600-mile flights. The market potential for HSR could be further enhanced by integrating long-distance commuter air service into the system, by serving metropolitan areas and other high-density regions, and by linking cities with major tourist attractions. Several states and regions are prime candidates for HSR, including Florida, California-Nevada (San Francisco-Los Angeles-Las Vegas), Pennsylvania, the Northeast Corridor (Boston-New York-Washington), Ohio, Michigan-Illinois-Wisconsin, and Texas. Moreover, other states such as Missouri, Washington, Georgia, upstate New York, New Mexico, and Louisiana would be more likely to improve overall rail-passenger service if they could "hub-and-spoke" into HSR service.

The biggest hurdle for HSR is mounting significant funds to cover the capital expenditures for new starts. A portion of the airline subsidies that are generated through the ticket tax should be reallocated to HSR projects. If just 1 percent of the 10-percent airline ticket tax were devoted to a new HSR Trust Fund, an estimated $1 billion a year would be available for HSR projects. These revenues could be used to leverage state and regional matching funds to build 2,000 miles of HSR infrastructure nationwide—enough to link the major cities within the high-density corridors—by the turn of the century.

Institute a Parking Pricing Policy. Charging for parking sends the clearest economic signal about the value of land used for parking and the cost of "free" parking to the transportation system. Charging employees for formerly free parking reduces VMT, energy use, and air pollution.

The money generated by these charges could be used as offsetting compensation to employees or to subsidize options to driving alone, such as vanpools and low-cost transit tickets.

OTHER PRICING SCHEMES. Economic and regulatory policies can be used in combination to create new marketable goods. Coordinating the two kinds of policies can yield a "carrot and stick" approach to policymaking, as in the examples of tradable CAFE credits, pay-as-you-drive insurance schemes, older vehicle scrappage programs, and congestion-regulation transfer schemes explained below.

Create a tradable CAFE-credit program. Under a tradable permit scheme, markets are created in which private interests can buy "rights" to use some public good and trade their rights away as they wish. Tradable permits are part economic and part regulatory in nature. The advantage of this hybrid policy instrument is that it can foster economic growth and innovation while reducing social costs. It can do this for CAFE standards in several ways: it can speed mandated improvements; it can create an incentive to do better than the standard requires; and it can help prove out new technologies more quickly, making it easier to revise the standard in the future.

Tradable permits are not common in the transportation sector today. One way to implement them would be to establish a market system for trading CAFE credits held by individual vehicle manufacturers. By linking the current CAFE standard to an economic incentive, the program would motivate some manufacturers to go beyond what the regulations require for their fleet's average fuel economy. CAFE credits would probably be priced just below the current penalty for not meeting the standard—$5 per tenth of a mile per gallon for each vehicle sold.

Because the standard itself serves as the floor, this would not weaken current regulations.[5] Instead, such a policy could use the market to provide economic advantage to those manufacturers who have innovative designs and bring improved vehicles to the marketplace. A federal clearinghouse would be needed to administer transfers.

Institute a pay-as-you-drive automobile-insurance scheme. Instead of paying for automobile insurance on an annual, fixed-fee basis, a more efficient scheme would be to pay for insurance incrementally as we drive. Pay-as-you-drive (PAYD) schemes would consist of a direct payment to any insurance carrier along with an equitable supplement consisting of an incremental charge either at the fuel pump or through odometer readings based on annual VMT. PAYD schemes would reduce vehicle miles traveled, thus reducing petroleum use, urban pollution, and carbon dioxide emissions.

When PAYD insurance is charged through gasoline prices, it has the additional benefit of removing uninsured motorists from the road (since all drivers buying gasoline are buying insurance as well), thus reducing the total amount of insurance motorists are required to buy. It is estimated that gasoline surcharges ranging from $0.50 to $0.75 per gallon would cover PAYD insurance rates.

Charging insurance based on odometer readings (or an on-board computer) is easy to implement with current vehicle technology, although computerized readings might be preferable in order to reduce odometer tampering. Since the current system of charging insurance as a fixed payment forces women to pay higher effective rates than men per mile driven, a PAYD scheme that charges insurance per mile driven would remove this inequity while reducing total miles traveled. PAYD insurance rates would be set at about $0.04 per mile.

Studies estimate that a PAYD program could reduce vehicle miles traveled by up to 15 percent in the short term and 40 percent in the long term (El-Gasseir 1990). However, distance-based PAYD schemes may be less effective than gasoline-based schemes because the latter provide more information to the driver since the fee is paid weekly, while the former is paid annually. Nevertheless, either form of PAYD is a more efficient means of purchasing insurance that the current method.

Old-vehicle recycling scrappage programs. Since pre-1971 vehicles emit an average of 60 times more pollutants per mile and are only half as fuel efficient as 1990 cars, there are energy and environmental benefits to removing these vehicles from the road. Union Oil Company (UNOCAL) recently implemented such a program in Southern California, known as SCRAP (South Coast Recycled Auto Project), in which 8,376 pre-1971 cars were scrapped. Los Angeles vehicle owners were offered $700 to sell their old vehicles for scrappage (enough to afford replacement with a cleaner, more fuel-efficient post-1978 car). The vehicles scrapped under the program were driven an average of 5,500 miles annually and emitted 10.7 million pounds of HC, CO, and NO_x and an estimated 80 million pounds of carbon dioxide each year (Rafuse 1990).

This industry-government cooperative experimental program was considered successful by all involved. Not only did the environment benefit directly, information was obtained on these old vehicles that will improve future regulatory efforts. Other polluted urban areas could also benefit from implementing a SCRAP-type program.

Develop a scheme of tradable commuting rights. A more futuristic scheme aimed at reducing congestion would be to give every commuter in a region the same rights to commute by car during rush hours (200 miles per week has been suggested for the San Francisco Bay area) and then allow individual commuters to trade with one another to buy or sell more rights.[6] Enforcing this scheme would require advanced technologies such as on-board computers and road sensors. In essence, a vending machine would enable a commuter either to trade in commute-mile allowances and receive credit or a check to purchase extra miles for a price that could be recomputed periodically to balance supply with demand for miles of travel. Such policies would have to be experimented with on a local level in extremely congested areas.

Information

Informational policies are designed to change behavior by educating consumers, producers, and even regulators themselves. These instruments can encourage changes in both consumer and producer behavior and can be used by the government to gather more facts before taking further regulatory action.

Information can benefit the public, the government, and the private sector, but it may not be enough on its own to inspire rational decision making. In some cases there will never be enough information to change consumer purchasing decisions, and in other cases there is evidence that some decisions may be too complicated to evoke rational consumer behavior (for example, determining where to live in order to minimize commuting costs while maximizing all other criteria—good schools, low taxes, best housing location and price, etc.).

Nevertheless, getting the facts out is crucial to the success of transportation policies. Without information about the social costs of individual transportation decisions, consumers cannot be expected to change their behavior. Moreover, informational policies can convince consumers that the nation's transportation problems are not solved merely by government regulation of private industry, but that the consumer is also part of the solution. Once informed, consumers may be willing to modify their behavior—a critical step in the right direction. Examples of such policies include testing, labeling, advertising, and public education.

TESTING AND DEMONSTRATION PROGRAMS. Before the government can set effective economic or regulatory policies, extensive testing and demonstration programs may be required for gathering data. Then, when regulations are enacted, testing may be mandated for proof of compliance. The government or the private sector, separately or jointly, can undertake these information-gathering programs.

Institute regional RD&D programs to fully assess the advantages of each alternative fuel prior to imposing nationwide standards and requirements. One important provision of the amended Clean Air Act requires that alternative-fueled vehicles be manufactured and sold in California by 1996. California has also set new standards that will encourage the introduction of alternative-fueled vehicles between 1994 and 1996. Other states may follow suit.

Unfortunately, there is still some uncertainty about the specific environmental effects of alternative fuels. In order to assess the cumulative impacts of burning each new fuel, a demonstration program is warranted. Such a program could be undertaken by the Environmental Protection Agency in conjunction with the Departments of Energy and

Transportation as a means of implementing alternative-fuel requirements, or established separately and funded by new taxes on vehicle emissions. (See Table 13 for nonquantitative measures of evaluating these fuels.)

Because environmental problems are often regional in nature, as with smog or carbon monoxide violations, and different fuels are indigenous to different regions, a regional focus makes sense. Moreover, a regional alternative-fuel demonstration program could also provide a boost to local economies and create the kind of federal, state, and local partnership that the Department of Transportation has referred to in its National Transportation Policy.

Specifically, this demonstration program would obtain comparable data on the following for each alternative fuel:

■ In-use emissions of hydrocarbon, NO_x, CO, SO_x, and particulates for the full fuel cycle (emissions from fuel production, distribution, and from the vehicle itself)

■ Actual CO_2 emissions (full fuel cycle)

■ Effects of toxic emissions on air, water, and land

■ Vehicle maintenance requirements and performance characteristics

■ Supply availability

■ Costs for heavy-duty and passenger-vehicle fleet retrofits, for new optimized vehicles, and for fuel-marketing system retrofit

■ Consumer acceptance

This program could apply to all commercial fleet and municipal-government vehicles, so that different regions could be charged with demonstrating different alternatives over the course of a few years. For example, the various regions could demonstrate the following fuels in local fleets: Midwest—ethanol, South—natural gas, Pacific Northwest—electricity, Northeast—LPG, Mid-Atlantic—fuel cells, Mountain States—oxygenates, California—methanol, and Southwest and Hawaii—solar energy and hydrogen fuels. By using indigenous resources, the program could directly involve local private-sector interests.

Alternative fuels are much more likely to come to market if local, state, and federal governments forge a strong partnership with the private sector. The most comprehensive effort to date involves an alternative-fuels evaluation system for fleet vehicles compiled by Public Technology, Inc., and the City of Denver. This tool is "fuel-neutral" and can produce comparisons based on available data and a weighting priority assigned subjectively. This model will be a valuable decision-making tool as soon as better comparable data on different alternative fuels is collected. A regional demonstration program could fill the data void and refine the value of this new model.

Improve transportation RD&D efforts and foster technology transfer. Transportation RD&D programs are essential for gathering more information to assist in sound policymaking. Intermodal freight, high-speed rail, and innovative infrastructure maintenance and repair technologies all merit attention. There are common elements to solving transportation problems whether they are international, federal, state, or local in scope. Thus transportation RD&D efforts must be furthered and, in turn, shared through enhanced technology transfers. Also, partnerships between the public and private sectors could promote further RD&D.

LABELING. Labeling conveys information to the consumer prior to a purchase. Without labeling, it may be difficult to provide consumers with more complete information so that they can make as rational a decision as possible.

Increase distribution of the EPA Gas Mileage Guide to new-vehicle purchasers, and include emissions information for cleaner vehicle models. One example of successful labeling in the transportation sector is the *Gas Mileage Guide,* which compares the fuel efficiencies of all models of new cars, light trucks, and vans. Based on legislation passed in 1975, dealers are required to make this guide available to consumers on the showroom floor. And the vehicles themselves must prominently display a fuel-economy sticker for easy comparison between models. Distribution of the guide was significantly reduced under the Reagan administration. To promote informed consumer decision making, increased distribution of the guide is essential.

To the extent that manufacturers offer cleaner alternative-fueled vehicles in the future, information should be distributed to consumers evaluating these new fuels and comparing not only fuel economy but emissions as well. Both mileage guides and vehicle stickers could be easily modified to incorporate the new emission information.

ADVERTISING/PROMOTIONAL PROGRAMS. Both industry and the government can influence consumers by waging public campaigns. Today companies recognize that their public image can be a substantial asset to them in the marketplace and that promoting their social achievements can be advantageous. Likewise, government can inform consumers through advertising that builds understanding about the public sector's role in solving transportation problems.

It will take a lot of prodding to get individuals out of their single-occupancy vehicles, and every little bit will help. Information campaigns can do their part to improve the image of mass transit, ridesharing, cycling, and walking in the public's eye. Moreover, a sense of duty can accompany campaigns. Following are examples of educational promotional programs.

Launch statewide promotional campaigns for transit and high-occupancy-vehicle (HOV) programs. State and local governments are in a good position to change the way their residents view public transit and HOVs. Transportation operators can market public transit and other HOV programs such as ridesharing.

According to a case study of transit promotion in Minnesota (which has succeeded in increasing transit ridership statewide), a number of barriers may be encountered in creating such informational policies (Works and Ellison 1990). First, a decision must be made as to the appropriateness of spending public funds on marketing public services. Second, there is concern that if the campaign is unsuccessful, there could be a backlash in future appropriations. Third, given transit's negative public image, the question remains whether a new statewide campaign can deliver long-term positive results. Finally, staff usually have limited time and resources for special projects, which makes it difficult to fit a marketing program into the routine workload. Nevertheless, each of these obstacles can be surmounted.

The most effective campaign strategies include catchy names and slogans, redesigned logos, distributing "how-to-ride" instructions, and establishing local telephone contacts with whom prospective passengers can discuss optimal routes. Print ads, press releases, radio spots, promotional items (buttons), posters, system brochures, direct mail, driver uniforms, staff/customer incentive programs, marketing training, media planning, public relations, and improved vehicle appearance can all be effective. Similar campaigns can be undertaken for ridesharing programs.

Regional-transit authorities can also use employees to market public transit. Promotional programs such as transit "report cards" can use teams of front-line employees who have authority to create projects aimed at increasing ridership. Where these have been established, ridership has in fact increased, employee morale has improved, interdepartmental cooperation has been fostered, customer relations have improved, and public relations has been enhanced (Brogan et al. 1990).

Use the media to encourage shifts in travel behavior. Developing a TV-based traffic-mitigation campaign for a metropolitan region could encourage shifts in travel behavior. Cooperative ventures between the media and local governments can be an important component of a comprehensive transportation plan. These promotional campaigns should focus on explaining problems and helping individuals find appropriate personal solutions.

The media can be especially helpful when new transportation services are put into effect. Because of TV's popularity, an entire community can be informed about transportation-system improvements and new transit options.

PUBLIC EDUCATION AND OUTREACH. To encourage individuals to examine their actions, educational programs can play a key role. They can help solve an array of problems associated with driving automobiles and light trucks. Both the public and fleet operators should be aware that their driving habits affect the environment.

Driver and cyclist training. Training for the general public and fleet operators should include information on what techniques reduce emissions and energy use, as well as safe bicycling techniques. There are a few simple things drivers can do that would reduce the amount of pollution their vehicles produce and the energy they use. Cyclists can also take measures to operate their vehicles more safely and efficiently. These lessons should be taught when individuals are learning how to drive or cycle. They include:

- getting the vehicle tuned-up and changing motor oil regularly
- checking for correct tire pressure and wheel alignment
- using radial tires
- inspecting the emission system regularly
- driving at a steady speed within the legal limit
- avoiding both idle and stop-and-go driving conditions by selecting nonpeak travel times and using alternate routes whenever possible
- minimizing air-conditioner use
- avoiding short trips in a motor vehicle when combined trips and walking or bicycling will do
- providing tips to both cyclists and drivers on safely sharing the road

Fleet drivers in particular spend a significant portion of their time in a vehicle. It is important that these drivers make an effort to operate their vehicles responsibly as detailed above.

Quasi-Governmental Measures

By creating new levels of authority that mix government, the public, and the private sector, policymakers can involve citizens and businesses in transportation decision making. Greater individual involvement makes for more successful—and often more creative—policies. Some examples of quasi-governmental transportation measures are ridesharing agencies, transportation-management agencies, regional development commissions, and organized citizen involvement in transportation planning.

PUBLIC AND/OR PRIVATE RIDESHARING AGENCIES. Ridesharing agencies can provide free assistance to persons interested in carpooling and vanpooling. These information services match persons with similar commuting patterns through questionnaires and computerized data bases. Ridesharing agencies could also publish commuter registers to help people make their own contacts and form carpools individually.

TRANSPORTATION-MANAGEMENT ASSOCIATIONS. These can promote private-sector involvement in transportation. They give the business community a voice in local transportation decision making and provide an organizational framework for private-sector participation and negotiations on transportation programs. The functions of transportation-management associations include:

■ engaging in public-information and educational activities concerning the area's transportation services

■ assisting members in carrying out regulatory requirements assumed as conditions of development

■ conducting "travel audits" for local employers

■ planning for the long-range transportation needs of their members

■ organizing and operating common transportation services, such as park-and-shuttle systems and contract buses

Because these associations are not bound by bureaucratic constraints, they would be freewheeling agents able to devise solutions that might be difficult to implement in the more constrained environment of local government. To the extent that these groups evolve into a local "shadow government" of policymakers who don't have strict governmental authority, they may gain political and organizational acceptance.

TRANSPORTATION FUNDING FOR REGIONAL DEVELOPMENT COMMISSIONS.
To stimulate local input on transportation issues and to provide a focal point for coordination of state/regional planning activities, states could fund regional development commissions. These bodies would initiate general transportation-planning activities. The specific priorities earmarked for funding would be financed by a competitive study grant program to allow maximum flexibility to the commissions. Such a program is currently under way in Minnesota (DOT 1988d).

CITIZEN INVOLVEMENT IN THE TRANSPORTATION PLANNING PROCESS.
It is important to involve citizens in the transportation planning process because each of us pays the costs and enjoys the benefits of transportation services. Case studies have shown that working closely with the community in developing transportation plans, and using a task-force structure to continue community involvement as development proceeds, are crucial to reducing a project's transportation impacts (Nash 1990).

Many citizen-participation processes end after the project is approved. Continued administrative support is needed to maintain adequate levels of citizen involvement.

When citizens are given a vested interest in determining the regulatory requirements that a local development will adhere to, they are more likely to accept the development and want it to be a success. Thus citizen involvement throughout the term of a project is vital.

Comprehensive Policy

Policy instruments can also be combined to create comprehensive transportation strategies. Because the transportation sector has so many varying elements, a comprehensive set of policies is essential. Such policies should include a national fuel-use policy, a model bicycle and pedestrian program, transportation-management programs, and a national transportation policy.

DEVELOP A NATIONAL FUEL-USE POLICY. The Department of Transportation, the Department of Energy, and the Environmental Protection Agency should establish a national fuel-use policy to simultaneously reduce consumption, diversify fuel use, and reduce the environmental impacts of the transportation sector. Transportation's dependence on oil—most of which is imported—and its excessive emissions cause a host of problems. The US needs a comprehensive policy to evaluate the potential for reduction of energy use, improvements in environmental quality, cost-effectiveness, equity, and political and administrative feasibility.

A fuel-use policy would coordinate the efforts of the federal agencies that regulate portions of the transportation sector. The policy could provide broad-based goals—i.e., elements of the National Energy Strategy, the Statement of National Transportation Policy, and the federal Clean Air Act; provide a forum to debate specific criteria; establish means of evaluating policies; and create momentum for implementation of sound policies. The benefit of a national fuel-use policy is that Congress could enact energy legislation in a coordinated manner rather than in its typical piecemeal fashion.

DEVELOP A MODEL BICYCLE AND PEDESTRIAN TRANSPORTATION PROGRAM. Encouraging people to get out of their cars (and all motorized transport) and walk or bicycle can reduce energy consumption, pollutant emissions, and traffic congestion. There are several components to integrating bicycling and walking into comprehensive transportation programs. These include the following actions:

■ construct bikeways and secure storage facilities at transit stations

■ ensure that all development and road construction provides new or expanded bicycle facilities and sidewalks

■ create an Office of Nonmotorized and Neighborhood Transportation to ensure that funds are appropriated to integrate and market bicycles and to encourage walking

■ improve bicycle and pedestrian access routes

■ analyze the benefits of using nonmotorized transport as a means of alleviating the social costs associated with automobile use (MCPD 1986)

Bicycling and pedestrian plans can enhance cycling and walking safety as well as secure bike parking; disseminate route information; and influence the private sector to encourage employees to cycle and walk instead of driving to work.

DEVELOP TRANSPORTATION SYSTEM MANAGEMENT PROGRAMS. These fall loosely under comprehensive strategies because they require several policy instruments in order to be effective. State and local governments, for example, can require or encourage the private sector to offer incentives to their employees to lure them out of single-passenger vehicles. Such programs include:

■ establishing a priority parking system that allows vehicles used for ridesharing to have preferential parking spaces

Overview of Environmental and Energy Objectives in the Bush Administration Statement of National Transportation Policy

The *Statement of National Transportation Policy* (NTP) was initiated by Transportation Secretary Samuel Skinner at the request of President Bush upon his taking office. Following 34 field hearings throughout the country and extensive review by the administration, DOT delivered its policy statement in early 1990. The recommendations for national transportation policy are captured under six major themes: system maintenance and expansion; provision for a sound financial base; competitiveness; public safety and national security; environmental protection; and further technological expertise.

According to the NTP, a major goal of federal transportation policy must be to minimize the negative side effects of our transportation system. DOT must continue to coordinate its efforts with those of other federal agencies to ensure effective environmental review of transportation projects and to guarantee that environmental policies are reflected in transportation programs and decisions. Specifically, the NTP states that it is federal transportation policy to:

■ support fully the administration's efforts to update the Clean Air Act, including federal initiatives necessary to enforce the transportation-related aspects

■ participate in national and international research on transportation-related environmental issues, such as global climate change

■ ensure that measures are taken to minimize the adverse environmental effects of transportation construction activities

■ encourage the design and building of transportation facilities that fit harmoniously into communities and the natural environment, and preserve scenic and historic sites

■ develop improved procedures for ensuring expeditious environmental review and timely decisions on transportation projects and programs at the federal level, through coordination among all federal agencies involved

■ foster development and use of more fuel-efficient and lower-emitting vehicles and transportation operations

■ promote increased bicycling and encourage planners and engineers to accommodate bicyclist and pedestrian needs in designing transportation facilities for urban and suburban areas

■ offering employees vans for vanpooling (and subsidizing this effective form of ridesharing)

■ authorizing workers to adopt flexible work hours to encourage employee ridesharing

■ providing company vehicles for ridesharers' mobility in the event of an emergency during work hours

■ limiting the amount of free, abundant parking spaces available for employees

Conclusion

The question of government authority is critical to US transportation policymaking efforts. Some combination of federal, state, and local governments must assume the principal responsibility as transportation policymaker.

Because transportation activities comprise almost one-fifth of GNP and one out of 10 jobs in the US economy is transportation-related, the federal government of necessity plays a prominent role in transportation policy (Cole 1989, Chao et al. 1990). While several federal agencies both directly and indirectly control transportation activities, the federal government to date has not adopted a coordinated national transportation policy. However, authorizations for the Department of Transportation's highways, aviation, and mass-transit programs will soon expire. Thus a comprehensive, unified policy is needed to address these and other transportation issues.

The federal government is in the process of formulating a comprehensive policymaking plan through its *Statement of National Transportation Policy* (NTP), which was previewed by the Department of Transportation in early 1990. The policy sets out several sound goals in an effort to reduce the high social costs of the transportation sector (see sidebar). But the most important elements, the policies themselves, are not specified in the NTP. Unless and until the federal government adopts such environmental- and energy-related transportation policies, social costs will continue to mount.

Policymakers face a big challenge in implementing the NTP's goals. User fees, modest increases in state and local funding, and further transportation R&D—the only recommendations set out by the Department of Transportation—are not enough to solve all of our transportation-related problems. Now, more than ever, there is a need for a national transportation plan. In formulating such a plan, the Department of Transportation and the administration should carefully consider the policy recommendations set out in the final chapter of this study.

State governments are in an ideal position to assess the failures of their transportation networks and take a more detailed look at solving their problems. Because they are wedged between federal decision makers and local interests, state governments are centrally positioned to form a partnership on transportation issues. Also, states have a better idea of their specific transportation needs than does the federal government.

Population shifts and regional growth are probably the most important factors affecting statewide transportation needs. Both current and projected growth must be incorporated into state policymaking decisions. The states that grew the fastest throughout the 1980s were Nevada, Arizona, Florida, and Alaska, and the fastest-growing regions were the West and Pacific Northwest. Transportation officials throughout the nation should watch these high-growth areas, for it is here that the most aggressive transportation-policy actions will be required in the near future to accommodate rapid growth.

Increasingly, the burden of solving the nation's transportation problems is being handed down to regional and local governments. It is true that land-use and transportation planning may best be coordinated at this level. Yet planners at this level lack the fiscal resources to make needed improvements. Local governments may have to take the lead in forming a coalition between federal and state governments, the private sector, and citizens in order to address transportation problems. If this is the new model, the shift of responsibility must be accompanied by the commitment of federal (as well as any available state) funds. If adequately supported, local governments can leverage the resources available to them and fit solutions to their specific problems.

Notes

1. The Senate defeated a cloture vote that would have ended an auto industry-inspired filibuster against S.1224, the Motor Vehicle Fuel Efficiency Act of 1989, introduced by Sen. Richard Bryan (D-NV). Thus the bill died in the 101st Congress.

2. An NBC news poll in June 1990 found that 44 percent of Americans favor raising the gas tax if new transportation revenues are needed. As evidence of this, California voters passed a doubling of their state gasoline tax, revenues from which will be spent on the state transportation system.

3. This analysis uses a long-run elasticity of -0.5.

4. Assuming that an individual commutes 15 miles a day round trip (300 miles a month) in an inefficient car getting 20 miles to a gallon, then he or she pays about $25 a month to commute by private auto. Thus a subsidy of $50 a month more than compensates for substantial gasoline taxes.

5. In order to prevent deterioration of the on-road fuel economy of the new fleet, only CAFE credits obtained after enactment of this policy could be traded.

6. This idea is attributed to the Environmental Defense Fund in Oakland, CA.

9 Summary of Recommendations

This book has addressed the environmental, energy, and congestion problems attributable to the US transportation sector. No single policy can solve these problems; rather, a comprehensive solution will require an array of creative policies.

Accordingly, the recommendations detailed below are offered as a "master list." Federal policies are applicable across the board; however, not all state and local policies will work everywhere. Thus state, regional, and local policymakers can choose options that seem most likely to work in their area, based on several criteria:

- Does the policy reduce energy consumption, emissions, and congestion (as it realizes other social benefits)?
- Does it minimize net costs?
- Is it equitable by income, region, and other classifications?
- Can it be administered easily?
- Is it politically feasible?

The answers to these questions will determine the ultimate success or failure of each policy.

The overall goals for the US transportation sector are aimed at improving vehicles and influencing how they are used. They include:

- increase energy efficiency
- commercialize clean-burning fuels
- increase vehicle occupancy
- reduce vehicle miles of travel
- improve intercity rail
- increase mass-transit ridership
- promote intermodal freight

What follows are detailed objectives followed by specific policy recommendations needed to achieve these goals. The recommendations are grouped according to the level of government—federal, state, or local—that should have primary responsibility for their implementation.

Although the benefits of these policies are difficult to quantify exactly, they should produce energy savings by the year 2005 of about 20 percent compared with current levels. Transportation emissions can be expected to drop by about 20 percent over current levels nationwide, even more in regions with poor air quality. Traffic congestion should, at the least, be stabilized at current levels.

Federal Policies

OBJECTIVE: *Increase the energy efficiency of the transportation system by increasing the fuel efficiency of new vehicles (cars, light trucks, heavy-duty trucks, trains, and aircraft) sold in the US by 50 percent by 2005 and by switching to more energy-efficient transport modes, such as mass transit and ridesharing.*

POLICIES:

■ *Raise CAFE.* Adopt a new corporate average fuel economy (CAFE) standard of 40 mpg for cars and 30 mpg for light trucks and vans by 2001. Review progress toward the end of the decade to identify additional goals beyond the year 2000.

■ *Raise fuel taxes.* Phase in an increase of $0.25 per gallon in federal fuel taxes for gasoline, diesel, and jet fuels by 2000. Allocate a significant portion of the revenues to alternative-transportation strategies.

■ *Raise and extend the gas-guzzler tax.* Revise the federal gas-guzzler tax on the least-efficient new cars by raising the minimum from 22.5 to at least 27 mpg as the CAFE standard is increased to 40 mpg. Extend the tax to new light trucks and vans by setting a target of 20 mpg. Increase mpg targets as CAFE standard increases.

■ *Create tradable CAFE credits.* Create a tradable CAFE-credit program in which vehicle manufacturers would receive monetary rewards for exceeding minimum CAFE standards.

■ *Enforce speed limits.* Require strict enforcement of national highway speed limits.

■ *Expand mass-transit and high-occupancy-vehicle (HOV) programs.* Increase capital and operating expenditures on transit; increase tax-free employee mass-transit allowance to at least $50 a month; give employers tax credits for establishing HOV programs; and increase transportation R&D funding.

■ *Establish a high-speed-rail trust fund.* Devote 1 percent of total receipts from the current airline-ticket tax to fund new high-speed rail start-ups between the most heavily traveled cities from 100 to 600 miles apart, and link the new system into existing rail networks.

OBJECTIVE: *Commercialize clean alternative fuels in heavy-duty and passenger vehicles by 2005.*

POLICIES:

■ *Increase funding for alternative-fuels R&D.* Provide increased funding for continued federal R&D on alternative fuels such as hydrogen, fuel cells, woody-biomass ethanol, and solar energy, and demonstrate these ultra-clean fuels in fleet vehicles.

■ *Fund alternative-fuel demonstration programs.* Institute regional demonstration programs to fully assess the advantages and disadvantages of alternative fuels by 1995.

■ *Encourage states to adopt California's stricter tailpipe-emission standards.* Consider future amendments to the act that would use the results of a regional alternative-fuel demonstration program to set requirements for clean fuels in all "non-attainment" areas throughout the country.

■ *Tax owners for tailpipe emissions.* Levy pollutant excise taxes based on vehicle tailpipe emissions (new vehicles would be taxed at time of sale and old vehicles could also be taxed according to smog-check results) and use these revenues to fund the regional alternative-fuel demonstration program.

OBJECTIVE: *Promote intercity-rail enhancements and upgrade systems to high-speed rail in highly traveled US corridors by 2005.*

POLICIES:

■ *Upgrade Amtrak.* Fund necessary capital improvements to the Amtrak network—estimated at $250 million annually.

■ *Fund high-speed rail.* Provide federal investments in high-speed rail (which is integrated into the current Amtrak and mass-transit network) to serve as a catalyst to attract stable, reliable financial commitments from state and local government and the private sector. Increased fuel taxes can provide a portion of the funds (estimated at $6 million per mile of new track).

■ *Stop rail abandonment.* Require federal government approval of all rail abandonments, leases, and sales, and impose fines if regulatory requirements are not abided by, to preserve the option of reinstituting rail service along old lines in the future.

■ *Tax heavy trucks.* Establish weight/distance taxes (based on payload weight and distance hauled) for heavy-duty trucks to reflect their actual cost to society.

As a result of the five-year budget agreement approved by Congress and the Bush administration in 1990, it is likely that any increases in federal transportation expenditures will have to be drawn from transportation-related revenues. An example of how the above policies might be implemented consistent with this approach follows.

Federal gas-tax increases, when fully phased in, could provide about $25 billion annually, over and above the $10 billion per year that now goes to the Highway Trust Fund. Other taxes on pollutants and heavy-duty trucks could provide an additional $5 billion in new revenues.

A significant share of these revenues could be allocated to repair of existing highways and bridges (total projected needs have been estimated at $250 billion through 2000). Remaining revenues could be targeted for:

■ partial funding of the program to integrate high-speed rail into the Amtrak system (about $6 million per mile)

■ transit improvement and expansion and other high-occupancy-vehicle programs ($5-12 billion per year)

■ increases in transit operating assistance ($750 million to $1 billion)

■ increases in the tax-free employee mass-transit allowance to at least $50 per month (estimated at $1 billion per year)

■ increases in transportation R&D ($100 million per year)

■ upgrading of the Amtrak system (about $250 million)

The public is well aware of transportation-system problems—they breathe the dirty air, sit in traffic jams, and pay dearly for militarizing the Middle East to protect our essential oil imports. Thus there is much evidence that voters will support higher transportation taxes and user fees if they know that the revenues will be used to address these problems.

State Policies

OBJECTIVE: *Increase motor-vehicle fuel efficiency and reduce passenger-vehicle emissions.*

POLICIES:

■ *Make state vehicles more efficient.* Establish state fuel-economy purchasing standards that require new government vehicles to be even more fuel efficient than federal standards require.

■ *Increase state fuel taxes.* Phase in an increase to state gasoline and diesel taxes of $0.25 to $0.50 per gallon by 2000. Revenues should be used to repair and maintain infrastructure as well as fund policies detailed below. (This will increase the combined state and federal gas tax $0.50 to $0.75 per gallon.)

■ *Offer rebates for buying fuel-efficient vehicles.* Institute a program whereby consumers purchasing clean, fuel-efficient vehicles receive a rebate or reduction in sales tax that is paid for by a surcharge on consumers buying high-polluting, inefficient vehicles.

■ *Strictly enforce speed limits.* Provide stricter enforcement of high-way speed limits.

■ *Adopt California's standards for tailpipe emissions.*

OBJECTIVE: *Increase average passenger-vehicle occupancy by 20 percent and increase use of alternative-transportation modes such as mass transit and intermodal freight by 2000.*

POLICIES:

■ *Charge user fees for the transportation system.* Adopt user fees and variable-pricing schemes for roadways, airports, and mass transit in order to internalize social costs of various transportation services (e.g., time-of-day and distance-based charges and pay-as-you-drive insurance through gasoline taxes).

■ *Offer tax relief for ridesharing, transit, bicycling, and pedestrians.* Make employee commuting allowances for ridesharing, mass transit, bicycling, and walking nontaxable for state-tax purposes.

■ *Promote alternatives to the single-occupant auto.* Provide incentives to rideshare and use transit (e.g., preferential parking spaces, shuttles to transit, emergency ride services, and flexible work hours); adopt parking policies that discourage auto use; promote telecommuting, and provide HOV facilities.

■ *Reward high-ridership transit systems.* Provide monetary rewards to local transit systems that increase ridership while keeping operating costs down (funds can come from increased state gasoline taxes).

■ *Limit heavy-truck size.* Promote intermodal freight transport by not permitting an increase in truck size and weight standards on highways.

OBJECTIVE: *Commercialize alternative fuels in state-government-owned fleet vehicles by 1995.*

POLICIES:

■ *Use alternative fuels in state vehicles.* Work with the federal government on cost-sharing programs to demonstrate clean alternative fuels for state-owned fleet vehicles, and collect and share data.

Regional and Local Policies
OBJECTIVE: *Double mass-transit ridership in urban areas by 2005.*

POLICIES:

■ *Subsidize mass-transit passes.*

■ *Advertise regional transit services.*

■ *Zone for mass transit.* Adopt local zoning ordinances that take land-use and transportation planning into account. Promote mixed-use development, tighten commercial zones to safeguard against overdevelopment in some areas and low-density sprawl in others, and establish targets for regional job/housing balances.

■ Improve pedestrian and cyclist access to transit, including bike parking and well-lit transit stops.

OBJECTIVE: *Stabilize regional VMT levels by 2000.*

POLICIES:

■ *Promote link between transportation planning and land-use development.* Coordinate land-use and transportation planning through regulatory requirements that promote development in areas with existing mass-transit services. Promote development that offers alternatives to the automobile (e.g., transit, bicycles, and walking). Promote housing construction in job-rich areas and employment opportunities in residential areas.

■ *Build bike and pedestrian facilities.* Build safe, convenient routes for cycling and walking, along with secure bicycle-storage facilities.

■ *Raise parking fees and adopt parking-management strategies.* Establish user fees based on variable pricing for parking and institute other policies that regulate parking.

■ *Educate the public about alternatives to the single-occupant auto.* Educate citizens (through advertising and outreach programs) about the benefits of ridesharing, transit, bicycling, and walking.

OBJECTIVE: *Commercialize alternative fuels in municipal fleet vehicles by 1995.*

POLICIES:

■ *Promote alternative fuels for fleet vehicles.* Work with state and federal governments and local business interests to demonstrate regionally available, clean alternative fuels for heavy-duty fleet vehicles, and collect and share data.

Comprehensive Transportation Policy in the Long Term

The United States has little experience in comprehensive transportation policymaking. Yet this kind of planning is vital to the health of our economy and society. Policies that set out broad-based goals along with the means of achieving them are needed well before a crisis arises; once an Arab oil embargo or an Iraqi invasion occurs, it is usually too late to act in a measured way.

The transportation policies adopted today will determine the fate of our transportation system for decades to come. Those decisions will determine whether we continue to depend exclusively on the gasoline-powered automobile, which has provided unprecedented mobility along with unparalleled pollution and congestion, or whether we will find better alternatives.

To guarantee that the best alternatives will be considered, the US must establish comprehensive transportation policies. Implementing them will not be easy. The changes required will no doubt affect the fabric of American society. Without such policies, however, the social costs of pollution, traffic congestion, and dependence on imported oil may well rise to intolerable levels.

The following long-term objectives merit action:

■ Formulate a national transportation policy based on the goals set out in the Department of Transportation's NTP and flesh it out with the specific actions discussed herein to achieve these goals.

■ Formulate and adopt a federal fuel-use policy aimed at diversifying the energy sources used for transportation.

■ Strengthen the coordination of land-use and transportation planning to promote sustainable development.

■ Integrate transportation requirements into the regulatory process at all levels of government to take account of the social costs of transportation.

■ Bolster transportation research, development, and demonstration efforts and encourage technology transfer of transportation innovations, especially those that increase system-wide efficiency.

■ Coordinate federal, state, and local policymaking efforts to ensure that policies work together to achieve desired goals.

❖ ❖ ❖

Americans cherish their freedom, and to most of us this means the freedom to choose. But for passenger transportation in the 1990s, there is no true choice: most of us are limited to the gasoline-powered automobile. While the car once provided cheap, nearly unlimited mobility, today it is the cause of pollution, congestion, and a nationwide addiction to ever greater oil imports. Moreover, our hundreds of millions of passenger vehicles, each emitting its weight in carbon annually, are threatening climate stability by adding dangerous levels of carbon dioxide to the atmosphere.

The time is overdue for addressing these issues. As the problems caused by our inefficient use of transportation resources mount, we will pay a high price in reduced productivity, damage to the environment, and diminished human health and welfare. Transportation policy must steer a new course; we cannot afford to wait.

Glossary

Amtrak: An agency created by Congress in 1970 to operate the national railroad passenger system. It also operates commuter-rail service under contract, usually to metropolitan transit agencies. (Also called *intercity rail*.)

Autoignition temperature: The temperature beyond which a mixture will automatically ignite.

Automated Guideway Transit (AGT): Any guided transit mode with fully automated operation. The term includes personal rapid transit concepts and group rapid transit or people-mover systems.

Biofuel: Fuel made from biomass.

Biomass: Biological matter that can be used as a source of energy, including wood and other plant matter, municipal wastes and methane produced from landfills, and food crops and other grain surpluses.

Busway: A special roadway designed for exclusive use by buses. It may be constructed at, above, or below grade and may be located in separate rights-of-way or within highway corridors.

Carpool: A term used loosely to describe a shared car carrying two or more persons to work on a regular basis.

Commuter rail: A passenger-railroad service that operates within metropolitan areas on trackage that usually is part of the general railroad system. The operations, primarily for commuters, are generally run as part of a regional system that is publicly owned or by a railroad company as part of its overall service. (Also called *regional rail*.)

Dedicated-fuel vehicle: Alternative-fuel vehicles that run on a single fuel other than gasoline.

Dual-fuel vehicle: An alternative-fuel vehicle capable of using both gasoline and alternative fuels, one at a time.

Externalities: Spillovers or side effects that arise whenever the actions of one economic agent affect another agent directly (not through priced transactions). Common examples of externalities are pollution and traffic congestion.

Feedstock: The primary ingredients of a substance produced by a chemical, physical, or other reaction.

Flammability limits: The range of mixtures of fuel in air that will result in fire or explosion.

Flashpoint: The temperature beyond which combustible mixtures form just above the liquid surface of the fuel.

Flexible-fuel vehicle: An alternative-fuel vehicle capable of using both gasoline and alternative fuels mixed together in varying proportions.

Gross heating value: A measure of the standard heat of combustion of fuels containing hydrogen, assumes that all the water formed in the combustion process is condensed into the liquid state. (Also called *higher heating value*.)

Heavy rail: A transit system that generally serves one urban area, using electrically powered passenger-rail cars operating at speeds of 70 mph in exclusive rights-of-way, without grade crossings and with high platforms. The tracks may be any combination of underground, elevated, and surface level. (Also called *rapid rail, metro, subway,* and other local names.)

High Occupancy Vehicle (HOV): A passenger vehicle that meets or exceeds a certain predetermined minimum number of passengers—for example, more than two or three people per automobile. Buses, carpools, and vanpools are HOV vehicles.

High-occupancy-vehicle lane (HOV lane): A highway or street lane reserved for the use of high-occupancy vehicles (HOVs). Priority HOV lanes are generally reserved during specific hours for one or more specified categories of vehicles, such as buses, carpools, and vanpools.

High-speed rail: Steel-wheel trains operating on traditional train tracks at speeds of 80–200 mph (although France's TGV attained a record speed of 320 mph in a recent trial). These trains have been operating in France, Germany ("ICE"), and Japan ("Bullet") for over a decade.

Hybrid electric vehicle: A dual-fuel vehicle that combines electric motors with small internal-combustion engines or fuel cells to allow extended driving range.

Intercity rail: Rail transit service between cities and towns operating on private rights-of-way that are physically separated from other traffic (by curbs, barriers, grade separations, etc.) but have grade crossings for other vehicles and pedestrians, including regular street intersections.

Light rail: A metropolitan electric railway system that operates as single cars or short trains along exclusive rights-of-way at ground level, on aerial structures, in subways or occasionally, in streets, and boards and discharges passengers at track or car-floor level. Light-rail transit (LRT) systems can be defined broadly to include trolleys and streetcars.

Magnetic levitation (maglev) train: A train powered by electromagnets that raise rail cars about six inches above a guideway and propel them at speeds of up to 300 mph.

Minivans: Small buses seating 10–20 passengers.

Mode: A means of transportation. Mass or public transit may be considered a mode, with bus, subway, and commuter rail as submodes. Walking and bicycling are considered passenger modes, along with traditional modes like cars, light trucks, and utility vehicles.

Multimodal trips: Trips that combine modes as a means of door-to-door transportation, such as auto to bus to train.

Net heating value: A measure of the standard heat of combustion of fuels containing hydrogen; assumes that all the water formed in the combustion process remains in the vapor state (also called *lower heating value*). The net heating value is a closer measure of real combustion processes than the gross heating value.

On-road vehicles: The set of transportation vehicles used for road-based travel, such as cars, light trucks, heavy-duty trucks, and buses.

Passenger-miles traveled: The distance covered by passengers (in miles) over a certain time frame (usually one year).

Passenger vehicles: Cars, light trucks (less than 3,750 gross vehicle weight, in pounds), vans, and utility vehicles.

Personal rapid transit: A concept for an automated guideway transit system that would operate small units (2-6 passengers) under computer control over an elaborate system of guideways for travel between origin and destination stations without stopping.

Rail: Any of the family of transit modes using rail technology. The major ones, generally in ascending order of performance, are streetcars, light rail transit, heavy-rail transit, and commuter, or regional, rail.

Reid Vapor Pressure (RVP): The measure of a petroleum product's ability to evaporate or a measure of a fossil fuel's volatility.

Renewables: Energy that is replenished from a virtually inexhaustible source at a rate equal to the rate at which it is consumed, such as energy in sunlight, wind, rivers, plants, and tides.

Reverse commute: A term denoting travel of center city residents to suburban work locations in the opposite direction of the main volume of traffic.

Rideshare: A term used to describe both carpools and vanpools.

Telecommuting: A means of transmitting information without transporting people. This includes working at home instead of in the office, teaching by TV instead of in a classroom, and using other electronic communications for transactions formerly done in person.

Traditional commute: The pattern of commuting from a suburblike area outside a city to a downtown work location.

Transportation demand management (TDM): Transportation strategies aimed at influencing people to shift out of inefficient transportation modes into more efficient modes and to travel during off-peak hours.

Transportation system management (TSM): That part of the transportation planning process undertaken to improve the efficiency of the existing transportation system. The goal is to make better use of the existing system by using short-term, low-capital transportation improvements that generally cost less and can be implemented more quickly than system-development actions.

Trolley system: A street transit system consisting of electrically powered rail vehicles operating in one- to three-car transit units, mostly on surface streets with mixed traffic. (Also called *streetcar, street railway, or tramway*.)

Vanpool: A term used to describe a shared van carrying from 9–13 persons to work on a regular basis.

Vehicle miles of travel (VMT): On highways, a measure of the total miles traveled by all vehicles in the area for a specified time period. It is calculated by the number of vehicles multiplied by the miles traveled in a given area or on a given highway during the time period. In transit, the number of vehicle miles operated on a given route, line, or network during a specified time period.

Vehicle occupancy: The number of occupants in a vehicle, including the driver.

[For more detailed definitions of public-transit terms, refer to the *Urban Public Transportation Glossary*. Washington, DC: Transportation Research Board, 1989.]

List of Acronyms

AASHTO American Association of State Highway and Transportation
            Officials
ADIS Advanced driver information system
APTA American Public Transit Association
ATMS Advanced traffic management system
AVCS Advanced vehicle control system
AVHS Advanced vehicle/highway system
      (also IVHS Intelligent vehicle/highway system)
AVI Automated vehicle identification
AVL Automated vehicle location
Bpd Barrels per day (MBpd = million bpd unless otherwise stated)
Btu British thermal unit of heat energy (kBtu = 1000 Btu)
CARB California Air Resources Board
CEC California Energy Commission
CFC Chlorofluorocarbons
CH_4 Methane
CNG Compressed natural gas
CO_2 Carbon dioxide
CO Carbon monoxide
CPI Consumer price index
CRS Congressional Research Service
CVT Continuously variable transmission
°C Degrees Centigrade
°F Degrees Fahrenheit
DOE Department of Energy
DOT Department of Transportation
EIA Energy Information Administration
EIS Environmental Impact Statement
EPA Environmental Protection Agency
EPCA Energy Policy Conservation Act
EPRI Electric Power Research Institute
ETBE Ethyl tertiary butyl ether
EV Electric vehicle (EVs = electric vehicles)
FHWA Federal Highway Administration

GAO   General Accounting Office
gbh   Grams per brake–horsepower hour
gpm   Grams per mile
HC   Hydrocarbons
HOV   High-occupancy vehicle
HSR   High-speed rail
IEA   International Energy Agency
kWh   Kilowatt-hours
LEV   Low-emitting vehicle
LNG   Liquid natural gas
LPG   Liquefied petroleum gas
LTV   Light truck/van
MIS   Motorist information system
mpg   Miles per gallon
mph   Miles per hour
MSOFC   Monolithic solid oxide fuel cell
MTBE   Methyl tertiary butyl ether
MW   Megawatts
NARP   National Association of Railroad Passengers
NEPA   National Environmental Policy Act
NO_x Oxides of nitrogen
N_2O Nitrous oxide
NRC   National Research Council
NTP   National Transportation Policy
OECD   Organization for Economic Cooperation and Development
ORNL   Oak Ridge National Laboratory
OTA   Office of Technology Assessment
PEM   Proton exchange membrane
PM_{10} Particulate matter less than 10 microns in size
PMT   Passenger miles of travel
ppm   Parts per million
PRT   Personal rapid transit
psi   Pounds per square inch
PURPA Public Utility Regulatory Policy Act
PV   Photovoltaic
Quad   Quadrillion Btu (10^{15} Btu)
R&D   Research and Development
RD&D   Research, Development, and Demonstration

ROG   Reactive organic gases

RVP   Reid Vapor Pressure

SCAG   South Coast Association of Governments

SCAQMD South Coast Air Quality Management District

SO_x Sulfur oxides

TCM   Transportation control measure

TDM   Transportation demand management

TMT   Ton per mile traveled

TRB   Transportation Research Board

TSM   Transportation system management

TSP   Total suspended particulates

UHB   Ultra-high bypass

UMTA Urban Mass Transit Administration

VMT   Vehicle miles of travel

VOC   Volatile organic compounds

WIM   Weight in motion

Conversion Factors

Length
1 inch	2.54	centimeters
1 foot	30.48	centimeters
1 yard	91.44	centimeters
1 meter	39.37	inches
1 mile	5280	feet
1 kilometer	0.6214	miles

Area
1 square mile	640	acres

Mass
1 pound	453.6	grams
1 kilogram	2.205	pounds
1 ton (short)	2000	pounds
1 ton (metric)	2200	pounds

Volume
1 cubic inch	16.39	cubic centimeters
1 liter	61.03	cubic inches
1 liter	1.057	quarts
1 cubic foot	7.481	US gallons
1 US gallon	4.0	quarts
1 US gallon	3.785	liters
1 barrel	42	US gallons

Density
1 gram per cubic centimeter	62.43	pounds per cubic foot
1 gram per cubic centimeter	8.345	pounds per US gallon

1 pound mole of an ideal gas at 0 degrees C and 760 mm Hg is equivalent to 359.0 cubic feet.

Pressure
1 pound per square inch	51.71	millimeters of mercury
1 atmosphere	760	millimeters of mercury
1 atmosphere	2116.2	pounds per square foot
1 atmosphere	14.7	pounds per square inch

Temperature Scales
Degrees Fahrenheit (F)	1.8	(degrees C + 32)
Degrees Centigrade (C)	1/1.8	(degrees F - 32)

Degrees Kelvin (K) .... degrees C + 273.16
Degrees Rankine (R) .... degrees F + 459.7

Power

1 kilowatt	1000	joules per second
1 kilowatt	56.87	Btu per minute
1 kilowatt	1.341	horsepower
1 horsepower	0.707	Btu per second
1 horsepower	745.7	watts
1 megawatt	1000	kilowatts

Heat, Energy, or Work Equivalents

ft-lb	kWh	hp-hr	Btu	calorie	joule
0.7376	2.773×10^{-7}	3.725×10^{-7}	9.478×10^{-4}	0.2390	1
7.233	2.724×10^{-6}	3.653×10^{-6}	9.296×10^{-3}	2.3438	9.80665
1	3.766×10^{-7}	5.0505×10^{-7}	1.285×10^{-3}	0.3241	1.356
2.655×10^{6}	1	1.341	3.4128×10^{3}	8.6057×10^{5}	3.6×10^{6}
1.98×10^{6}	0.7455	1	2.545×10^{3}	6.4162×10^{5}	2.6845×10^{6}
74.73	2.815×10^{-5}	3.774×10^{-5}	9.604×10^{-2}	24.218	1.0133×10^{2}
3.086×10^{3}	1.162×10^{-3}	1.558×10^{-3}	3.9657	1×10^{3}	4.184×10^{3}
7.7816×10^{2}	2.930×10^{-4}	3.930×10^{-4}	1	2.52×10^{2}	1.055×10^{3}
3.086	1.162×10^{-6}	1.558×10^{-6}	3.97×10^{-3}	1	4.184

Analysis of Air

By weight: oxygen, 23.2%; nitrogen, 76.8%
By volume: oxygen, 21.0%; nitrogen, 79.0%
Average molecular weight of air on above basis =
        28.84 (usually rounded off to 29)
True molecular weight of dry air (including argon) = 28.96

Bibliography

Advanced Transit Association (ATA). 1988. "Personal Rapid Transit (PRT): Another Option for Urban Transit?" *Journal of Advanced Transportation*, Vol. 22, No. 3.

American Association of State Highway and Transportation Officials (AASHTO). 1988. *Keeping America Moving: The Bottom Line.* Published as part of AASHTO's Transportation 2020 Project. Washington, DC. September.

American Public Transit Association (APTA). 1989. *Managing Mobility: A New Generation of National Policies for the 21st Century.* A report of the Transit 2000 Work Force, Washington, DC. November.

Andrle, S., J. Kraus, and F. Spielberg. 1990. *Lessons from the Broome County Distance-Based Fare Demonstration.* Presented at 69th Annual Transportation Research Board Meeting, Transportation Research Board Paper No. 890260. Washington, DC. January.

Barber, Kenneth. 1990. *Fuel Cells and Batteries for Transportation Prospects.* US Department of Energy—Electric and Hybrid Propulsion Division: Washington, DC. Presentation before the Environment and Energy Study Institute. Washington, DC. July.

Behnke, Robert W. 1991. *Trips: Transportation Resources Information Processing System.* Aegis Transportation Information Systems, Inc., Portland, OR. March.

Bicker, William. 1990. Transportation Coordinator to the Mayor of Los Angeles, CA. Personal communication.

Bicycle Institute of America (BIA). 1990. *Bicycling Reference Book.* Washington, DC: BIA.

Black, A. 1990. "Analysis of Census Data on Walking to Work and Working at Home." *Transportation Quarterly*, Vol. 44, No. 1. January.

Bleviss, Deborah L. 1988. *The New Oil Crisis and Fuel Economy Technologies: Preparing the Light Transportation Industry for the 1990s.* New York: Quorum Press.

Blum, Wilfried. 1990. Verbound Schweizer Elektric Werke, Bahnhef Platz 3, 8023 Zurich, Switzerland. Personal communication.

Bottles, Scott. 1987. *Los Angeles and the Automobile: The Making of the Modern City.* Berkeley: University of California Press.

Bouley, Jean. 1989. "Breaking the Sound Barrier in Europe." *TR News.* Transportation Research Board Publication No. 145. Washington, DC. November/December.

Brogan, R., H. Stamm, and J. Hamm. 1990. *Drive for Excellence.* Presented at 69th Annual Transportation Research Board Meeting, Transportation Research Board. Washington, DC. January.

Brower, Michael. 1990. *Cool Energy: The Renewable Solution to Global Warming.* Cambridge, MA: Union of Concerned Scientists.

Buchholz, R.A. 1982. *Business Environment and Public Policy: Implications for Management.* Englewood Cliffs, NJ: Prentice-Hall.

Burke, M.C. 1989. *High-Occupancy-Vehicle Facilities: General Characteristics and Fuel Savings Potential.* Washington, DC: American Council for an Energy-Efficient Economy. September.

Burnham, John C. 1961. "The Gasoline Tax and the Automobile Revolution." *Mississippi Valley Historical Review.* December.

California Assembly Office of Research (AOR). 1989. *California 2000—Exhausting Clean Air.* Report #0289-A. October.

California Energy Commission (CEC). 1989. *AB234 Report: Cost and Availability of Low-Emission Motor Vehicles and Fuels.* Draft Staff Report. April.

———. 1990. *Transportation Issues—1990 Conservation Report.* Documentation for the CEC Conservation Report Committee public hearings. Sacramento, CA. May.

Callahan, Kateri. 1990. Electric Transportation Coalition, Washington, DC. Personal communication.

Cannon, J.S. 1990. *The Health Costs of Air Pollution.* New York: The American Lung Association.

Carlsmith R.S., W.U. Chandler, J.E. McMahon, and D.H. Santini. 1990. *Energy Efficiency: How Far Can We Go?* Oak Ridge National Laboratory, Oak Ridge, TN. TM-11441.

Casler, Stephen. 1990. Allegheny College, Meadville, PA. Personal communication.

Casler, Stephen, and B. Hannon. 1989. "Readjustment Potentials in Industrial Energy Efficiency and Structure." *Journal of Environmental Economics and Management,* Vol. 17, pp. 93-108.

Chandler, William U., and A.K. Nicholls. 1990. *Assessing Carbon Emissions Control Strategies: A Carbon Tax or a Gasoline Tax?* Batelle Memorial Institute. ACEEE Policy Paper No. 3, American Council for an Energy Efficient Economy. Washington, DC. February.

Chao, Elaine, Thomas D. Larson, Anthony R. Kane, and Wallace Burnett. 1990. "Development of a National Transportation Policy: The Process and the Product." *TR News,* No. 149. July/August.

Christiansen, D.L. 1990. *The Status and Effectiveness of the Houston High-Occupancy-Vehicle Lane System, 1988.* Presented at 69th Annual Transportation Research Board Meeting, Transportation Research Board Paper No. 890048. Washington, DC. January.

Clarke, Andy. 1990. "Gridlock 2020." *TR News.* No. 146. Transportation Research Board. Washington, DC. January/February.

———. 1990a. Bicycle Federation of America, Washington, DC. Personal communication.

Cochran, Thomas C. 1972. *Social Change in America: The Twentieth Century.* New York: Harper & Row.

Colberg, C., and K. Jacobson. 1988. "Evaluation of the Cost-Effectiveness of HOV Lanes." *Urban Traffic Systems and Parking: Transportation Research Record 1181.* Transportation Research Board. Washington, DC.

Cole, L.M. 1989. *Transportation: National Plans and Policies.* Proceedings of a Congressional Research Service Seminar. CRS#89-559E. September 15.

Crandall, Robert W., and John D. Graham. 1989. "The Effect of Fuel Economy Standards on Automobile Safety." *Journal of Law and Economics.* Vol. XXXII. April.

CRC Press. 1976. *Handbook of Chemistry and Physics.* 57th ed. Cleveland, OH.

Dallos, Robert E. 1990. "Pay as They Go—Faster." *Los Angeles Times,* August 14, p. A-1.

Davis, Stacy C., D.B. Shonka, G.J. Anderson-Batiste, and P.S. Hu. 1989. *Transportation Energy Data Book: Edition 10.* ORNL-6565. Oak Ridge National Laboratory, Oak Ridge, TN. September.

Deakin, Elizabeth. 1988. *A Look Ahead: Year 2020, Special Report 220.* Transportation Research Board, National Research Council. Washington, DC.

Deakin, John F., Calvin Broomhead, and Raymond R. Sullivan. 1989. *The Sustainable City: Phase II.* City and County of San Francisco, Bureau of Energy Conservation.

DeJarnette, K.R. 1989. "Changing Regulation of Surface Transportation: Development and Implications of Current Policies." *Transportation in the United States: Perspectives on Federal Policies.* US Congressional Research Service. February.

DeLuchi, Mark A. 1989. "Hydrogen Vehicles: An Evaluation of Fuel Storage, Performance, Safety, Environmental Impacts, and Cost." *International Journal of Hydrogen Energy,* Vol. 14, No. 2.

DeLuchi, Mark A., Quanlu Wang, and Daniel Sperling. 1989b. "Electric Vehicles: Performance, Life-Cycle Costs, Emissions, and Recharging Requirements." *Transportation Research,* Vol. 22A, No. 5. May.

DeLuchi, Mark A., Daniel Sperling, and Robert A. Johnson. 1987. *A Comparative Analysis of Future Transportation Fuels.* Research Report UCB-ITS-RR-87-13. Institute of Transportation Studies, University of California, Berkeley.

————. 1988a. *Methanol vs. Natural Gas Vehicles: A Comparison of Resource Supply, Performance, Emissions, Fuel Storage, Safety, Cost, and Transitions.* Society of Automotive Engineers (SAE) Technical Paper Series, 881656. November.

————. 1989a. "Transportation Fuels and the Greenhouse Effect." *Transportation Research Record 1175.* Transportation Research Board, Washington, DC.

Difiglio, Carmen. 1989. "Timing of Methanol Supply and Demand: Implications for Alternative Transportation Fuel Policies." *Transportation Research.* Vol. 23A, No. 3, p. 234.

Ditlow, Clarence M. 1990a. *Testimony on H.R. 5560 before the House Subcommittee on Energy and Power.* Washington, DC: Center for Auto Safety, September 15.

————. 1990b. *Statement on Safety and Fuel Economy.* Press Release. Center for Auto Safety, Washington, DC. September 24.

Doniger, David. 1990. Natural Resources Defense Counsel, Washington, DC. Personal communication.

Dower, Roger, and Robert Repetto. 1990. *Testimony on the Use of the Federal Tax System to Improve the Environment before the House of Representatives Committee on Ways and Means.* Washington, DC: World Resources Institute. March 6.

Dunn, James A., Jr. 1981. *Miles to Go: European and American Transportation Policies.* Cambridge, MA: The MIT Press.

Egan, J. 1989. "California Company Bets that PV's Future Is in Autos." *Energy Daily,* July 25.

————. 1990a. "Will Arco Have to Reformulate EC-1 Gasoline?" *Energy Daily,* April 4.

————. 1990b. "PG&E Takes on Chicken-And-Egg Problem." *Energy Daily,* September 26.

El-Gasseir, Mohamed M. 1990. "The Potential Benefits and Workability of Pay-As-You-Drive Automobile Insurance." *1990 Conservation Report.* Docket No. 89-CR-90. State of California Energy Resources Conservation and Development Commission. Sacramento, CA. June 8.

Electric Power Research Institute (EPRI). 1989. *Electric G-Van.* Palo Alto, CA. Spring.

Energy Information Administration (EIA). 1990a. *Monthly Energy Review February 1991.* DOE/EIA(91/02). November.

———. 1990b. *Monthly Energy Review May 1990.* DOE/EIA-0035(90/05). August.

———. 1990c. *Annual Energy Review 1989.* DOE/EIA-0384(89). May.

———. 1989. *Annual Energy Review 1988.* DOE/EIA-0384(88). May.

———. 1988. *International Energy Outlook 1989—Projections to 2000.* DOE/EIA-0484(89). May.

Environment. 1989. "A New Gas for Old Cars." Vol. 31, No. 9, p. 23. November.

Environmental and Energy Study Institute (EESI). 1990. *The Senate-Passed and House Energy Clean Air Bills: A Comparison.* Special Report. Washington, DC. April 16.

Ewell, W.E. 1989. "A Freeway Traffic Management System and Team." *Transportation Quarterly,* Vol. 43, No. 4. October.

Feder, B.J. 1989. "Building a Flying Train." *New York Times,* December 13, p. D6.

Ferguson, Erik. 1990. *The Influence of Household Composition on Residential Location and Journey to Work in the United States.* Presented at 69th Annual Transportation Research Board Meeting. Transportation Research Board Paper No. 890769. Washington, DC. January.

Fisher, Lawrence M. 1990. "Rehabilitating the Image of the Two-Stroke Engine." *New York Times,* July 8, p. F9.

Flink, James J. 1988. *The Automobile Age.* Cambridge, MA: The MIT Press.

Foster, Mark S. 1982. *From Streetcar to Superhighway: American City Planners and Urban Transportation, 1900-1940.* Philadelphia: Temple University Press.

Fwa, T.F., K.C. Sinha, and S.K. Saha. 1990. *Update Analysis of Highway Cost Allocation.* Presented at 69th Annual Transportation Research Board Meeting. Transportation Research Board Paper No. 890067. Washington, DC. January.

Giuliano, G., and T.F. Golob. 1990. *Staggered Work Hours for Traffic Management: A Study Case.* Presented at 69th Annual Transportation Research Board Meeting. Transportation Research Board Paper No. 890703. Washington, DC. January.

Gold, Allan R. 1990. "After Years of Becoming Cleaner, New York City Air Grows Dirtier." *New York Times,* April 18, p. A1.

Goodman, E. 1989. "James Worden's Solar Cars." *Washington Post,* June 3, p. A15.

Greene, David L. 1989. *Energy Efficiency Improvement Potential of Commercial Aircraft to 2010.* Oak Ridge National Laboratory, Oak Ridge, TN. October 13.

Gushee, David, and Sandra Sieg-Ross. 1988. *The Role of Transportation Controls in Urban Air Quality.* 88-101-S. US Congressional Research Service, Washington, DC. January 28.

Hansson, L. 1990. *The Swedish Approach to Multi-modal Transportation Planning.* Association of American Railroads 1990 Intermodal Policy Conference, Key Largo, FL. April 6.

Hartgen, D.T., and M.A. Casey. 1990. *Using the Media to Encourage Changes in Urban Travel Behavior*. Presented at 69th Annual Transportation Research Board Meeting. Transportation Research Board Paper 890423. Washington, DC. January.

Hawthorne, Gary. 1988. *The Role for Transportation Control Measures in the Post '87 Era*. US Environmental Protection Agency, Washington, DC.

———. 1989. *Clean Air Legislation and Future Emissions/Congestion Problems*. US Environmental Protection Agency, Office of Mobile Sources. Presented at the 1989 AASHTO Annual Meeting.

Higgins, Thomas. 1990a. *Guidelines for Developing Local Demand Management or Trip Reduction Policies*. Presented at 69th Annual Transportation Research Board Meeting. Transportation Research Board Paper No. 890052. Washington, DC. January.

———. 1990b. *The Effectiveness of Employer-Based Transportation Control Measures in Suburban Areas: National Review Findings*. Presented at 69th Annual Transportation Research Board Meeting. Transportation Research Board Paper No.890736. Washington, DC. January.

High Speed Rail Association (HSRA). 1990. *TGV Atlantique Sets New Record at 320.2 MPH*. Pittsburgh, PA: HSRA.

Hillsman, Edward L., and F. Southworth. 1990. *Factors That May Influence Responses of the U.S. Transportation Sector to Policies for Reducing Greenhouse Gas Emissions*. Oak Ridge National Laboratory, Oak Ridge, TN. Presented at 69th Annual Transportation Research Board Meeting. Transportation Research Board Paper No. 890776. Washington, DC. January.

Hirst, Eric. 1989. *Federal Roles to Realize National Energy-Efficiency Opportunities in the 1990s*. Oak Ridge National Laboratory, Oak Ridge, TN. ORNL/CON-290. October.

Institute for Transportation Research and Education (ITRE). 1989. *1988 Annual Report*. Research Triangle Park, NC: University of North Carolina.

Institute of Transportation Engineers (ITE). 1989. *A Toolbox for Alleviating Traffic Congestion*. Washington, DC.

Interrante, Joseph. 1983. "The Road to Autopia: The Automobile and the Spatial Transformation of American Culture." *The Automobile and American Culture*, David L. Lewis and Laurence Goldstein, eds. Ann Arbor: University of Michigan Press.

Johnson, Larry R. 1990. "Putting Maglev on Track." *Issues in Science and Technology*. Vol. VI, No. 3 (Spring). National Academy of Sciences. Washington, DC.

Katauskas, Ted. 1989. "Maglev Will Fly in the U.S." *Research & Development*, November, p. 22.

Khisty, C.J. 1990. *Non-Motorized Transportation in Developing Countries*. Presented at 69th Annual Transportation Research Board Meeting. Transportation Research Board Paper No. 890242. Washington, DC. January.

Kitamura, R., H. Zhao, and R. Gibby. 1990a. *Evaluation of Truck Impacts on Pavement Maintenance*. Presented at 69th Annual Transportation Research Board Meeting. Transportation Research Board Paper No. 890658. Washington, DC. January.

Kitamura, R., J.M. Nilles, P. Conroy, and D.M. Fleming. 1990b. *Telecommuting as a Transportation Planning Measure: Initial Results of State of California Pilot Project*. Presented at 69th Annual Transportation Research Board Meeting. Transportation Research Board Paper No. 890753. Washington, DC. January.

Kitsock, G. 1990. "The Cell of a New Machine." *City Paper* (Washington, DC). April 13.

Komanoff, Charles. 1990. *Bicycle Group Hits Chemical Company Claims on Oil Savings.* Press release by Transportation Alternatives, New York, NY. June 29.

———. 1990a. Komanoff Associates, New York, NY. Personal communication.

Lafen, Peter. 1990. Law firm of Hoffman, Williams, Lafen, and Fletcher, Arlington, VA. Personal communication.

Lancaster, Ann, and Timothy Lomax, eds. 1987. *Second National Conference on High-Occupancy Vehicle Lanes and Transitways.* Conference Proceedings, Houston, TX. October 25-28.

Langer, B. 1990. National Highway Traffic Safety Administration. Washington, DC. Personal communication.

League of American Wheelmen (LAW). 1989. *Basic Bicycle Facts.* Baltimore, MD.

Ledbetter, Marc. 1989a. *Testimony on Global Warming and the CAFE Standards before the Senate Consumer Subcommittee.* American Council for an Energy-Efficient Economy. Washington, DC. May 2.

———. 1989b. *Automobile Safety and Fuel Economy—Information Brief.* American Council for an Energy-Efficient Economy: Washington, DC. September.

———. 1990. Testimony on Light-Vehicle Fuel Economy before the House Subcommittee on Energy and Power. American Council for an Energy-Efficient Economy. Washington, DC. September 15.

Ledbetter, Marc, and Marc Ross. 1990. *Supply Curves of Conserved Energy for Automobiles.* Prepared for Lawrence Berkeley Laboratory—Applied Science Division, Berkeley, CA. March.

Lee, Patrick. 1989. "Arco Keeping Cap on New Unleaded Fuel." *Los Angeles Times,* December 27, p. D1.

Lemov, Penelope. 1989. "Buck Rogers Doesn't Live Here Anymore." *Governing.* November, p. 28.

Leuchtenburg, William E. 1958. *The Perils of Prosperity, 1914-32.* Chicago: University of Chicago Press.

Levenson, Leo, and Deborah Gordon. 1990. "DRIVE+: Promoting Clean and Fuel Efficient Motor Vehicles Through a Self-Financing System of State Sales Tax Incentives." *Journal of Policy Analysis and Management.* Vol. 9, No. 3 (Summer), pp. 409-15.

Lippman, Thomas W. 1990. "More Use of Natural Gas as Motor Fuel Explored." *Washington Post,* February 14, p. A16.

Lomax, T.H., D. Bullard, and J. Hanks, Jr. 1989. *The Impact of Declining Mobility in Major Texas and Other US Cities.* Texas Transportation Institute, State Department of Highways and Public Transportation, and US Department of Transportation, Federal Highway Administration. Research Report 431-1F. September.

Lomont, D. 1989. "Power from the Sun." *Honolulu.* May.

Lowry, Ira S. 1988. "Planning for Urban Sprawl," *A Look Ahead: Year 2020, Special Report 220.* Transportation Research Board, National Research Council, Washington, DC.

Lynd, Lee R. 1989. "Large-Scale Fuel Ethanol from Lignocellulose: Potential Economics and Research Priorities." Hanover, NH: Thayer School of Engineering, Dartmouth College.

Lynd, Robert S., and Helen Merrell Lynd. 1929. *Middletown: A Study in Modern American Culture.* New York: Harcourt, Brace and World, Inc.

―――. 1937. *Middletown in Transition: A Study in Cultural Conflicts.* New York: Harcourt, Brace and World, Inc.

Machalaba, D. 1990. "Mobile Homes: Transit Systems Face Burden of Providing Last-Resort Shelter." *Wall Street Journal,* July 18, p. A1.

MacKenzie, James J. 1989. Testimony before the Consumer Subcommittee of the Senate Committee on Commerce, Science, and Transportation. Washington, DC: World Resources Institute. September 7.

―――. 1990. *Why We Need a National Energy Policy.* World Resources Institute. Washington, DC. August.

Markow, M.J., E.L. Seguin, E.F. Ireland, and D.M. Freund. 1990. *Feasibility Study of Changes to the Highway Maintenance and Operations Cost Index.* Presented at 69th Annual Transportation Research Board Meeting, Washington, DC. Transportation Research Board Paper No. 890758. January.

Maskery, M.A. 1990. "Battery Jolt." *Automotive News.* April 26.

Mathews, Jay. 1990. "Severe Smog-Control Law Enacted in California." *Washington Post,* September 29, p. A3.

McGill, R. 1985. *Fuel Consumption and Emission Values for Traffic Models.* Oak Ridge National Laboratory, Oak Ridge, TN. FHWA/RD-85/053 (NTIS 018430223). May.

McGreer, Patrick L., and Enoch H. Durbin. 1990. "Natural Gas in Cars—And Step on It." *New York Times,* October 2, p. A27.

McNutt, Barry, and David L. Greene. 1989. Department of Energy, correspondence to Lynda T. Carlson re: *The Need for Gasoline Purchase Diary Survey Data.*

Metz, B. 1990. *The Dutch Policy on Global Warming.* Testimony for the Standing Committee on the Environment by the Counselor for Health and Environment, Royal Netherlands Embassy. January 23.

Mintz, Marianne Miller, and Anne M. Zerega. 1989. *Transportation Projects with Energy, Economic, and Environmental Benefits: Innovative Uses of Oil Overcharge and Other Funds.* ANL/ESD-2. Argonne National Laboratory, Argonne, IL. October.

Montgomery County Planning Department (MCPD). 1986. *Montgomery County, Maryland: Interim Growth Policy.* The Montgomery County Planning Board Maryland-National Capital Park and Planning Commission. Silver Spring, MD. June 26.

―――. 1989. *Montgomery County, Maryland, Comprehensive Growth Policy Study, Volume 3: Global Factors.* (One volume of a four-volume set.) The Maryland-National Capital Park and Planning Commission. Silver Spring, MD. July.

Montgomery, W.D., and R.D. Marcuss. 1990. *Testimony before the House Ways and Means Committee on Environmental Taxes.* US Congressional Budget Office. Washington, DC. March 7.

Moore, Curtis A. 1990. "Electric Cars: Against the Current?" *Washington Post,* March 11, p. B3.

Mydans, S. 1990. "Rail Line Makes Debut Where Car Is Supreme." *New York Times,* July 16, p. A8.

Nakadegawa, R. 1990. *Considerations for Cost-Effective Transit.* Presented at 69th Annual Transportation Research Board Meeting. Transportation Research Board Paper No. 890419. Washington, DC. January.

Nash, A.B. 1990. *Effective Citizen Participation in Transportation Planning.* Presented at 69th Annual Transportation Research Board Meeting. Transportation Research Board Paper No. 890252. Washington, DC. January.

National Academy of Science (NAS). 1989. *The Infinite Voyage: Crisis in the Atmosphere.* Television series on WQED, Pittsburgh, PA. Televised on December 14.

National Academy of Sciences, Committee on Science, Engineering, and Public Policy. 1991. *Policy Implications of Greenhouse Warming.*

National Association of Railroad Passengers (NARP). 1989. *Light Rail Transit: A Cost-Effective and Successful Transit Mode.* Washington, DC: NARP. April 20.

———. 1990. Press Release #90-5, June 25.

National Journal. 1990. "Opinion Outlook: Views on the Economy." October 16, p. 2426.

Neff, John. 1990. American Public Transit Association, Washington, DC. Personal communication.

Nice, D.C. 1989. "Stability of the Amtrak System." *Transportation Quarterly*, Vol. 43, No. 4. October.

Nicholas, C.J. 1989. "Double-Stack Container Trains' Potential for Agricultural Exports." *Ports, Waterways, Intermodal Terminals, and International Trade Transportation Issues.* Transportation Research Circular No. 350. May.

Ogden, Joan M., and Robert H. Williams. 1989. *Solar Hydrogen: Moving Beyond Fossil Fuels.* Washington, DC: World Resources Institute. October.

Organization for Economic Co-operation and Development (OECD). 1986. *Environmental Effects of Automotive Transport: The OECD COMPASS Project.* Paris, France.

———. 1988a. *Transport and the Environment.* International Energy Agency, Paris, France.

———. 1988b. *Energy Statistics 1985-1986.* International Energy Agency, Paris, France.

———. 1989. *Energy and the Environment: Policy Overview.* International Energy Agency, Paris, France.

———. 1989a. *Energy Policies and Programmes of IEA Countries: 1988 Review.* International Energy Agency, Paris, France.

Orski, C.K. 1987. "Managing Suburban Traffic Congestion: A Strategy for Suburban Mobility." *Transportation Quarterly.* Vol. 41, No. 4. October.

Owen, Wilfred. 1985. "Transportation and World Development." *Transportation Quarterly.* July.

———. 1988. "The View From 2020: Transportation in America's Future." *The Brookings Review.* Fall.

Pane, Frank. 1990. US Technologies-Pratt and Whitney, East Hartford, CT. Personal communication.

Parcells, Harriet. 1990. National Association of Railroad Passengers, Washington, DC. Personal communication.

Parody, T.E., M.E. Lovely, and P.S. Hsu. 1990. *Net Costs of Peak and Off-Peak Transit Trips Taken Nationwide by Mode.* Presented at 69th Annual Transportation Research Board Meeting. Transportation Research Board Paper No. 890405. Washington, DC. January.

Passell, Peter. 1990. "Economic Scene: Sticky Traffic, Slick Fixes," *New York Times,* July 25, p. D2.

Percy, Charles H. 1990. "The Broad Benefits of a Gasoline Tax Hike." *New York Times,* July 8, p. A25.

Platte, Lois. 1990. US Environmental Protection Agency, Ann Arbor, MI. Personal communications.

Plotkin, Steven E. 1989. *Increasing the Efficiency of Automobiles and Light Trucks—A Component of a Strategy to Combat Global Warming and Growing U.S. Oil Dependency.* Statement on behalf of OTA before the Senate Consumer Subcommittee. May 2.

———. 1990. Presentation on electric vehicles before the Environment and Energy Study Institute. Washington, DC. July.

Postma, A.D. 1990. *Chlorofluorocarbons Elimination.* General Motors Corporation press release. Washington, DC. April.

Public Technology, Inc., and City of Denver. 1990. *An Alternative Fuels Evaluation System For Fleet Vehicles.* Public Technology, Inc. Energy Task Force of the Urban Consortium, Washington, DC. November.

Pucher, J. 1988. "Urban Travel Behavior as the Outcome of Public Policy: The Example of Modal-Split in Western Europe and North America." *Journal of the American Planning Association.* Autumn.

Rae, John B. 1984. *The American Automobile Industry.* Boston: Twayne Publishers.

Rafuse, John L. 1990. "Data and Lessons from UNOCAL's South Coast Recycled Auto Project (SCRAP)." Testimony before the US House of Representatives Committee on Energy and Commerce, Subcommittee on Energy and Power. October 1.

Renewable Fuels Association (RFA). 1989. *Ethanol Report: Ozone and Global Warming.* Vol. III, Issue 1. Washington, DC. August 10.

Reno, A.T. 1988. "Personal Mobility in the United States." *A Look Ahead: Year 2020, Special Report 220.* Transportation Research Board, National Research Council. Washington, DC.

Replogle, Michael A. 1984. *Bicycle Access: New Boost for Transit Performance.* Presented at the Conference of the American Association of Civil Engineers. Knoxville, TN. July.

———. 1988. *Bicycles & Public Transportation: New Links to Suburban Transit Markets.* Washington, DC: The Bicycle Federation, 1983 and 1988.

———. 1990. Director of Transportation and Modeling, the National-Capital Park and Planning Commission, Montgomery County, Maryland. Personal communication.

Research/Strategy/Management Inc. (RSM). 1989. *Global Warming and Energy Priorities: A National Perspective.* Study for the Union of Concerned Scientists. November.

Rind, David. 1989. "The Greenhouse Effect: How It Can Change Our Lives—A Character Sketch of Greenhouse." *EPA Journal*. Vol. 15, No. 1. January/February.

Rollcall: The Newspaper of Congress. 1990. "Transportation." Rollcall Policy Briefing No. 17. Washington, DC. July 23.

Rosenberg, W.G. 1990. *Clean Air Act testimony before the Senate Committee on Environment and Public Works*. January 11.

Ross, Marc. 1989. "Energy and Transportation in the United States." *Annual Review of Energy 1989,* Vol. 14, pp. 131-71.

Rote, Donald M. 1990. *Maglev Comparative Energy Efficiency and Market Potential*. US Department of Energy, Argonne National Laboratory. Presented at the Transportation Research Board Committee on Energy Conservation and Transportation Demand, Washington, DC. January.

Rothenberg, M. 1988. "Urban Congestion in the United States: What Does the Future Hold?" *Strategies to Alleviate Traffic Congestion*. Proceedings of Institute of Transportation Engineers 1987 National Conference, p. 374.

Rothschild, Edwin. 1990. *Testimony before the House Ways and Means Committee on environmental taxes*. March 7.

Rowand, R. 1989. "You Sit, and You Wait, and You Boil," *Automotive News*. December.

Saricks, Christopher L. 1990. *Technological and Policy Options for Mitigating Greenhouse Gas Emissions from Mobile Sources*. Argonne National Laboratory, Argonne, IL. Presented at 69th Annual Transportation Research Board Meeting. Transportation Research Board Paper No. 890794. Washington, DC. January.

Schlesinger, James. 1989. "So Hungry for Oil." *Washington Post,* October 24, p. A25.

Schumann, J.W. 1989. "What's New in North American Light Rail Transit Projects?" *TRB Special Report 221*. Transportation Research Board. Washington, DC.

Segal, Migdon R. 1988. *Alcohol Fuels*. US Congressional Research Service. IB74087. May.

Shreve, R.N., and Joseph A. Brink, Jr. 1977. *Chemical Engineering Process Industries*. New York: McGraw-Hill.

Sims, Calvin. 1989. "New Step for Clean Air: A Natural Gas Bus." *New York Times,* September 27, p. D6.

South Coast Air Quality Management District (SCAQMD) and Southern California Association of Governments (SCAG). 1989. *The Path to Clean Air: Attainment Strategies—Summary of 1989 Air Quality Management Plan*. El Monte, CA. May.

Southern California Association of Governments (SCAG). 1989a. *Regional Growth Management Plan*. Los Angeles, CA. February.

———. 1989b. *Air Quality Management Plan*. Los Angeles, CA. March.

Sperling, Daniel. 1989c. *Alternative Transportation Fuels*. New York: Quorum Books. P. 312.

Sperling, Daniel, D. Hungerford, and K. Kurani. 1989a. *Consumer Demand for Methanol*. December. Baltimore: Johns Hopkins University Press.

Sperling, Daniel, and Mark A. DeLuchi. 1989b. "Is Methanol the Transportation Fuel of the Future?" *Energy*. Vol. 14, No. 8.

Stammer, Larry B. 1990. "Health Trade-Off Surfaces in New Arco 'Clean' Gas." *Los Angeles Times,* September 25, p. B1.

Stevenson, Walt. 1990. US Environmental Protection Agency, Research Triangle Park, NC. Personal communication.

Stowers, J.R. 1988. "Organizing and Funding Transportation for 2020." *A Look Ahead: Year 2020, Special Report 220.* Transportation Research Board, National Research Council, Washington, DC, p. 483.

Stowers, J.R., and W. Boyar. 1985. *Energy Conservation in Transportation.* Transportation Research Board Report No. 121. Transportation Research Board, Washington, DC. December.

Sweeney, James L. 1990. *Projected Costs of Alternative Liquid Transportation Fuels.* Stanford University Center for Economic Policy Research, Energy Natural Resource and Environment Program. January.

Tax Foundation, Inc. (TFI). 1989. *Monthly Tax Features.* Washington, DC. June.

Thompson, S., and L. Sek. 1989. "Surface Transport Carriers: Deregulation Effects and Prospects." *Transportation in the United States: Perspectives on Federal Policies.* Washington, DC: Congressional Research Service. February.

Tilley, C.R. 1990. "Clean Air and Natural Gas Vehicles." *Public Utilities Fortnightly,* September 13, p. 31.

Totten, Michael. 1989. *Energywise Options for State and Local Governments.* Washington, DC: Center for Policy Alternatives. November.

Transportation Research Board (TRB). 1985. *Highway Capacity Manual.* TRB Special Report 209. National Research Council. Washington, DC.

———. 1987. *Research Priorities in Transportation and Energy.* Transportation Research Circular No. 323. September.

———. 1988a. *A Look Ahead: Year 2020.* Special Report 220. National Research Council. Washington, DC.

———. 1988b. *Bicycling and Bicycle Facilities: Research Problem Statements.* Transportation Research Circular No. 337. Washington, DC. October.

United States Congress, Office of Technology Assessment (OTA). 1982. *Increased Automobile Fuel Efficiency and Synthetic Fuels.* Washington, DC: US Government Printing Office. September.

———. 1988. *Gearing Up for Safety: Motor Carrier Safety in a Competitive Environment.* OTA-SET-382. Washington, DC: US Government Printing Office.

———. 1989a. *Catching Our Breath: Next Steps For Reducing Urban Ozone.* OTA-O-412. Washington, DC: US Government Printing Office. July.

———. 1989b. *Advanced Vehicle/Highway Systems.* Washington, DC: US Government Printing Office. September.

———. 1990. *Replacing Gasoline: Alternative Fuels for Light-Duty Vehicles.* OTA-E-364. Washington, DC: US Government Printing Office. September.

United States Department of Commerce (DOC). 1982. *Truck Inventory and Use Survey.* Bureau of the Census: Census of Transportation.

United States Department of Energy (DOE). 1986. *Energy Security: A Report to the President of the United States.* DOE Energy Report to President Ronald Reagan. Fall.

———. 1988a. *Assessment of Costs and Benefits of Flexible and Alternative Fuel Use in the U.S. Transportation Sector—Progress Report One: Context and Analytical Framework.* DOE/PE-0080. January.

———. 1988b. *Assessment of Costs and Benefits of Flexible and Alternative Fuel Use in the U.S. Transportation Sector—Progress Report Two: The International Experience.* DOE/PE-0085. August.

———. 1988c. *Assessment of Costs and Benefits of Flexible and Alternative Fuel Use in the U.S. Transportation Sector—Technical Report One: Study Objectives and Methodologies.* DOE/PE-0086. June.

———. 1989a. *Hydrogen Energy Coordinating Committee Annual Report—Summary of DOE Hydrogen Programs for Fiscal Year 1988.* DOE/CE-0242. January.

———. 1989b. *Electric and Hybrid Vehicles Program: 12th Annual Report to Congress for Fiscal Year 1988.* February.

———. 1991. *Posture Statement and Fiscal Year 1992 Budget Overview.* DOE/CR-0002. February.

United States Department of Transportation (DOT). 1980. *Bicycle Transportation for Energy Conservation.* DOT Program Statement. Washington, DC.

———. 1987a. Federal Highway Administration, *Urban Traffic Congestion: A Perspective to Year 2020.* September.

———. 1987b. *Encouraging Public Transportation Through Effective Land Use Actions.* DOT-1-87-35. May.

———. 1988a. *America's Challenge for Highway Transportation in the 21st Century.* FHA-PL-89-020, HPP-1-11-88. November.

———. 1988b. *The Status of the Nation's Local Mass Transportation: Performance and Conditions.* Department of Transportation Urban Mass Transit Association Report to Congress. June.

———. 1988c. *A Guide to Transportation Demand Management Plans for Employees.* September.

———. 1988d. *Transportation Innovation in the States: National Contest Entries for 1988.* Prepared for CENTRANS, the Council of State Governments, Washington, DC. August.

———. 1989. *An Assessment of Travel Demand Approaches at Suburban Activity Centers.* Urban Mass Transit Association #88-UMI. July.

———. 1990. *Highway Statistics 1989.* Federal Highway Administration. FHWA-PL-90-003.

United States Environmental Protection Agency (EPA). 1979. *Bicycling and Air Quality Information Document.* Washington, DC. September.

———. 1987. *Assessing the Risks of Trace Gases That Can Modify the Stratosphere, Volume II, Chapters 1-5.* EPA-400/1-87/001B. Office of Air and Radiation. Washington, DC. December 1987.

———. 1989. *Users' Guide to MOBILE4 (Mobile Source Emission Factor Model),* United States Environmental Protection Agency, EPA-AA-TED-89. February 1989.

———. 1989a. "The Greenhouse Effect: How It Can Change Our Lives." *EPA Journal.* Vol. 15, No. 1. January/February.

————. 1990. *National Air Quality and Emissions Trends Report*, EPA-450/4-90-002. Office of Air Quality Planning and Standards, Technical Support Division, Research Triangle Park, NC. March.

————. 1991. Implementation Strategy for the Clean Air Act Amendments of 1990. EPA. Office of Air and Radiation. January 15.

United States Environmental Protection Agency and US Department of Energy. 1989. *1990 Gas Mileage Guide: EPA Fuel Economy Estimates*. DOE/CE-0019/8. October.

United States General Accounting Office (GAO). 1989a. *Traffic Congestion: Trends, Measures, and Effects*. Report to the Chairman, Subcommittee on Transportation and Related Agencies, Committee on Appropriations, US Senate. GAO/PMED-90-1. November.

————. 1989b. *Traffic Congestion: Federal Efforts to Improve Mobility*. Report to the Chairman, Subcommittee on Transportation and Related Agencies, Committee on Appropriations, US Senate. GAO/PEMD-90-2. December.

————. 1989c. *Transportation Infrastructure: Reshaping the Federal Role Poses Significant Challenge for Policy Makers*. GAO/RCED-90-81A. December.

————. 1990a. *Gasoline Marketing: Uncertainties Surround Reformulated Gasoline as a Motor Fuel*. GAO/RCED-90-153. June.

————. 1990b. *Alcohol Fuels: Impacts from Increased Use of Ethanol Blended Fuels*. GAO/RCED-90-156. July.

————. 1990c. *Issues Related to DOT's Fiscal Year 1991 Budget Request*. Statement of Kenneth M. Mead, Director of Transportation Issues Resources, Community, and Economic Development Division, before the Senate Subcommittee on Transportation and Related Agencies. GAO/T-RCED-90-72. April 26.

————. 1990d. *Transportation Infrastructure: A Comparison of Federal and State Highway Laws*. GAO/RCED-90-157. June.

————. 1990e. *Operations of and Outlook for the Highway Trust Fund*. Statement of John W. Hill, Jr. Associate Director, Transportation Issues Resources, Community, and Economic Development Division, before the Subcommittee on Water Resources, Transportation, and Infrastructure. GAO/T-RCED-90-79. May 9.

United States House of Representatives (House). 1988. *Alternative Motor Fuels Act of 1988—Conference Report*. Report 100-929. September 16.

————. 1990. *Department of Transportation and Related Agencies Appropriations Bill, 1990*. Report No. 101-183. H.R. 3015. July 26.

United States Senate (Senate). 1989. *Clean Air Act Amendments of 1989: Report of the Committee on Environment and Public Works—Calendar No. 427*. Report No. 101-228. December 20.

Vander Schaaf, Mary Beth. 1989. "Automotive News Staff Looks at 1999." *Automotive News*. December, p. 236.

Vuchic, Vukan R. 1990. *Urban Public Transportation Systems and Technology— Complete, Current Coverage of Modern Transit Systems and Technology*. Englewood Cliffs, NJ: Prentice-Hall International.

Wachs, Martin. 1989. "U.S. Transit Subsidy Policy: In Need of Reform." *Science*, Vol. 244, June 30.

Wald, Matthew L. 1990. "Science Learns to Catch a Polluting Car in the Act." *New York Times*, July 29, p. E20.

Walker, E.L. 1990. *Overview of Texas High Speed Rail Study*. Presented at 69th Annual Transportation Research Board Meeting, Washington, DC. January.

Walsh, Michael P. 1990. *Pollution on Wheels II: The Car of the Future*. Prepared for the American Lung Association. January 19.

Weiss, M.J. 1990. "The High Octane Ethanol Lobby." *New York Times Magazine Special Business Section*. April 1.

Weisskopf, Michael. 1990. "Quilt of Compromise Stitched on Clean Air." *Washington Post*, March 5, p. A7.

Wendling, Robert. 1990. US Department of Commerce, Washington, DC. Personal communication. (Citing data from US Department of Commerce, "Input/Output Structure of the US Economy, 1977," and "Bureau of Economic Analysis Detailed Input/Output Study 1977.")

Westbrook, Fred, and Phillip Patterson. 1989. *Changing Driving Patterns and Their Effect on Fuel Economy*. US Department of Energy. Presented at the Society of Automotive Engineers Meeting. May.

Wicker, T. 1990. "Escape from Gridlock?" *New York Times*, March 15, p. A23.

Willis, D.K. 1990. "IVHS Technologies: Promising Palliatives or Popular Poppycock?" *Transportation Quarterly*. Vol. 44, No. 1. January.

Winston, Clifford. 1990. "How to Ease Traffic Jams." *New York Times*, July 18, p. A21.

Winston, Clifford, and Associates. 1987. *Blind Intersection? Policy and the Automobile Industry*. Washington, DC: Brookings Institution.

Winston, Clifford, Thomas M. Corsi, Curtis M. Grimm, and Carol A. Evans. 1990. *The Economic Effects of Surface Freight Deregulation*. Washington, DC: Brookings Institution.

Woodruff, David. 1990. "Big Bets on a Little Engine." *Business Week*, January 15, p. 81.

Works, R.M., and J.A. Ellison. 1990. *Launching the Heartland Express: A Statewide Transit Marketing Program Making a Difference*. Presented at 69th Annual Transportation Research Board Meeting. Transportation Research Board Paper No. 890321. Washington, DC. January.

Yago, Glenn. 1984. *The Decline of Transit: Urban Transportation in German and US Cities, 1900-1970*. New York: Cambridge University Press.

Yesney, Michelle. 1989. *Conserving the Natural Environment—The Sustainable City: A Revolution in Urban Evolution*. Presented at Stanford University's Deciding Our Environmental Future Conference. January 29.

Zimmerman, Samuel L. 1990. *The Urban Mass Transportation Administration and Major Investments: Evaluation Process and Results*. Presented at 69th Annual Transportation Research Board Meeting. Transportation Research Board Paper No. 890801. Washington, DC. January.

Index

About the Author

DEBORAH GORDON is Senior Transportation and Energy Policy Analyst for the Union of Concerned Scientists. She previously worked at the Department of Energy's Lawrence Berkeley laboratory and at Chevron USA, where she was an environmental and regulatory engineer. She served as a Congressional Fellow in the office of Congressman David Skaggs. She coauthored the pending DRIVE+ Feebate legislation in California, which would give consumers economic incentives to buy cleaner, more fuel-efficient cars. Gordon holds a Masters in Public Policy from the University of California at Berkeley and a B.S. in Chemical Engineering from the University of Colorado at Boulder.

Also Available from Island Press

Ancient Forests of the Pacific Northwest
By Elliott A. Norse

Balancing on the Brink of Extinction: The Endangered Species Act and Lessons for the Future
Edited by Kathryn A. Kohm

Better Trout Habitat: A Guide to Stream Restoration and Management
By Christopher J. Hunter

Beyond 40 Percent: Record-Setting Recycling and Composting Programs
The Institute for Local Self-Reliance

The Challenge of Global Warming
Edited by Dean Edwin Abrahamson

Coastal Alert: Ecosystems, Energy, and Offshore Oil Drilling
By Dwight Holing

The Complete Guide to Environmental Careers
The CEIP Fund

Economics of Protected Areas
By John A. Dixon and Paul B. Sherman

Environmental Agenda for the Future
Edited by Robert Cahn

Environmental Disputes: Community Involvement in Conflict Resolution
By James E. Crowfoot and Julia M. Wondolleck

Forests and Forestry in China: Changing Patterns of Resource Development
By S. D. Richardson

The Global Citizen
By Donella Meadows

Hazardous Waste from Small Quantity Generators
By Seymour I. Schwartz and Wendy B. Pratt

Holistic Resource Management Workbook
By Allan Savory

In Praise of Nature
Edited and with essays by Stephanie Mills

The Living Ocean: Understanding and Protecting Marine Biodiversity
By Boyce Thorne-Miller and John G. Catena

Natural Resources for the 21st Century
Edited by R. Neil Sampson and Dwight Hair

The New York Environment Book
By Eric A. Goldstein and Mark A. Izeman

Overtapped Oasis: Reform or Revolution for Western Water
By Marc Reisner and Sarah Bates

Permaculture: A Practical Guide for a Sustainable Future
By Bill Mollison

Plastics: America's Packaging Dilemma
By Nancy Wolf and Ellen Feldman

The Poisoned Well: New Strategies for Groundwater Protection
Edited by Eric Jorgensen

Race to Save the Tropics: Ecology and Economics for a Sustainable Future
Edited by Robert Goodland

Recycling and Incineration: Evaluating the Choices
By Richard A. Denison and John Ruston

Reforming The Forest Service
By Randal O'Toole

The Rising Tide: Global Warming and World Sea Levels
By Lynne T. Edgerton

Saving the Tropical Forests
By Judith Gradwohl and Russell Greenberg

Trees, Why Do You Wait?
By Richard Critchfield

War on Waste: Can America Win Its Battle With Garbage?
By Louis Blumberg and Robert Gottlieb

Western Water Made Simple
From *High Country News*

Wetland Creation and Restoration: The Status of the Science
Edited by Mary E. Kentula and Jon A. Kusler

Wildlife and Habitats in Managed Landscapes
Edited by Jon E. Rodiek and Eric G. Bolen

For a complete catalog of Island Press publications, please write:
Island Press, Box 7, Covelo, CA 95428, or call: 1–800–828–1302